SEMEIA 75

POSTCOLONIALISM AND SCRIPTURAL READING

Guest Editor: Laura E. Donaldson
Board Editor: R. S. Sugirtharajah

© 1996
by the Society of Biblical Literature

SEMEIA 75

Copyright © 1996 by the Society of Biblical Literature

All rights reserved. No part of this work may be reproduced or transmitted in any form or by any means, electronic or mechanical, including photocopying and recording, or by means of any information storage or retrieval system, except as may be expressly permitted by the 1976 Copyright Act or in writing from the publisher. Requests for permission should be addressed in writing to the Rights and Permissions Office, Society of Biblical Literature, 825 Houston Mill Road, Atlanta, GA 30329, USA.

ISSN 0095-571X
ISBN 1-58983-198-5

Printed in the United States of America
on acid-free paper

Contents

Contributors to this Issue v

Postcolonialism and Biblical Reading: An Introduction
    Laura E. Donaldson 1

1. Postcolonialism and Imperial Motives for Canonization
    Jon L. Berquist 15

2. Reading for Decolonization (John 4:1–42)
    Musa W. Dube 37

3. A Canaanitic Word in the Logos of Christ; or The Difference the Syro-Phoenician Woman Makes to Jesus
    Jim Perkison 61

4. *The Gospel of Lucas Gavilán* as Postcolonial Biblical Exegesis
    Hector Avalos 87

5. "Everybody Talking about Heaven Ain't Going There": The Biblical Call for Justice and the Postcolonial Response of the Spirituals
    Kimberly Rae Connor 107

6. Green Ants and Gibeonites: B. Wongar, Joshua 9, and Some Problems of Postcolonialism
    Roland Boer 129

7. From I-Hermeneutics to We-Hermeneutics: Native Americans and the Post-Colonial
    Jace Weaver 153

8. Tropes of Travel
    Miriam Peskowitz 177

RESPONSES

El salto hermenéutico de hoy
    Elsa Tamez 199

The Hermeneutical Leap of Today
    Elsa Tamez 203
Response
    Robert Allen Warrior 207

Response to the Semeia volume on Postcolonial Criticism
    Kwok Pui-lan 211

The Ethics of Postcolonial Criticism
    Mark G. Brett 219

Mapping the Hybrid World: Three Postcolonial Motifs
    Susan VanZanten Gallagher 229

CONTRIBUTORS TO THIS ISSUE

Hector Avalos
  1215 Florida Ave. #405
  Ames, IA 50014-3064

Jon L. Berquist
  P.O. Box 17
  Lawrenceburg, KY 40342-0017

Roland Boer
  United Theological College
  16 Masons Drive
  North Parramatta, NS 2151
  Australia

Mark G. Brett
  Whitley College
  University of Melbourne
  271 Royal Parade
  Parkville, Victoria 3052
  Australia

Kimberly Rae Connor
  224 Country Club Drive
  San Francisco, CA 94132

Laura E. Donaldson
  English, Women's Studies, and
  American Indian/Native Studies
  202 Jefferson Building
  University of Iowa
  Iowa City, IA 52242-1418

Musa W. Dube
  Dept. of Theology and Rel. Studies
  University of Botswana
  Private Bag 0022
  Gaborone
  Botswana

Susan VanZanten Gallagher
  Professor of English
  Tiffany Hall
  Seattle Pacific University
  3307 Third Avenue West
  Seattle, WA 98119-1997

Jim Perkinson
  5540 S. Woodlawn
  Chicago, IL 60637

Miriam Peskowitz
  Department of Religion
  125 Dauer Hall
  University of Florida
  Gainesville, FL 32611

Kwok Pui-lan
  Episcopal Divinity School
  99 Brattle Street
  Cambridge, MA 02138

Elsa Tamez
  Seminario Biblico Latino Americano
  APDO 901
  1000 San Jose
  Costa Rica

Robert Allen Warrior
  English Department
  Stanford University
  Stanford, CA 94305-2087

Jace Weaver
  70 LaSalle Street #13-B
  New York, NY 10027

POSTCOLONIALISM AND BIBLICAL READING:
AN INTRODUCTION

Laura E. Donaldson
The University of Iowa

APOLOGIES NOT ENOUGH

In his essay "Critical Fanonism," Henry Louis Gates remarks that the current ascendancy of the colonial paradigm constitutes one of the most important developments in contemporary literary and cultural theory (457). Indeed, the past decade has witnessed a veritable explosion of publications and conferences about "postcolonialism" and its importance as an analytical and political tool. Yet, the postcolonial perspective is not entirely new. Within the Jewish and Christian religions, for example, some scholars have perceived parallels between the prophetic tradition of the Bible and the goals of emerging postcolonial literatures: both call individuals and societies to new ways of life and both proclaim the need for justice at all levels of society (Gallagher: 20). Or, to paraphrase Archbishop Desmond Tutu, the prophetic—and, I would add, the postcolonial—urges us to condemn "as worthless religiosity a concern with offering God worship when we were unmindful of the sociopolitical implications of our religion" (29). However, a crucial difference between these two positions emerges from the prophetic tradition's awakening of its followers to a heterogenous group of socio-ethical concerns, whereas postcolonialism specifically addresses the historical, textual, discursive and epistemological legacies of colonialism.

This issue of *Semeia* attempts to document what postcolonial criticism might mean for biblical studies, not only as a practice of interpretation but also as a challenge to the disciplinary history of the religious academy. Its scope is interdisciplinary and multifaceted, ranging from Latin American rewritings of Luke's Gospel and the postcolonial response of African-American spirituals to the importance of the Syro-Phoenician woman and the formation of the Hebrew canon. What links this diverse group of essays together, however, is a critical focus on imperialism, neo-colonialism, and Eurocentrism as well as an investigation of how these processes are embodied in literary and theological forms. The urgency of developing a postcolonial perspective, particularly within the Christian tradition, is amply demonstrated by Edward Said's *Orientalism* (1978), a text which has profoundly influenced the colonial turn described above.

In his meticulous analysis, Said details how the eighteenth-century revolution in biblical studies constituted one of the most important motivations for studying the "Orient"—one of the West's deepest and most recurring images of the Other (1978:17). He specifically identifies Bishop Robert Lowth, Johann Gottfried Eichhorn, Johann Gottfried von Herder, Johann David Michaelis and, later, Ernest Renan as progenitors of the ideological discourse and scientific methodology called "Orientalism," i.e. the production of the "Orient" as an object of knowledge for the Occident. The fascination these scholars exhibited for biblical lands and languages—echoed in the travel literature of pilgrims (see Peskowitz, this issue)—imagined a geography that not only maintained the epistemological distinction between the West and the Rest of Us, but also imbued the "East" with strategic Anglo-European interests.

Significantly, the century of Orientalism's most intense institutional growth also corresponded precisely with the globalization of European imperialism. From 1815 to 1914, the powers of Europe—primarily England and France—expanded their domination from 35 percent of the earth's surface to a staggering 85 percent. For Said, this is no historical coincidence; it instead suggests that Orientalism "was a scientific movement whose analogue in the world of empirical politics was the Orient's colonial accumulation and acquisition by Europe" (1986:215). Orientalism functioned as a "saturating hegemonic system" that distributed Western geo-political concerns into aesthetic, scholarly, economic, sociological, historical, and philological texts (1978:12), and the role of biblical criticism in this immersion cannot be ignored.

A recent instance likewise emphasizes the necessity for the religious academy to develop a postcolonial critique. In the last few years, several Christian denominations have issued public apologies for their historical treatment of Native North Americans. Even though the official remorse expressed, for example, by Canadian Anglicans or the joint Protestant-Catholic declaration of the Pacific Northwest is a significant act, the inadequacy of these responses also foregrounds the need for a critical paradigm that would enable churches to confront their histories in a more direct manner. Clearly, apologies are not enough. As Dakota scholar Elizabeth Cook-Lynn notes, "Some may say that there is great sympathy for the dreadful situation in which Indians find themselves politically and economically. Certainly that is true of many churchgoing people . . . but they have developed *no active intellectual position* beyond the pledges of support" (59). Postcolonial criticism helps to fill this intellectual and ethical void, since it would require not only a systematic accounting of Christianity's participation in imperialism, but also that individual congregations actively become involved in the work of decolonization. However, in order to investigate how postcolonialism facilitates such atonement, we first need to map its geo-critical territories and explore its sometimes contradictory meanings.

"Post-colonialism Is Dead; Long Live Postcolonialism"

Perhaps the most difficult issue facing this volume as well as the larger field of postcolonial studies is how, exactly, to delineate the term "postcolonial." In *The Empire Writes Back: Theory and Practice in Postcolonial Literatures*, Bill Ashcroft, Gareth Griffiths, and Helen Tiffin offer one of the most widely cited definitions in their affirmation that the "post-colonial" encompasses all the culture affected by the imperial process from the moment of colonization to the present day: "This is because there is a continuity of preoccupations throughout the historical process initiated by European imperial aggression. We also suggest that it is most appropriate as the term for the new cross-cultural criticism which has emerged in recent years and for the discourse through which this is constituted" (1989:2). Tiffin further clarifies this double-edged definition by distinguishing between different archives of the postcolonial: the historical and the discursive. The former constructs postcolonialism from aesthetic production constituted by the "subordinating power of European colonialism—that is, as writing from countries of regions which were formerly colonies of Europe" (1990:vii), while the latter conceives of postcolonialism "as a set of discursive practices, prominent among which is *resistance* to colonialism, colonialist ideologies, and their contemporary forms and subjectificatory legacies" (1990:vii).

The Empire Writes Back was one of the first attempts to summarize postcolonial literatures and theory, and it has been helpful in clarifying this very complex field. In the years following the book's publication, however, its framing of the issues has proven to be primarily useful for the critical conversation it has engendered. While some scholars have questioned the way it collapses the experience of white settler colonies such as Australia, Canada, and the United States with that of indigenous peoples (Shohat and Weaver, this issue), others have castigated its assumption that colonialism automatically spawns resistance and the seeds of its own demise (Williams and Chrisman). The missionary efforts that accompanied Anglo-Europe's colonization of Africa offer a brilliant illustration of the problematic assumptions involved in this second point.

In her insightful introduction to *Postcolonial Literature and the Biblical Call for Justice*, Susan VanZanten Gallagher acknowledges the complicity of the Christian missionary enterprise with the structures of colonial oppression. In spite of this complicity, she argues, colonial institutions such as the mission school also possessed "positive" effects: "Despite its chauvinistic cultural limits, such education eventually provided the means by which significant indigenous leaders were formed. The political leaders who were to take the lead in the postwar decolonization process were invariably educated in mission schools. And the leading figures in literature, such as Ngũgĩ [Wa Thiongo], also first struggled with the issue of finding a voice with the benefit of their mission school educations" (22). However, I would recontextualize this statement, since I believe what Gallagher describes as the allegedly "positive" effects of an imperial Christianity actually connotes the possibility of the colonized's resistance to their own oppression.

We should instead consider how the apparatuses of imperialism such as the mission school sometimes, *but not always*, contribute to its destruction. For example, one of the most effective strategies of colonization was the suppression of indigenous languages and the imposition of imperial ones—and the best means of implementing this translation existed in the mission school. In the schools of the English colonies, students were usually punished for speaking their native tongues and forced to adopt the English-only ambience of these educational institutions. Such linguistic and cultural deracination had (and continues to have) severe consequences:[1] children often lost the ability to communicate with parents who did not speak English; the disappearance of aboriginal languages hastened the disruption of indigenous social structures and non-European knowledge systems; and, perhaps most painfully, many individual children were so traumatized by their experience that they suffered from depression, alcoholism, and high rates of suicide. However, the imposition of English also produced results that were completely unexpected, since it facilitated interaction among students of different tribes and language groups who had been heretofore unable to talk with each other and share information as well as support. In what one can only call poetic justice, the imposition of an imperial language ironically created a common *lingua franca* and thus, the enabling conditions for the emergence of contemporary pan-African movements for decolonization.

Is the fact that many students utilized English to construct a counter-hegemonic discourse a "positive" outcome of the mission school? I would emphatically reply: "Absolutely not." What it does show, though, is that imperializing strategies such as language suppression frequently enabled the colonized to resist colonization in some very surprising ways. This contradiction also reveals that many First World theorists consistently undervalue the ability of the oppressed to negotiate colonial structures and appropriate them for their own purposes. The example of the mission school teaches us that colonized peoples often utilized the master's—and the mistress's—tools to at least partially dismantle the colonizer's house.

Even more troubling than the problematic of resistance is the way that the presentation of postcolonialism in *The Empire Writes Back* (as well as by other scholars) provides a last bastion for the dream of a "global theory" (Gates: 469–70). In a gesture that I have sometimes called "re-orientalism," the very critique posed by postcolonialism risks merely substituting one to-

---

[1] "To deracinate" stems from the Latin verb meaning to pull up by the roots and to uproot. By extension, it connotes the process of extirpation or eradication.

talizing framework for another. As Anne McClintock notes in her essay, "The Angel of Progress: Pitfalls of the Term 'Post-colonialism'":

> If 'post-colonial' *theory* has sought to challenge the grand march of western historicism with its entourage of binaries (self-other, metropolis-colony, center-periphery, etc.), the *term* 'post-colonialism' nonetheless re-orients the globe once more around a single, binary opposition: colonial/post-colonial. Moreover, theory is thereby shifted from the binary axis of *power* (colonizer/ colonized—itself inadequately nuanced, as in the case of women) to the binary axis of *time*, an axis even less productive of political nuance since it does not distinguish between the beneficiaries of colonialism (the ex-colonizers) and the casualties of colonialism (the ex-colonized). (1994:292)

In their reply to McClintock's criticism, i.e. that postcolonialism subsumes a disparate collection of histories under the binary opposition colonialism/ postcolonialism, some have argued that, when differently defined, postcolonialism contests this very dichotomy. For example, Bob Hodge and Vijay Mishra's concept of "oppositional" postcolonialism designates the potentially insurgent underside of any colonial context—a potential vividly dramatized by the Christian mission school—and thus disrupts any construal of colonialism and postcolonialism as rigidly separated entities or eras.

Biblical scholar R. S. Sugirtharajah presents the project of oppositional postcolonialism as involving the search for protesting voices (see Avalos, this issue). To illustrate this point, he argues that the Parable of the Tenants in the Gospels of Matthew, Mark, and Luke is usually read from an "overly Christological" viewpoint or from the property owner's perspective; interpreters have rarely focused upon the people who were part of the parable's textual and actual audience (Sugirtharajah: 25). When the audience learns that the owner plans to destroy the tenants and lease the land to others, they respond "Heaven forbid!" (Lk 20.16b)—an expression of shock acknowledging that they are the inheritors of Yahweh's allotment of land, which has now been stolen from them. According to Sugirtharajah, "people know at once the land is gone, [and that] they lose not only income but are also at the mercy of the owner for new working arrangements. What post-colonial criticism will do is bring to the front such marginal elements in the texts, and in the process subvert the traditional meaning. It will engage in an archival exegesis as a way of rememorialising the narratives and voices which have been subjected to institutional forgetting" (25).

Oppositional postcolonialism also contests the hyphenation of "post" and "colonial" as implying a transcendence of colonialism and a movement somehow "after" and "beyond" the past. Although the following passage insightfully interrogates the logic of modernism and postmodernism, it also captures the imbricated and overdetermined relationship between colonialism and postcolonialism: "Once we view . . . [it] not in terms of a succession of ideas and concepts only, but as the staggering of legacies and symptoms at their different stages of articulation, then the 'displacement' of modernism by postmodernism [or colonialism by postcolonialism] becomes a complex matter and can vary according to the objective for which that displacement is argued" (Chow: 56). What does this staggered inheritance imply for the religious academy as well as the theory and practice of scriptural reading? One certain implication within biblical studies is the necessity of re-visiting the so-called "Great Commission" in Matthew 28.19–20.[2]

"Go Therefore and Make Disciples of All Nations"

One of Christianity's most urgent priorities should be investigating how Matthew's directive has been mobilized as a justification of conquest. And perhaps a story about a recent journey to the national American Academy of Religion/Society for Biblical Literature conference will illustrate why. On one occasion in the not too distant past, my flight to the national meeting routed me through Atlanta. A soberly dressed, middle-aged gentleman occupied the seat next to me and for most of the trip we did not speak. When he pulled out an AAR/SBL program, however, I casually asked if he were going to the conference. "Why yes," he replied, "and how about you?" From that modest beginning, we began a conversation, the memory of which still enrages, amuses, and instructs me about the desperate need for a postcolonial consciousness amongst Christians. He was fascinated by the family history I spoke about in the paper I was going to present and wanted me to tell him more about my Cherokee heritage. I asked him why he was so interested. "Because," he intoned, "I teach at a small seminary (in a large Southern city) that has a very active missiology department. We want to avoid some of the mistakes you've talked about and train missionaries who are culturally sensitive."

"Hmm." My mother had always taught me never to be rude to strangers, so I tried to answer with an ambiguous exclamation that would hopefully end the conversation. He, unfortunately, took it as an invitation to chat further.

"We want to teach our students how to appreciate and be responsive to the cultures of indigenous peoples."

"Why?" I asked.

He answered: "All the better to bring them to Christ."

"Why," I asked.

---

[2] "Go, therefore, and make disciples of all nations, baptizing them in the name of the Father and the Son and of the Holy Spirit, and teaching them to obey everything that I have commanded you. And remember, I am with you always, to the end of the age" (Matt 28.19–20 NRSV). Many scholars believe that these verses were actually an editorial addition by the writer of Matthew.

"Because we believe that Christ is the final end for all cultures, whatever and wherever they are."

"Even if these cultures say that He isn't?"

"If a culture isn't of God, then it can't be good in and of itself," he replied.

(In other words, I thought, it's of Satan.) "But that's delusional," I said in my most sincerely diplomatic and objective tone.

He started in his seat, turned to me and said (in a voice tight with astonishment and forced politeness), "Could you please explain that to me?"

"Of course," I answered affably. "Look at the history—what civilization invented the most brutal system of conquest and exploitation the world has ever known? Christian. Who made slavery into the basis for capitalist expansion? Christians. What religion has been most responsible for the genocide of aboriginal peoples? Christianity. In my view the Christian church has a much more substantial record of pure evil than of any final good." And, I should have added, apologies are not enough.

With a strained smile, my neighbor said, "Well, you know it's good to talk about these things in a civil conversation. I guess we'll just have to agree to disagree." At that point, the flight attendant cautioned all of us to put our trays in the upright and locked position and fasten our seatbelts for landing. I directed my attention to the aisle and he determinedly stared out the window. Our short encounter was mercifully over.

The interpretation of the Great Commission evidenced by my fellow passenger (and many Christians like him) has too often unleashed the lethal weapons of the Word and the European world against aboriginal peoples and creating "responsive" agents cannot alter this fact. A postcolonial perspective would rigorously interrogate its use in support of imperialist agendas and offer an alternative reading through such biblical figures as the Syrophoenician woman seeking healing for her daughter (see Perkinson, this issue) and the Canaanite woman seeking water from the well (see Dube, this issue). In her book, *Discovering the Bible in the Non-Biblical World*, Kwok Pui-lan observes that the Church has traditionally interpreted the encounter of the Syrophoenician woman with Jesus (Mk 7.24–30; Matt 15.21–28) as a basis for missions to the Gentiles. Indeed, she notes, most interpreters uncritically follow the "salvation history" model by arguing that the Syrophoenician woman's story legitimizes admitting Gentiles into the Christian community—a model with strongly anti-Jewish and Christian imperialist overtones. Furthermore, the woman herself possesses an intricate positionality: marginalized because she is a woman and a Gentile, but privileged because she is Greek-speaking and urban (Kwok: 75). A postcolonial reading must attend to all these complexities, that is, it "must expose and investigate the intersection of anti-Judaism, sexism, and cultural and religious imperialism in the history of the text's interpretation" (Kwok: 79). For Kwok, this means that a "single-axis" approach—one that separates culture, race, class and gender—can no longer suffice. Instead, postcolonialism demands that we adopt a "multiaxial frame of reference" (Kwok: 79) and re-configure biblical reading through a multi-dimensional perspective.

In the final section of this introduction to postcolonialism and biblical studies, I want to articulate just such a multiaxial framework through a case study of Judges Chapters 19 and 20.

THE MIRANDA COMPLEX

Feminist biblical critics have identified Chapter 19 of the book of Judges as a "text of terror" whose brutalizing violence exposes the Bible's patriarchal attitudes toward women: an unnamed concubine is sacrificed so that her master can avoid sexual assault by the men of Gibeah. In his stead, she is raped to death, dismembered, and the pieces of her body sent "throughout all the territory of Israel" (Judg 19:29). Phyllis Trible interprets this narrative as depicting "the horrors of male power, brutality, and trimphalism; of female helplessness, abuse, and annihilation" (65); Danna Nolan Fewell, writing in the more recent *Women's Bible Commentary*, argues that this, as well as other stories in Judges, speak of "women betrayed" in the perpetuation of male self-interest (74). While no one should underestimate the importance of such anti-misogynist readings, it is also symptomatic that no feminist scholars look further than the single axis of women's estate in their interpretations of the violence perpetrated against the "unnamed concubine." If they had looked further, they might have noticed that this story frames yet another "text of terror"—Chapter 20 of Judges, which provided the early settlers of New England with all the legitimation they needed to wage war against the Pequot.

Before the First Puritan Conquest, the Pequot—whose name translates loosely as "the destroyers" or "manslayers"—were among the Northeast's most powerful and influential American Indian nations. After the war, their population of 13,000 had been reduced to 1,000, and they became the first Native culture subjected to governmental termination. On May 26, 1637, the English setters massacred 700 elderly men and defenseless women and children (their sons and husbands were largely absent) who resided in a village on the banks of the Mystic River. In less than an hour, Pequot hegemony in the region was broken (Hauptman and Wherry: xiv) and the soul of the People put to the test. John Underhill, the soldier who trained the Connecticut militia, was a participant in this action, and his eyewitness account stunningly catalogues the horrors of that day:

> But seeing the fort was too hot for us, we devised a way how we might save ourselves and prejudice them. Captain [John] Mason entering into a

wigwam, brought out a firebrand, after he had wounded many in the house. Then he set fire on the west side, where he entered; myself set fire on the south end with a train of powder. The fires of both meeting in the center of the fort blazed most terribly, and burnt all in the space of half an hour . . . Many were burnt in the fort, both men, women, and children. Others were forced out, and came in troops to the Indians, twenty and thirty at a time, which our soldiers received and entertained with the point of the sword. Down fell men, women, and children . . . It is reported by themselves [the Pequot] that there were about four hundred souls in this fort, and not above five of them escaped out of our hands. (Segal and Stineback: 136–37)

Under the terms specified by the 1638 Hartford Treaty, the Pequot were officially suppressed (almost 300 years before the United States implemented its policy of "termination") and its members forbidden to speak the name of their tribe. Like all societies dependent upon oral tradition, they stood only one generation away from silence, so the intent of the Treaty remains clear: in the words of Captain John Mason, the architect of the Mystic village raid, it was "to cut off the Remembrance of them from the Earth."

A seventeenth-century apologia justifying such actions begins where contemporary feminist biblical criticism ends: in the aftermath of the anonymous woman's heinous dismemberment. According to its author, John Higginson, who delivered his treatise to Governor John Winthrop at the time of the Mystic village massacre, Judges 20 offers the Pequot war's most extensive "vindication," and its parallels with the Puritans' own New World struggles are exceedingly clear. Just as the war between the Israelites and the Benjaminites of Gibeah was precipitated by the latter's murder of the unnamed concubine, the war between Massachusetts Bay Colony and the Pequot was started by the Pequot murders of Captains John Stone and John Oldham;[3] just as the Benjaminites refused to give up the responsible parties, so the Pequot refused to give up the murderers of Stone and Oldham, thus making war inevitable; just as the Benjaminites won early skirmishes in the military campaign, so were the Pequot relatively successful in the first stages of the Puritan War; just as God delivered the Benjaminites into the hands of the Israelites, so He delivered the Pequot to the Massachusetts Bay Colony; just as the Israelites "put the whole [Benjaminite] city to the sword" and burned it to the ground, so did the Massachusetts Bay militia burn Mystic Fort and slay all its inhabitants. And, I would add, this text of terror subjected the Pequot to a fate just as terrible as that of the unnamed concubine.

---

[3] This accusation turned out to be factually inaccurate. John Oldham was most probably killed on Block Island by Western Niantics, a tributary tribe of the Pequot. And, as Francis Jennings has documented, the real motives for the war involved the Pequot's negotiation of the 1634 peace treaty with Massachusetts Bay and the early colonization of the Connecticut Valley by the English—and not these murders (1976:190).

A postcolonial approach to biblical studies would demand that we read chapters 19 and 20 in the context of each other and regard them as a cluster of stories exploring how violence against women is linked to violence against Native peoples.[4] Indeed, postcolonialism interrupts what I have in earlier work identified as "the Miranda Complex" (16–17). Inspired by the relationship between Caliban (the disenfranchised Native) and Miranda (the Anglo-European daughter) in Shakespeare's *The Tempest*, the Miranda complex examines why these two figures—who are both victims of Prospero—have such trouble "seeing" each other and forging a politics of coalition against white supremacist, masculinist, and colonialist hegemony. One might ask a similar question of feminist biblical critics: why have they failed to read further in both the biblical and social text? Why have they failed to "see" the presence of Caliban, or in this case the Pequot, in their texts of terror? One answer would be that, like the character of Miranda, the largely Anglo-European community of feminist biblical scholars displays a disturbing myopia concerning colonialism and its entanglements within their own interpretive enterprise.[5]

However, chapters 19 and 20 also state the need for a gendered postcolonialism, i.e. a recognition that "the task of the postcolonial cannot be restrained within the specular master-slave enclosure" (Spivak: 279). Reading these two texts in isolation vividly embodies the central problem of the Miranda complex, i.e. "the dangers of monotheistic reading, that is, reading structured so tightly by a single principle (whether emanating from the West or the Rest of Us) that it excludes all other interpretive categories" (Donaldson: 17). Postcolonialism instead calls for a *proliferation* of historically nuanced theories and strategies which may more effectively engage with the "calamitous" dispensations of power in past and present societies (McClintock: 303).

Reading Like a Canaanite

The implications of postcolonialism for biblical studies are immense. Its broad parameters encompass the effects of the Anglo-European as well as Roman and Israelite imperial projects (see Dube and Berquist in this issue). And, although it lacks a unified field, postcolonial criticism powerfully

---

[4] I do not wish to resurrect here the very problematic and frequently cited homology, man=colonizer and woman=colonized. This parallel uncritically and ethnocentrically appropriates the experience of the colonized as a metaphor for gender oppression. It not only trivializes the experience of colonized peoples, but also lacks any awareness of gender—or colonialism for that matter—as a contested field whose identities are often contradictory.

[5] There are some exceptions, of course. For example, Elsa Tamez, Kwok Pui-lan, both respondents for this issue, and Musa Dube, author of an essay for this issue—have made anti-colonialism a central feature of their feminist work.

enunciates the need for biblical critics to engage with colonialism as well as its "posts"—not just as official topics of inquiry, but also as present within their own practices of reading. It teaches us, in other words, to read like Canaanites.

> The Lord said, "I have indeed seen the misery of my people in Egypt. I have heard them crying out because of their slave drivers, and I am concerned about their suffering. So I have come down to rescue them from the hand of the Egyptians and to bring them up out of that land into a good and spacious land, a land flowing with milk and honey—the home of the Canaanites . . . . (Exod 3:7–8)

The scriptural vision of coming home to a "good and spacious" land has generated and sustained many different peoples in the throes of oppression. Yet, the actual realities of liberation are much more ambiguous.

As Mark Walhout remarks, for the colonizer "the biblical conquest of the Promised Land is part and parcel of a national-religious ideology that was central to the founding of a modern state. For the native inhabitant, on the other hand, it is the suppressed subtext of Canaanite experience that is the key to the Exodus narrative . . ." (206). The Canaanites are, of course, the much vilified people who occupied the "promised land" before the arrival of the wandering Israelites. Yet they also stand in for all peoples whose lands have been conquered and expropriated. In the work of Edward Said, for example, the plight of the Canaanites stands in for the plight of present-day Palestinians struggling to retain their ancestral homeland. In the nineteenth-century sermons of the Reverend Nahum Gold, the "red Canaanites"—his term for American Indians—stand in for all that America must reject; in fact, he preached, ridding the country of its first peoples was the only way to prevent them from "trampling down" the vineyard God had so graciously planted there. America must emulate Yahweh's directive to smash the Canaanites' altars, break down their Asherah poles, and kill the people themselves. Indeed, when we listen to the voices which are silenced by canonical readings of the story, the Exodus loses its appropriateness as a model for human liberation (see Warrior).

Such a paradigm shift exists at the heart of oppositional postcolonialism. As Kwok Pui-lan movingly writes:

> I first became aware that other people might look at the Exodus story differently when I listened some years ago to C. S. Song, a Presbyterian theologian from Taiwan. From the perspective of the tribal people in Taiwan, Song explained, the Exodus story is oppressive because the Canaanites were treated badly. Later, as I had opportunities to visit the Maoris in New Zealand and the Aborigines in Australia, they shared similar insights. I had never read the story from the perspective of the Canaanites and the experience was shocking to me. (98)

It is shocking and disorienting to be confronted with angles of vision that contest dominant assumptions, making it impossible to interpret a story in familiar ways. However, the defamiliarization of the Exodus story through the witness of its Canaanite victims functions as a microcosm of the impact postcolonialism should have on biblical critics and readers. They could no longer ignore either the existence of the colonized within the texts of the Bible or promote reading practices and interpretations which erase their existence.

Although reading like a Canaanite will not correct colonialism's past catastrophic intentions, it might help the religious academy not to repeat them. It—as well as this issue of *Semeia*—might help to prepare the way for a new sort of liberation whose promised land fulfills its commitments to *all* of its inhabitants.

WORKS CONSULTED

Ashcroft, Bill, Gareth Griffiths, and Helen Tiffin
    1989   *The Empire Writes Back: Theory and Practice in Post-Colonial Literatures.* New Accents. London and New York: Routledge.

Chow, Rey
    1993   *Writing Diaspora: Tactics of Intervention in Contemporary Cultural Studies.* Bloomington and Indianapolis: Indiana University Press.

Cook-Lynn, Elizabeth
    1996   *Why I Can't Read Wallace Stegner and Other Essays: A Tribal Voice.* Madison: The University of Wisconsin Press.

Donaldson, Laura E.
    1992   *Decolonizing Feminisms: Race, Gender, & Empire-Building.* Chapel Hill and London: The University of North Carolina Press.

Fewell, Danna Nolan
    1992   "Judges." Pp. 67–77 in *The Women's Bible Commentary.* Ed. Carol A. Newsom and Sharon H. Ringe. Louisville and London: Westminster/John Knox and SPCK.

Gallagher, Susan VanZanten
    1994   "Introduction: New Conversations on Postcolonial Literature." Pp. 3–33 in *Postcolonial Literature and the Biblical Call for Justice.* Ed. Susan VanZanten Gallagher. Jackson, MS: University Press of Mississippi.

Gates, Henry Louis, Jr.
    1991   "Critical Fanonism." *Critical Inquiry* 17:457–70.

Hauptman, Laurence M. and James D. Wherry
    1990   "Preface." Pp. xiii–xix in *The Pequots in Southern New England: The Fall and Rise of an American Indian Nation.* Ed. Laurence M. Hauptman

and James D. Wherry. Norman and London: University of Oklahoma Press.

Hodge, Bob, and Vijay Mishra
    1990   *Dark Side Of The Dream: Australian Literature and the Postcolonial Mind.* Australian Cultural Studies. Sydney: Allen & Unwin.

Jennings, Francis
    1975,   *The Invasion of America: Indians, Colonialism and The Cant of Conquest.*
    1976   New York and London: W.W. Norton & Company.

McClintock, Anne
    1994   "The Angel of Progress: Pitfalls of the Term 'Post-colonialism.'" Pp. 291–304 in *Colonial Discourse and Post-Colonial Theory: A Reader.* Ed. Patrick Williams and Laura Chrisman. New York: Columbia University Press.

    1995   *Imperial Leather: Race, Gender and Sexuality in the Colonial Conquest.* New York and London: Routledge.

Said, Edward W.
    1978   *Orientalism.* New York: Vintage.

    1986   "Orientalism Reconsidered." Pp. 210–29 in *Literature, Politics and Theory: Papers from the Essex Conference 1976–84.* Ed. Frances Barker, Peter Hulme, Margaret Iversen, and Diana Loxley. London and New York: Methuen.

Segal, Charles M. and David C. Stineback
    1977   *Puritans, Indians, and Manifest Destiny.* New York: G.P. Putnam's Sons.

Shohat, Ella
    1996   "Notes on the Post-colonial." Pp. 332–34 in *Contemporary Postcolonial Theory.* Ed. Padmini Mongia. London and New York: Arnold.

Spivak, Gayatri Chakravorty
    1996   *The Spivak Reader: Selected Works of Gayatri Chakravorty Spivak.* Ed. Donna Landry and Gerald MacLean. New York and London: Routledge.

Sugirtharajah, R. S.
    1996   "From Orientalist to Post-Colonial: Notes on Reading Practices." *Asia Journal of Theology* 10:20–27.

Tiffin, Helen
    1990   "Introduction." Pp. vii–xvi in *Past the Last Post: Theorizing Post-Colonialism and Post-Modernism.* Ed. Ian Adam and Helen Tiffin. Calgary: University of Calgary Press.

Trible, Phyllis
    1984   *Texts of Terror: Literary-Feminist Readings of Biblical Narratives.* Philadelphia: Fortress.

Tutu, Desmond
    1994   *The Rainbow People of God: The Making of a Peaceful Revolution.* Ed. John Allen. New York and London: Doubleday.

Walhout, Mark
    1994   "The *Intifada* of the Intellectuals: An Ecumenical Perspective on the Walzer-Said Exchange." Pp. 198–217 in *Postcolonial Literature and the Biblical Call for Justice*. Ed. Susan VanZanten Gallagher. Jackson, MS: University Press of Mississippi.

Warrior, Robert Allen
    1989   "Canaanites, Cowboys, and Indians: Deliverance, Conquest and Liberation Theology Today." *Christianity and Crisis* 49 (September 11):261–65.

Williams, Patrick and Laura Chrisman
    1994   "Colonial Discourse and Post-Colonial Theory: An Introduction." Pp. 1–19 in *Colonial Discourse and Post-Colonial Theory: A Reader*. Ed. Patrick Williams and Laura Chrisman. New York: Columbia University Press.

POSTCOLONIALISM AND IMPERIAL MOTIVES FOR CANONIZATION

Jon L. Berquist

ABSTRACT

Postcolonialism offers several distinct advantages to the biblical interpreter wishing to understand the process of canonical formation. Because of its focus on imperial practices, including the imperial production of culture, postcolonial theory can shed light on the ways that empires used texts to expound and expand their imperializing ideologies. This essay considers the early stages of Hebrew Bible canonization as an imperial production of ideology during the reign of the Persian Empire over colonial Yehud. In one sense, the canon is a colonial text, representing the colonizing intentions of the empire. At the same time, the social location of the text's production reflects a group wedged between empire and colony, and so there are postcolonial opportunities embedded within the text itself.

Postcolonial discourse enables interpreters to expose colonial realities and to direct our gaze upon the imperializing practices involved in the creation of a colony. Without this attachment to specific colonial-imperial relations, postcolonialist theory becomes utopic. Postcolonialism, just like the structures of the colony itself, cannot come into existence without the empire. Of course, the colonized peoples existed prior to the colonization, and they may have organized themselves in any of a number of social forms, but they were not a colony before the imperial intrusion. In order to explore the benefits of postcolonial discourse, I wish to examine the specific colonization of Yehud, the area around Jerusalem, in relation with the Persian Empire that created and named this colony. I will first trace the lines of imperial power between Persia and Yehud, in order to sketch the shape of Yehud's colonial form, with some attention to the ideological tools of imperialization. Because the notions of imperialization and colonization cross between postcolonial theory and sociological analysis, they allow opportunities for theoretical parallax and the chance for a more multidimensional understanding. I wish to explore the ways in which postcolonial discourse can benefit the understanding of colonial Yehud and its nascent canon. My goal is to describe the relationship of colonizing forces to the canon (as it was developed within the period of the Persian Empire). In what sense is the Yehudite canon a colonial and colonizing literature, and/or in what sense is it a postcolonial document? I will argue that the canon is strangely both.

Sociology and Colonial Yehud

Study of Persian-period Yehud or Second Temple Judaism usually commences with a quick refresher on its background (Berquist, 1995a:3–19). If the retelling of Jerusalem's history/narrative does not start even earlier, it at least includes Judah's monarchy, its Babylonian defeat and captivity, Persia's conquest of Babylonia and the subsequent inheriting of the areas formerly under Babylonian rule, and the restoration of Judah as a colony within the Persian Empire. Thus the history becomes a narrative of Judah as nation, as exiles, and as restored community. The focus on imperialization, however, redirects the gaze away from Judah. Instead, our travel must begin in the Persian Empire, not in one of its small western provinces.

Persia's imperial conquest of Babylonia is usually assigned the date of 539/538 BCE, although their competition had already lasted several years while Persia gradually assumed greater influence over Babylonia's previous territories and holdings. Persian power over the area of Mesopotamia entered into a relatively uncontested period at the same time that its imperial domination manifested itself; the two processes are not distinct. By 539, when modern historiography claims that Persia "became" the ruling "world" empire, it had already begun its imperializing practices. This notion of imperialization provides a starting point for sociological investigation, which can produce a description of the social process that together make up the imperialization. But the interpreter working with sociological analysis must exercise due caution, for sociology is not a unified discipline. Some forms of sociology, especially theories connected to the writings of Marx, prove very congenial to postcolonial theorists; in fact, much postcolonial theory to date is visibly indebted to Marxist sociology. On the other hand, other sociologies are less directly helpful. The range of functionalist and anthropological approaches may be quite useful in the *description* of a colonial situation's social relations, but their frequent desire to be "value neutral" belies a deep commitment to social stability. These functionalist paradigms are still worth postcolonialists' consideration, but only insofar as interpreters are aware of the methods' ideological investments.

Social theorists have described imperialism as a social process involving the asymmetrical distribution of resources and power to create a centralized imperial core and a number of peripheral colonies that serve to support and finance the imperial power and expansion. Functionalist sociological discourse defines an empire as a large-scale social unit that extracts resources (including labor) from other social units, the colonies. Thus, an empire must always be in relationship with one or more colonies. An empire is not a static social unit, or a category that a social unit attains once it reaches a certain size and power as compared to its neighbors, or once its military defeats another empire. In this sense, it is more correct (or at least more advantageous) to discuss the process of imperialization than the social unit of the empire, since the empire exists only insofar as it *continues* to extract resources.

Empires construct multiple modes of extraction. Conquest is a straightforward example of resource extraction. When an empire defeats the people of a region and takes a bounty of food, products, or humans, it performs an essential task of imperialization. But within the larger context of modes of extraction, conquest is a relatively clumsy affair. Military solutions are notoriously expensive. The expansion of an area shrinks the proportion of the area that is on the periphery; thus the empire's force becomes spread over a greater area and does not increase fast enough to cover the expanded area. Logistically, larger empires have greater problems with funding the movement, feeding, and provisioning of ever-larger armies. A further problem is that empires often conquer wealthier areas first, and so further expansion by conquest is a matter of diminishing returns (especially in proportion to the imperial wealth). Worse yet, large-scale military endeavors tend to decrease the labor supply available for other economically productive activities, and so empires must consider conquest to be an inefficient mode of extraction, especially over time as the geographic size of the empire grows.

Empires must therefore turn to other sources of extraction. Methods such as taxation are slower and more subtle than conquest, but no less imperialistic. In this environment, the empire creates colonies, that is, defined social units administered by the empire and given the specific task of sending money, goods, and/or services to the imperial core. Different forms of colonialism may be distinguished based on the rate of extraction and the ability of the colony to maintain that level of pay-out. The empire may extract a high amount, leading to a decreasing colonial ability to survive. Alternately, the empire may extract little, allowing the colony some modicum of self-control as well as sufficient resources to attain partial autonomy and to grow; the empire then gains over a long span of time as a result of the increased resources within the colony that the empire can extract. The empire may use its army along with other more bureaucratic measures to intensify local production in order to increase extraction. In these and many other ways, as well as in differing combinations of these modes over time and across geography, imperialization means the empire's removal of resources from colonies.

The Persian Empire monopolized the physical resources of a large geographic area over more than two centuries. As such, it was a highly successful empire that extracted a great deal of wealth and resources from its colonies through a variety of strategies. After its first half-century, it experienced only small and temporary success at conquest, and so it relied on other modes of extraction. Darius, the third emperor, reigned from 522 to 486 BCE, and in his time the empire made important shifts from conquest extraction to other forms more suited to long-term imperialization. Although

Darius participated in military endeavors, he is remembered more for his innovations in social organization and legal administration.

Darius's involvement with Yehud included the appointment of governors, some of whose names the Hebrew Bible has preserved. During this time, the empire funded the construction of a temple in Jerusalem to function not only as a religious site but also as a political administrative site and perhaps even as a storehouse for goods to be delivered to the empire. Darius invested resources in Yehud in order to maintain Yehud as a colony for long-term extraction, not only for short-term imperial benefit. Thus, the effects of imperialization and colonization occur not only on the materialist, infrastructural, economic level; there are also important effects in social structure and in the ideological superstructure of the society. Yehud was organized as a colony, experiencing a certain level of independence but still subject to strict imperial controls. The goal of the colonial administration was to maintain the imperial extraction and to reproduce the conditions of imperialization. In other words, the local governor and his administration not only had to pay taxes and tribute to Persia on a set schedule, but they also had to control the Yehudites and their ideology so that they saw the benefit of remaining loyal colonials of the Persian Empire. I have argued elsewhere about the specific conditions that this imperialization produced within Yehud (1995a, 1995c).

One must see the ideological production of Yehud within this context. Although I wish to maintain the social and materialist definition of imperialization as a process of resource extraction, it is vital to recognize the ideological ramifications of such a system. This is the move that functionalist sociology fails to make. Christopher Hampton describes ideology, from a Marxist standpoint, as "a justifying veil for the repressive process by which the system enforces the submission of majorities into acquiescence and conformity with minority will" (Hampton: 3; cp. Miller: 63). In a colonial setting, this refers to the ideology expressed by the imperialists and other Persian agents while they were in the midst of and outnumbered by the natives whose society was being made into a colony. Persia constituted Yehud as a colony; that is, as a social unit the extraction of resources from which the empire wished to maintain over multiple generations. Keeping Yehud as a functioning colony required, in a sense, its continual recolonization. With each new birth, the empire gained a new worker if and only if the colony, on the empire's behalf, socialized the youngster into a colonial. This process required a complex set of social institutions to maintain and reinforce the ideology of colonialism through measures of "domination, accommodation and resistance" (Hodge: 203; cp. Gledhill: 70–71; Memmi: 91).

Persia's imperial activity involved a variety of ideologically colonizing features. At a minimum, a list of Persian strategies should include the common language of Imperial Aramaic (Memmi: 106–7), the construction of provincial bureaucracies, the appointment of Persians to roles within colonial governmental structures, military control of vast regions, taxation and other redistribution of resources, conscription of various persons into imperial service (whether at local levels or within the imperial core), and the ideologies of race and ethnicity within the empire (Sowell: 373). Social processes and ideologies merged to produce the phenomenon of overdetermination, by which the empire provides multiple causations for each effect on the colonized society (Ricoeur). Part of the (re)production of the colony involved Persia's imperial creation and imposition of official documents, legal and otherwise. In this context, it is not surprising that the Emperor Darius was remembered as a law-giver. During his administration, the empire encouraged and required its provinces and colonies to develop written documents that explained each colony's past history and current legal traditions, along with cultic practices. In each region, this was proclaimed as the King's Law—the emperor's own statement of imperial goals in each social unit's own language and custom (Berquist, 1995a:110–12; Dandamaev and Lukonin: 116–18). The imperial administration in Darius's time appears uninterested in standardizing worship throughout the empire, or introducing a single language or coinage system, or adjusting colonial customs to match imperial dress or pottery. Instead, Darius allowed each colony to establish its own legal system, its own history, and its own traditions. Of course, these documents were required to pass imperial review, at least. One could reason a high probability that the documents were written with the assistance of imperial scribes.

Imperial Uses of Ideology

Darius's imperial administration did the same in Yehud as in other regions of the empire; that is, the empire published documents in Yehud, containing laws and narrative material, known as the King's Law, consisting of previous local traditions, with an unknown amount of imperial censorship, editing, or fabrication. Current evidence leaves this assertion both unprovable and unfalsifiable, but it would parallel the empire's known activity in other areas. A Persian publication of Yehudite traditions in written form, whether during Darius's rule or a subsequent time with the same imperial conditions, would be consistent with several other historical realities: the reference to the King's Law in extant Hebrew Bible texts (Ezra 7:26), the emphasis on public proclamation of the law (Deut 4:44–5:1; Josh 24:1–28; Neh 8:1–18), and the use of Aramaic similar to the imperial language in some texts (Gen 31:47; Jer 10:11; Dan 2:4–7:28; and Ezra 4:8–68, 7:12–16), as well as the perhaps too obvious reality of the existence of a large body of literature from the Yehudite community and its successors. The literature now extant must have derived from some time during the Persian or Hellenistic periods

(Davies: 94–133). If there was a large amount of literature available before 539 BCE, it probably was not complete at that point and thus would undergo at least one major redaction, which may well have been in this middle period of the Persian Empire. On the other hand, there are parts of the current canon that postdate the Maccabean era. The identification of these passages as Maccabean or later in date requires the supposition that the surrounding material was unlike it, and therefore earlier. In any case, it is difficult to imagine the entire composition of the Hebrew Bible in Hebrew and Aramaic at a time during or later than the second or first centuries BCE, when the use of Greek had become widespread in the Jewish communities. It is thus more reasonable to think of any Maccabean materials as additions to a previously recognized body of literature.

Such a body of literature would consist of narrative material explaining the roots of the Yehudite community and justifying its status as a colony, as well as legal material that explained how the community should function. Albert Memmi notes that imperialists construct an image of the colonized, and they use this image as justification for their own colonizing activity. "More surprising, more harmful perhaps, is the echo that [this image] excites in the colonized himself. Constantly confronted with this image of himself, set forth and imposed on all institutions and in every human contact, how could the colonized help reacting to his portrait?" (87). This is only a hint about what such a fifth-century canon (or pre-canon) would include, but it is interesting that such a description would rule out hardly anything in the current canon, and that a body of literature corresponding to the Primary History (Genesis–2 Kings) and including the Latter Prophets (Isaiah–Malachi) could function quite well as imperial ideology in the Persian period.

The dating of all texts from the Hebrew Bible is under debate, but the date of first composition is not the issue at present. If there was material considered to be canonical in monarchic or exilic times, this literature continued its transmission through the Persian period and might have been the core of the imperially propagated canon. Whether the empire fabricated texts or slavishly followed older traditions, the fact of their publication and official imperial status remains unchanged. Certainly the Persian Empire did not publish the Hebrew Bible in its current form; there were texts added later. The question of what material was available in the fifth century BCE and what was a later addition is not at stake here. Even if none of the canonical literature existed in the fifth century and was entirely the production of, for instance, Hellenistic historians, the cultural milieu of Hellenization would present a number of social forces quite parallel to the Persian ideology of imperialization.

What would be the function and characteristics of the Persian imperial promulgation of some early canon for Yehud? First of all, this canon would not have been religiously motivated. It was a politically constructed document for the purposes of advancing an imperializing ideology. But that does not mean that it was anti-religious, or even neutral. The connection with family rituals and religion as a function of priests more than kings reflects the colonizing attitudes of the empire (Memmi: 100). In fact, the construction of religion may well have been one of the chief functions of the imperialist canon. Memmi notes:

> With its institutional network, its collective and periodic holidays, religion constitutes another refuge value, both for the individual and for the group. For the individual, it is one of the rare paths of retreat; for the group, it is one of the rare manifestations which can protect its original existence. Since colonized society does not possess national structures and cannot conceive of a historical future for itself, it must be content with the passive sluggishness of the present. (Memmi: 101)

The ideology of the empire must have depended for some of its authority upon a base within the previously existing beliefs of the populace. The canon was, after all, the story of Yehud's history as Israel, not the story of Persian domination. It was not a canon to replace a history or to displace an established religion by establishing a new one. The canon gave expression to the understandings already present while at the same time modifying those understandings. The new literary context could accomplish much of this modification. The Persian-appointed governors and scribes produced the document and pronounced it from the midst of the imperially-funded temple. That act in itself blurred many of the distinctions between old and new, between religion and politics. To believe in this past was to know why Israel did not have its own king, and why it was right to worship at the Jerusalem temple, the proceeds from which supported the Persian Empire. The imposition of canon occurred within a wider context of social and cultural change as the empire intruded to extract; canon is thus contemporaneous with a moment of economic and political force and violence.

Furthermore, the nascent canon had to involve familiar aspects. The populace had to grant authority to the canon in order for its ideology to be effective; it is difficult to imagine an effective and accepted canon that was an entire fabrication, altogether new, to the inhabitants of Yehud, both immigrants and natives. The canon connects the great tradition and the local tradition (Wolf). The empire was constructing a great tradition, in which subject peoples had lost legitimate claim upon their lands and yet still had a vital legal tradition to cast them as law-abiding citizens of the new empire. At the same time, Yehud had local traditions of various ages, which were woven together in such a way as to emphasize the importance of keeping the law and recognizing the imperial rationale for the loss of the land.

A canon itself speaks to these very issues. By its nature, a canon—even one that is preliminary by our later standards of the "full" canon—creates a set of limits and boundaries. Canons obscure other literature through their constant and already self-falsifying claim to be the only text. A canon is a space defined from outside (*d'hors-texte, à la* Derrida) by the canonizers (Blanchot). As written word, it is a fixed and limited space; it is a ruly space, ruled from within by the logic of its own organization and ruled from without by the power that constitutes the literature as a published piece.

Canon may attempt to delineate itself as text, but in the act of doing so it fails; it is a text of self-contradictory assertion. Although it strives to be determinate, fixed, foundational, and stable, its existence as text denies this; the canonical text is a result of power and cannot exist without the continual application of that power. Even as is the case with any text, its act of constituting itself begins its process of self-destabilizing. Yet it continues to claim its univocality by its status as "a" text. The reference to this literature as the King's Law thus summarizes and presents both of these aspects; canon is a function of imperial power and is inherently orderly (at the same time that it is internally incoherent, because it is *text*). In a sense, Persia colonized the prior traditions of the Yehudites, making them controllable and exploitable. Persia claimed itself as the unwritten subject of the texts, infusing a new metanarrative into the text and turning the texts themselves into objects, written items that could be used and enforced (Blanchot: 202).

This canon contained legal materials. For the Yehudite community, these laws stated basic principles of social organization, such as the Decalogue, the incest and food laws, and the hierarchical arrangement of society under legitimate kings. In addition, the law states the conditions under which the earlier Israelites would lose their land, and the narrative materials in the Primary History document the fulfillment of these conditions and the subsequent removal of Judah's elites from the land. Robert Hodge points out the social connectedness of such narrative trajectories: "From this follows a basic premise for the social analysis of narrative: the social categories that organize the levels of narrative must first be understood in relation to the dominant categories and syntagmatic forms of social life, as these operate through the semiosic context of specific narratives" (175). If this nascent canon operated as Persian imperial ideology, the implications are clear. Israel and Judah lost their land by their own deeds, their own God removed them from the land and placed them under care of another, and now the other (about whom the historical texts are silent) rightfully rules. The prophets are even clearer about this ideological assertion that the Yehudites deserve their loss of land, even though a "remnant" will attain a modicum of control and power. Especially in texts such as Deutero-Isaiah, the Persian imperializing ideology is unmistakable: Cyrus is the messiah, the anointed one with God-given authority to rule over Yehud (Isa 44:24–45:8). This theological justification for political reality depicts Yehud as colony. The texts legitimate, authorize, and perpetuate the ideology of the colonized.

Refocusing Postcolonialism

The above analysis of the role of ideology and textual formation in imperial domination has been informed by sociology, but has not yet moved far beyond a functionalist paradigm. By failing to consider the values of imperialism, colonization, and oppression involved, this functionalist sociological perspective has obscured much. What, then, can postcolonialist theory add to this discussion? Or better, how does postcolonialism refocus the lens of interpretation to make new (in)sights visible? The variety of theories sharing the moniker of postcolonialism only complicates these questions, but the newness and fecundity of postcolonial theories argues for the embracing of a certain eclecticism. Postcolonialism can sharpen the analysis of Yehud's colonial situation in at least three ways: it can help to show the ways in which the empire dominates, it can help to show the colonizing functions of colonial life, and it can add an ideological emphasis that functionalist sociology misses.

First, postcolonialism emphasizes the imperial modes of domination. By casting light upon the colonizer-colonized relationship, it illuminates certain features of the colony. Postcolonial studies remove the supposed neutrality in which some functionalist sociology wraps itself. Within the postcolonial frame, one cannot consider Persia to be just an example of a large bureaucratic empire, analyzable as an isolated unit, nor can the interpreter take a simply functionalist sociological view of the imperialism's transfer of goods and resources. "Neither imperialism nor colonialism is a simple act of accumulation and acquisition. Both are supported and perhaps even impelled by impressive ideological formations that include notions that certain territories and people *require* and beseech domination, as well as forms of knowledge affiliated with domination" (Said: 9). One must constantly focus on the Persian Empire's modes of extraction; the colonies will be central to this analysis, as will be the colonizing ideologies employed by the empire and its servants. Functionalist and Marxist sociologies alike may focus too much on the activity within a single economic generation, but postcolonialism must always focus on the ways in which the populace becomes the colonized, to reproduce the economic relationships of extraction and oppression over multiple generations. "Ideology creates the type of subjects suitable to be 'supports' of social relations and inserts people into places predefined by the structures of social formation" (Miller, Rowland, and Tilley: 9).

Likewise, one cannot simply concentrate on "postexilic Judah" or some similar category; the colonial experience will be crucial to everything that occurs within Yehud. This flies in the face of much biblical scholarship that has tried to explain postexilic religion only in terms of Judean experience, without recognizing the massive economic, military, social, and ideological forces brought to bear on every aspect of Yehudite life (Berquist, 1995a:3–12).

This is postcolonialism's second great advance, and if taken seriously it would have an enormous impact upon Second Temple studies. The very titling of the period in terms of the "Second Temple" appears remarkably naive and obscurantist from this perspective, another example of the supposed neutrality of standard scholarship that results in missing the point of the object of study. The "Second Temple" terminology can lead interpreters to think that Judah controlled at least its religious development. A phrase such as "colonial Yehud" reflects a situation in which the people of the colony could not even name themselves without the name passing through the imperial filters.

Third, postcolonialist theory consistently concentrates on the conflicts that occur within the ideological space of the colony. Colonies are continually contested sites in every sense. Although sociology at its best provides as much attention to ideology as to economic and social realities, most sociological study has fallen short in this regard, and postcolonialism is a welcome addition. No longer can one speak of a textual ideology that is stable, for they are all already contested.

As an example of the ways that postcolonial discourse can improve the analysis of Yehud, consider the notion of empire as teacher. Jerry Phillips has examined the tendency of imperial cultures to understand their relationship to their colonized populations as a mode of instruction. In other words, the empire seeks to educate the "barbaric" colonies in order to "civilize" them.

> In its classic formulation the moment of imperialism is also the moment of education. Imperialism—a system of economic, political, and cultural force that disavows borders in order to extract desirable resources and exploit an alien people—has never strayed far from a field of pedagogical imperatives, or what might be called an ideology of instruction. (Phillips: 26)

Part of this instructional ideology is the assertion that there is a standard of education (Phillips: 34). This assumes that culture—defined as what the imperial core has that the colonial periphery lacks—is a script, a definable something, often a narrative (or a meta-narrative). One can see the Persian imperialist narrative (the "great tradition"), written upon the mountains for all to see, in the Behistun inscription. Depicting that the representatives of each colony approach Darius bowed, this carving shows the narrative in pictorial form. The inscription also offers the narrative in writing for those wishing the details (Kent: 107–8, 116–134).

Within the context of this concept of imperial education, Darius's creation of local canons comes even more sharply into focus. The colonies were not able to rule themselves; the local narratives prove that themselves, or at least they do within the redaction that the empire provides. Instead, the colonies require the civilization of the empire for their own protection. Perhaps this explains some of the fascination with Egypt within the canonical texts, since Egypt was Persia's chief rival on its western borders for the early part of the Persian Empire. Yehud thus is taught to fix its gaze upon Egypt, the great oppressor who remains a constant threat, morally if not militarily. By gazing upon Egypt with animosity, the text refocuses Yehudite social vision and obscures the domination that Persia plays in the present.

But the education of Yehud goes further. Yehud learns that it is inadequate by itself, that it needs its God's protection, and that God has given them into Persia's hand for protection. Persia teaches that God acts through Persian authority, since the Persian emperors are anointed by God for this purpose. God even demands in the law that tithes and offerings be given to the temple built and staffed by the empire. These are things that the Yehudites would not have known by themselves. The empire must educate them into being colonial citizens.

Many traditions of social thought (including functionalism and, in many ways, the Frankfurt school of critical social theory) understand states as rational systems, in which the ruled participate in their subjugation because they believe that the rulers are justified in their hegemony. The effects of ideology are much deeper. The colonized may be unaware of other social systems, or they may believe themselves to be in need of external social control, or they may be disinterested in taking charge of their own political lives. In any of these cases, the imperial-colonial pattern continues because the colonized do not rebel, and the lack of rebellion results from the imperial social and ideological practices that reproduce the imperialist system. The ideological components of this imperial reproduction tell individuals what exists, what is possible, what is right, and what is wrong (Therborn: 172).

These Marxist treatments of ideology have the value of connecting textual meaning with the social and historical forces of production. Nonetheless, postmodern sensibilities illuminate a problem within this definition of ideology. The existence of a false consciousness assumes the reality of a "true" consciousness; that is, a system of thinking that actually represents reality. Although ideology is a difficult concept to define, and perhaps an impossible one to discuss with immunity from critique, a working definition is necessary. I will use the term "ideology" to refer to patterned human discourse that privileges those persons in power who initiate that discourse. I understand this as closely related to Spivak's treatment:

> At its broadest implications this notion of ideology would undo the oppositions between determinism and free will and between conscious choice and unconscious reflex. Ideology in action is what a group takes to be natural and self-evident, that of which the group, as a group, must deny any historical sedimentation. It is both the condition and the effect of the constitution of the subject (of ideology) as freely willing and consciously choosing in a world that is seen as background. In turn, the subject(s) of ideology are the conditions and effects of the self-identity of the group as a group. It is

impossible, of course, to mark off a group as an entity without sharing complicity with its ideological definition. (Spivak: 118)

Canonical scripture can play a highly significant role in the ideology of imperialism, since religion and scripture also communicate the norms, values, and basic assumptions of a society's ruling class. This ideology inspires something beyond profit and extraction. According to Said, it involves "a commitment in constant circulation and recirculation, which, on the one hand, allowed decent men and women to accept the notion that distant territories and their native peoples *should* be subjugated, and, on the other, replenished metropolitan energies so that these decent people could think of the *imperium* as a protracted, almost metaphysical obligation to rule subordinate, inferior, or less advanced peoples" (Said: 10). In the case of Yehud, the Persian Empire's investment in such ideology is clear: the empire would benefit most from an ideology that emphasizes Yehud's inability to govern itself, to rebel against the imperial power, to expand itself beyond its current borders, or to ally itself effectively with other powers.

These insights are the results of a sociologically-informed postcolonial analysis. Such an analysis uses the descriptive powers of functionalism, the comparative value of anthropology (especially social and political anthropologies), the economic explanatory capability of (cultural) materialism, and the ideological insights of Marxism. In this way, postcolonialism combines these different sociological formulations in the service of understanding the empire in order to oppose it.

Implications of (Post)Colonialism

But doesn't postcolonialism add something even more than this? I believe that there is a greater value in postcolonial theory than those to which I have so far alluded, but it requires taking a step back to view the enterprise in a wider context. The goal of postcolonial study, in this perspective, is to create interpretations that illuminate the colonial and colonizing tendencies of the text's production and subsequent interpretations, while at the same time to suggest contemporary interpretations that have an effect of decolonizing the present world (including the world of biblical scholarship) (Spivak: 205). Gordon Collier describes this work as an ideological (mis)representation of the history, recognizing that there is no point of immaculate perception from which one's views can be objective. "So long as postcolonial analysts remain aware of the fact that they themselves are engaged in fruitful processes of mistranslations, mistranscription and misidentification not dissimilar to those they would expose, then the project's health will be safeguarded by its own antibodies" (Collier: xv). The point of postcolonialism, then, is not to achieve a new objectivity but to infuse the scholarly discourse with a new subjectivity, following a set of values that measure the new enterprise as "fruitful" rather than as imperializing. This understanding of postcolonialist discourse aligns it more closely with ideological criticism than with sociology.

With this concept of postcolonial study, the interpreter begins to search for canonical texts that can be used against the imperializing ideologies of the canon. Since the postcolonialist attitude is located in the interpreter rather than within the text itself (since texts do not have ideologies), this search is fruitful. As an example, I would point to texts in Third Isaiah such as Isaiah 66:1–5, a passage from the Persian imperial period where the interpreter can hear claims of God's displeasure with the temple and its supporters (Berquist, 1995b). Here God speaks (Hear God speak) against the interests of the imperial administration, repulsing them with vile epithets and accusations of evil. Also familiar are texts such as 1 Samuel 8 that argue against the rule of the king by showing that the hierarchies associated with royal or imperial rule will be costly and detrimental to the people.

Of course, the interpreter must be very careful in dealing with such texts from a postcolonial vantage, because it is difficult to hear the words of the colonized in texts subsumed by the colonists. Gareth Griffiths offers an important warning:

> Even when the subaltern appears to "speak" there is a real concern as to whether what we are listening to is really a subaltern voice, or whether the subaltern is being spoken by the subject position they occupy within the larger discursive economy. . . . In inscribing such acts of resistance the deep fear for the liberal critic is contained in the worry that in the representation of such moments, what is inscribed is not the subaltern's voice but the voice of one's own other. (75)

At the same time, the postcolonial interpreter can also break the bonds of the canon from outside, tracing the lines of power that formed the canon through exclusion, in order to find the texts outside the canon (Spivak: 118–33). Insofar as the canon insists that it is "the" text, the very presence of noncanonical texts begins to unravel the power systems of the canon and its colonizing. Said describes this as an act of postcolonial reading: "As we look back at the cultural archive, we begin to reread it not univocally but *contrapuntally*, with a simultaneous awareness both of the metropolitan history that is narrated and of those other histories against which (and together with which) the dominating discourse acts" (51). With texts such as these in hand, the interpreter can begin to break open the canon and its imperializing ideology from both within and without the canon itself.

> In the "post-colonial" moment, these transverse, transnational, transcultural movements, which were always inscribed in the history of "colonisation," but carefully overwritten by more binary forms of narrativisation, have, of

course, emerged in new forms to disrupt the settled relations of domination and resistance inscribed in other ways of living and telling these stories. (S. Hall: 251)

Postcolonial theory can gain here from postmodernist textual strategies. In a deconstructionist vein, the interpreter proceeds to the heart of the text and finds its inherent brokenness, a brokenheartedness and a heartfelt resistance familiar to postcolonial theorists. The canonical text is not a unified whole; it is not a body of literature at all. Instead, it is an assemblage held together only by the imperialist power that first created it. Although it is targeted against the colonies with an intention to subdue, this can(n)on cannot fire; it is powerless to conquer because of the weakness of its seams resulting from its mode of creation.

To say that the canon is held together only by imperialist power means several things. First, the historical circumstances of the canon's creation occurred only because of a historical empire used the canon as part of its ideology of imperialist instruction. Perhaps more importantly for the field of biblical studies, the canon can maintain the impression of a unified whole with a single ideology (or a center, or a single "biblical" or "canonical" theology) *only* by the continuing application of powerful imperializing ideologies. In order for canonical unity to remain, the interpreter must perceive that the canon has "a subject" which then organizes canonical meaning/theology/ideology around itself. The subject of the canon displaces the actual canon. In a sense, if canon has a subject, then it makes the rest of the canon into objects, mere evidence and example of the subject. To state this in postcolonial language: the continuance of the canon requires that contemporary canonical imperialists must impose their own metanarrative upon the canon in such a way that the canon becomes colony, a unit that exists only to be extracted and exploited for the imperialist's benefit. Canon is a function and expression of power, specifically imperial power. The imperial subject of the canon objectifies and colonizes.

I would consider these statements to be offensive accusations of many biblical scholars and their work, if I was able to imagine any of us approaching the text without this imperializing approach, if any of us were void of metanarratives. I realize that I myself am constructing a metanarrative in competition with other imperializing ones, and at that level this interpretation of canon is no different than the imperialists with whose interpretations I disagree. As I have insisted already, the Persian Empire created a canon out of earlier traditions, shaping it in order to fit their own imperialist ideology. Thus the canon was part of the creation of Yehud's colonial identity. The canon bounded the community, but the canon was not a coherent and consistent explication of imperialist desire, for at least two reasons. First, the canon was created as a patchwork of texts, held together by explicit ideological force. Even though the Persian redaction was done so that we can no longer reconstruct "sources" or prove definitively the words of imperial editing, the canon still represents and contains a variety of viewpoints, languages, geographies, classes, and ideologies. Thus it cannot be considered complete, coherent, or consistent. The second reason that this must be so is more abstract: the impossibility of creating systems (including texts and ideologies) that are both complete and coherent, as shown variously by Gödel and Derrida. The nature of language and even thought is such that complete coherence is impossible. So the canon—no matter what texts it contained in its first or any subsequent formulation—had gaps and differences, just as its producers' society did. In Said's words, "no vision, any more than any social system, has total hegemony over its domain" (186). The canon is a bricolage that presented and presents multiple views and ideologies.

The postcolonial interpreter faces this bricolage with sensitivity to the ideological use of these different texts. First the interpreter must transcend the contemporary imperializing ideologies to allow the text to deconstruct, but then the interpreter is faced with the variety of voices within the text. Again, postcolonialism provides a space in which to choose voices to construct interpretations that may have decolonizing effects in the contemporary world.

But what does this say about the text? It implies the insight already gained that imperialization had created a bifurcated social world that in turn created a fragmented text. The next interpretive step is to imagine the conflicting ancient worlds of the colonizer and the colonized that in/form the text of the canon. Here sociology once more enters into the interpretive fray, offering to describe these conflicting worlds and specifically the social mechanisms that reproduce the difference between the empire and the colony.

Who constructed the canonical texts in colonial Yehud? The empire funded the writing of a self-justifying ideological metanarrative that overlays and attempts to organize the canon. At the same time, the colonials had a repertoire of laws, stories, themes, customs, and genres that were the required raw materials for much of the canon. Therefore, asking whether the empire or the colony had the greater impact on the canon and its ideology is not a helpful question. Those who wrote the texts occupied a peculiar social location, partaking of the worldviews of colonizer and colonized at the same time. They were the scribes and the officials of Yehud, a class created and supported by the imperial powers and yet involved on a daily basis with the specificity of life in the colony Yehud. They received power from the empire and exercised power over the colony, but at the same time these administrators and scribes received their resources from the people of Yehud and controlled the flow of resources toward the Persian Empire (Berquist, 1995a; Davies). They were a ruling class within the colony, situated along the chasm between colonized and colonizer.

Postcolonial study must be informed by a careful class analysis if it is to succeed at its academic task of describing the effects of colonization or its ethical goal of decolonization in today's world. Even though postcolonial discourse rightly depicts the differences between the colonizer and the colonized as vast, the network of power relations cannot be reduced to such a simple dichotomy. One of the effects of colonization is a splitting of the colonized's population. In Eisenstadt's analysis, the existence of imperial power creates opportunities for the development of a local elite of collaborators and other administrators, just as the existence of colonial resources creates the opportunity for imperial extraction of those resources. Once the colony begins to feel the imperial power used to extract resources, a local elite begins to stratify the colonial social structure in new ways.

This local elite occupies a strange space within the colonial social world. In part, they are the colonized, but they are also active in the process of colonization and the reproduction of imperial/colonial ideology. Within the colony, they are the highest ranking local officials; within the empire, they are the lowest bureaucrats possible. Their position grows not only from the local resources but from the application of imperial power into the colony. The local official serving the empire often experiences the grudging and provisional acceptance of the imperial because "moving up" is, in some ways, the rhetorical goal for all colonials under imperial tutelage (Phillips). Said describes this position of ideological production:

> Moreover, the various struggles for dominance among states, nationalisms, ethnic groups, regions, and cultural entities have conducted and amplified a manipulation of opinion and discourse, a production and consumption of ideological media representations, a simplification and reduction of vast complexities into easy currency, the easier to deploy and exploit them in the interest of state policies. In all of this intellectuals have played an important role, nowhere in my opinion more crucial *and* more compromised than in the overlapping region of experience and culture that is colonialism's legacy where the politics of secular interpretation is carried on for high stakes. (36)

The effects of an empire upon a colony are much the same as the effects of any state upon its localities. To assume otherwise is to construct categories of benign state power *vs.* intrusive imperial power; that is, to privilege the state as a non-oppressive, non-coercive form of political and economic power. States and empires alike rule through the control of local resources, modes of production, and cultural modes of reproduction. In Göran Therborn's words, the exercise of state power is "a process of interventions in a given society effected by a separate institution which concentrates the supreme rule-making, rule-applying, rule-adjudicating, rule-enforcing, and rule-defending functions of that society" (144–45). In the colony of Yehud during the Persian period, this institution of state power was the Persian imperial administration. These statist interventions reproduce not only the social forces of production and the character of the state apparatus, but also the ideological superstructure that justifies the social system. Thus we can expect the Persian Empire to create ideologies that tend to reproduce the empire and to maintain the power of the ruling class. These ideologies are not a separate feature of society, somehow isolated from daily functioning; the imperialist ideology infuses itself throughout the various rules, norms, customs, and habits of the society (Gledhill: 76–78). The mode of reproduction for this ideology runs through the hands of the colonial administrators who formed the canon as an ideological device for perpetuating their privileged place within Yehudite culture and within the Persian Empire. These persons maintain a delicate balance being situated in the non-space between empire and colony. As Memmi vividly expresses the problem, "a man straddling two cultures is rarely well seated, and the colonized does not always find the right pose" (124).

There are further ambiguities imposed upon this social group of colonial administrators and canonizers. Their literary activities subject them to forces barely understood. In the midst of a social context in which they strive to find themselves a place of their own, their literature constructs the social bifurcation of the empire and belies the existence of themselves as authors. Perhaps no one speaks of this loss-of-self in the (non)space of writing as clearly as Maurice Blanchot:

> When to write is to discover the interminable, the writer who enters this region does not leave himself behind in order to approach the universal. He does not move toward a surer world, a finer or better justified world where everything would be ordered according to the clarity of the impartial light of day. He does not discover the admirable language which speaks honorably for all. What speaks in him is the fact that, in one way or another, he is no longer himself; he isn't anyone any more. (28)

This further expands the vastness of ambiguity for the canon and for its ideological creators and patrons. The canon can never be a truly Persian text; it never becomes a truly imperial artifact. Yet at the same time it is not equivalent to the colony; it does not speak the local vision as the locals would themselves voice it. The canon is part of a mediation between colonizer and colonized, but it is a troubled mediation, not a smooth dialectic synthesis. In the final analysis, the canon does not "possess" an ideology. Even though the canon was and still remains a construct of imperial ideological discourse, the canon is neither colonizing not decolonizing in any essentialist, ontological sense. Human systems of ideological thought cannot inscribe themselves that successfully. Instead of being a paradigm of colonization, the canon can only be seen as a site of contest and conflict. Conflict was present in the original inscription of the canon. Of course, this conflict is not only a function of the contemporary ideological pressures to be colonizing and/or decolonizing.

Is the Canon Postcolonial?

The canon is an example of postcolonial literature, despite its origins within a colony. At one level, we can affirm that the canon is always already postcolonial if interpreters treat it as such, and develop a decolonizing ideology from or with its texts. A historical argument arises at this point. The text itself was created as a bricolage of texts with immediately conflicting views. It was and is a diverse and pluralistic entity that exists in the spaces where the empire withdraws just enough to allow other voices, even if they are voices with imperial overtones. Persia never required the colonies to construct canons in the imperial language; the local vernacular was the right language for this canonical discourse. As the empire tried to bifurcate society, it failed, creating colonial governments as a wedge group between the colonized and the colonizer. Thus the fictions of an absolute empire begin to fall away within the text created by the one group that defies the splitting attempted by the empire.

Of course, to understand the canon as a postcolonial literature must first entail abandoning the absolutizing assertions about the developing canon. No longer can we assert that Judah's religious devotion was the ultimate force within the society; scholars must consciously move beyond notions of theocracy for the postexilic period. It was not the case historically, and the continued insistence on theocracy merely reaffirms the imperializing forces of the interpretive ideology. There was no one concept of God that emerged victorious to control the canon; the canon itself defies all attempts at control, even the attempts that brought the canon into being. Likewise, the fiction of a postexilic restoration must be rejected; there never was a single idea of the days before exile and there not a single or dominant concept of how Yehud should organize its own social existence after the exile. No one who went into exile "returned," although some of their children and grandchildren moved to Yehud as colonists. These colonists were not following some master plan that they developed as devout followers of the Yehudite God while in exile; there was no master plan, only a colonizing impulse that took many of the same forms as Persian imperialism did in other neighboring areas.

From a postcolonialist perspective, interpretation is not (only) a technical exercise, but a moral act of commitment. The commitments themselves, however, can shape the historical and sociological insights into the reality of Yehud, and can provide more adequate images for how Yehud operated as a colony. At the same time, I desire to resist the notions of postcolonial study that replicate old oppositions and dichotomies simply by revising or reversing them, since there is a danger within postcolonialist theory to embrace an idealism that serves as a thin mask for further imperialization. For a while, these oppositions may be necessary, but the interpreter must move beyond them.

> Reading (and writing) "against the grain" implies that there *is* a grain to work against. This entails the problem of counterdiscourse, which preserves a binary opposition and perpetuates the privileging of one of the poles even as it seeks to complicate and dismantle the basis for discriminatory contrast. (Sharrad: 201)

In other words, the old image of Judah the purified theocracy *vs.* the political powers of the contemporaneous world should not be replaced by either Yehud the colonized *vs.* the imperializing, colonizing behemoth of Persia, nor by Yehud, the sneaky colony of subversion *vs.* the monolithic culture of Persia. The insights of postcolonial study of colonial Yehud should be much more complex than such facile dichotomies as this. As Catherine Hall writes,

> Unpacking imperial histories, grasping the raced and gendered ways in which inter-connections and inter-dependencies have been played out, developing a more differentiated notion of power than that which focuses simply on coloniser and colonised, can have emancipatory potential. It is a history which involves recognition and the re-working of memory. A history which shows how fantasised constructions of homogeneous nations are constructed and the other possibilities which are always there. A history which is about difference, not homogeneity. (76)

The postcolonial canon remains a contested, conflicted site, inscribed with multiple layers of ideologically invested interpretation. It remains a place for interpreters' ideologies to work themselves out in textual strategies and in the present world, where colonialisms and decolonizing are still at work.

Works Consulted

Berquist, Jon L.
    1995a   *Judaism in Persia's Shadow: A Social and Historical Approach*. Minneapolis: Fortress.

    1995b   "Reading Difference in Isaiah 56–66: The Interplay of Literary and Sociological Strategies." *Method and Theory in the Study of Religion* 7:23–42.

    1995c   "The Shifting Frontier: The Achaemenid Empire's Treatment of Western Colonies." *Journal of World-Systems Research* 1.17:1–25.

Blanchot, Maurice
    1982   *The Space of Literature*. Trans. Ann Smock. Lincoln, NE and London: University of Nebraska Press.

Chambers, Iain, and Lidia Curti, eds.
    1996   *The Post-Colonial Question: Common Skies, Divided Horizons*. New York: Routledge.

Collier, Gordon, ed.
    1992   *Us/Them: Translation, Transcription and Identity in Post-Colonial Literary Cultures*. Cross/Cultures: Readings in the Post/Colonial Literatures in English 6. Atlanta: Rodopi.

Collier, Gordon
    1992   "Introduction." Pp. xii–xv in Collier 1992.

Dandamaev, Muhammad A. and Vladimir G. Lukonin
    1989   *The Culture and Social Institutions of Ancient Iran*. Cambridge: Cambridge University Press.

Davies, Philip R.
    1992   *In Search of 'Ancient Israel'*. JSOTS 148. Sheffield: Sheffield Academic Press.

Eisenstadt, S. N.
    1969   *The Political Systems of Empires: The Rise and Fall of the Historical Bureaucratic Societies*. Rev. ed. New York: Free.

Gledhill, John
    1994   *Power and Its Disguises: Anthropological Perspectives on Politics*. Anthropology, Culture and Society. London and Boulder, CO: Pluto.

Griffiths, Gareth
    1994   "The Myth of Authenticity: Representation, Discourse and Social Practice." Pp. 70–85 in Tiffin and Lawson 1994.

Hall, Catherine
    1996   "Histories, Empires and the Post-Colonial Moment." Pp. 65–77 in Chambers and Curti 1996.

Hall, Stuart
    1996   "When was the 'Post-Colonial'? Thinking at the Limit." Pp. 242–60 in Chambers and Curti 1996.

Hampton, Christopher
    1990   *The Ideology of the Text*. Buckingham and Philadelphia: Open University Press.

Hodge, Robert
    1990   *Literature as Discourse: Textual Strategies in English and History*. Parallax: Re-visions of Culture and Society. Baltimore: The Johns Hopkins University Press.

Kent, Roland G.
1953   *Old Persian: Grammar, Texts, Lexicon.* 2d ed., rev. American Oriental Series 33. New Haven, CT: American Oriental Society.

Memmi, Albert
1965   *The Colonizer and the Colonized.* New York: Orion.

Miller, Daniel
1989   "The Limits of Dominance." Pp. 63–79 in Miller, Rowland, and Tilley 1989.

Miller, Daniel, Michael Rowland, and Christopher Tilley, eds.
1989   *Domination and Resistance.* One World Archaeology 3. London and New York: Routledge.

Miller, Daniel, Michael Rowland, and Christopher Tilley
1989   "Introduction." Pp. 1–26 in Miller, Rowland, and Tilley 1989.

Phillips, Jerry
1993   "Educating the Savages: Melville, Bloom, and the Rhetoric of Imperialist Instruction." Pp. 25–44 in *Recasting the World: Writing after Colonialism.* Ed. Jonathan White. Parallax: Revisions of Culture and Society. Baltimore: The Johns Hopkins University Press.

Ricoeur, Paul
1994   "Althusser's Theory of Ideology." Pp. 44–72 in *Althusser: A Critical Reader.* Ed. Gregory Elliott. Oxford: Blackwell.

Said, Edward W.
1993   *Culture and Imperialism.* New York: Vintage.

Sharrad, Paul
1994   "Speaking the Unspeakable: London, Cambridge and the Caribbean." Pp. 201–17 in Tiffin and Lawson 1994.

Sowell, Thomas
1996   *Migrations and Cultures: A World View.* New York: Basic.

Spivak, Gayatri Chakravorty
1988   *In Other Worlds: Essays in Cultural Politics.* New York: Routledge.

Therborn, Göran
1978   *What Does the Ruling Class Do When It Rules? State Apparatuses and State Power under Feudalism, Capitalism and Socialism.* London: NLB.

Tiffin, Chris, and Alan Lawson, eds.
1994   *De-Scribing Empire: Post-colonialism and Textuality.* London and New York: Routledge.

Wolf, Eric R.
1966   *Peasants.* Foundations of Modern Anthropology. Englewood Cliffs, NJ: Prentice-Hall.

READING FOR DECOLONIZATION
(JOHN 4:1–42)

Musa W. Dube
University of Botswana

ABSTRACT

Post-colonial theories highlight that imperialism is a military exercise as it is a textual project. Imperial traveling agents employ texts to subjugate foreign geographical spaces, to colonize the minds of native inhabitants, and to sanitize the conscience of the colonizing nations. This paper discusses some post-colonial investigation into empires and texts; it inquires into the role of the Bible in empire-building and the foundation of its role by reading Jn 4:1–42. The paper expounds on the imperial setting, the construction of hidden interests, travelers, geographical spaces, expansion, and the Samaritan woman/people/land in Jn 4:1–42 The reading highlights that mission texts tend to befriend imperializing ideologies by authorizing the cultural subjugation of foreign lands and people. Its conclusion presents one re-writing of the story that proposes the Samaritan identity as an ideal space for contemporary post-colonial subjects and era.

"When the white man came to our country he had the Bible and we had the land. The White man said to us, 'let us pray.' After the prayer, the white man had the land and we had the Bible."
                                                A popular African saying

Modern imperialism was so global and all-encompassing that virtually nothing escaped it; besides, as I have said, the nineteenth-century contest over empire is still continuing today. Whether or not to look at the connections between cultural texts and imperialism is therefore to take a position in fact taken—either to study the connection in order to criticize it and think of alternatives for it, or not to study it in order to let it stand....
                    Edward Said, *Culture and Imperialism*, 68

INTRODUCTION: IMPERIALISM(S), SPACE AND TEXTS

Imperialism is an ideology of expansion that takes diverse forms and methods at different times, seeking to impose its languages, its trade, its religions, its democracy, its images, its economic systems, and its political rule on foreign nations and lands.¹ The victims of imperialism become the colonized, that is, those whose lands, minds, cultures, economies, and political institutions have been taken possession of and rearranged according to the interests and values of the imperializing powers.² Imperialism is, therefore, about controlling foreign geographical spaces and their inhabitants. By its practice and its goals, imperialism is a relationship of subordination and domination between different nations and lands, which actively suppresses diversity and promotes a few universal standards for the benefit of those in power. It involves the colonized and the colonizer, the ruler and the ruled, the center and the periphery, the First World and the Two-Thirds World, relationships which define our current world; and relationships that are closely related to, although not identical to, particular physical places of the earth.

In this introduction, I briefly discuss different imperialist movements and cultural strategies of dominating foreign spaces, as well as the Bible and empire-building, before I turn to John 4. Throughout this paper, the term "imperializing texts" designates those literary works that propound values and representations that authorize expansionist tendencies grounded on unequal international/racial relations. "Decolonizing" defines awareness of imperialism's exploitative forces and its various strategies of domination, the conscious adoption of strategies for resisting imperial domination, as well as the search for alternative ways of liberating interdependence between nations, races, genders, economies, and cultures.

Imperialism is certainly an ancient institution. The Babylonian sovereign Hammurabi, for example, "gave himself the title of "King of the Four Corners of the World" to describe his profession of disavowing boundaries (Maunier: 19). The Babylonian empire had a line of successors in the Assyrian, Hellenistic, and Roman Empires. In a tradition akin to Hammurabi, Roman emperors were called "Savior(s) of the World" (Cassidy : 6–16, Koester : 666–68, Talbert : 118–19). "World" in these titles symbolizes the claim to unlimited access to foreign geographical spaces. "King" and "Savior" articulate the claims of power by certain subjects and their followers (races and nations) over unlimited geographical spaces—over the world and its inhabitants. While "King" implies dominion over space and people, which may be just or unjust, "Savior" also implies power; further it carries an imperial ideology that came to a full-fledged maturity in modern centuries, whereby the violence of imperialism was depicted as a redeeming act for the benefit of subjugated, the so-called "duty to the natives."

---

1 For different types, methods, motivations, and definitions of imperialism(s), from ancient to contemporary times, see Manuier: 133–260; Delavignette: 1–46; Said: 9–13; Snyder: 40–44; Ngungi: 1–3.

2 Mudimbe (1988:1–2) describes modern imperialism as the tendency to "organize and transform non-European areas into fundamentally European constructs" and holds that it consists of three actions: "the domination of physical space, the reformation of natives' minds, and the integration of local economic histories into the Western perspective."

In Alexander the Great we encounter a well known and ancient example of what it takes to be a king or savior of the world. His career makes it evident that military might is as central to empire building as are cultural texts. According to David Quint, Alexander drew his inspiration from the literary characters of *The Iliad* (1–18). Alexander reportedly carried *The Iliad* in his conquest journeys and "kept it under his pillow together with a dagger" (Quint: 4). Prior to his attack on Persia and Asia, he visited Troy where he "honored the memory of the heroes who were buried there, with solemn libations; especially Achilles, whose grave he anointed" (4). In so doing, Alexander was making the literary character of "Achilles at Troy a model for the conquests carried out by his armies" (Quint: 4). Here a literary text that glorifies military might and conquest legitimates and furthers imperial agendas in a different history. Conquest in empire building then becomes a strategy of becoming king or savior over the world by annihilating its inhabitants, or demonstrating a viable death threat to them.

Quint concludes that the travel and triumph of epic heroes through untold dangers, the characterization of its heroes as people immensely favored by divine powers, and the characterization of foreigners as either dangerous, evil cyclopes, or women/goddesses desperate to hold on to traveling heroes have provided imperial travelers of different centuries and empires with a language of representing every land and people until the introduction of the novel. Imperial traveling agents and heroes drew their inspiration from epic characters and plots to endure their travel tribulations, and to regard themselves as divinely favored, destined, and chosen to survive and to conquer against all odds.

Not only do certain values of cultural texts inspire imperialism, cultures of the empire are used to maintain power over the colonized. Alexander's empire building project thus entailed an elaborate program of Hellenizing his conquered subjects. Alexander "established a network of routes from Egypt to India and sprinkled cities throughout Asia to radiate Greek culture" (Roetzel: 2). He founded Greek cities at "strategic points, to serve as administrative centers but also to provide a focus as beacon of Greek culture in the alien lands of the Orient" (Stambaugh and Balch: 14). The three generals who succeeded him "encouraged solidarity of Greek culture by building cities on the old model, just as Alexander had done" (Stambaugh and Balch: 14). Even the Roman Empire pursued the program of "instilling a sense of pride in traditional Greek civilization" (Stambaugh and Balch: 17). These ancient cases indicate that a cultural program serves to tame both the physical and mental space of the colonized. They also indicate that traveling and travelers are not neutral subjects (Blunt: 15–19). Imperial travelers depart from their familiar places to unfamiliar people and lands with goals of subjugating the latter. As indicated by the titles of King and savior of unlimited spaces, the colonizing travelers construct themselves in particular fashions to validate their travel and to confront unfamiliar places and people. Physical lands and minds are thus "spaces" that are subject to remolding through cultural texts and structures, such as cities, gymnasiums, markets, and so on.

In contemporary times, Spain, Belgium, Portugal, Russia, Germany, France, and Britain established empires of unparalleled magnitude, leaving little or no part of the earth untouched. Modern empires took different forms and methods from the ancient empires. Their unique strategies assumed the sophistication of disguising military might and economic greed under the guise of evangelical zeal, moral-rhetorical claims, and technological, racial, and cultural claims of superiority. Modern empires also differed according to each colonizing country as well as according to the particular culture and geographical area of the colonized. Temperatures that were similar or hospitable to the colonizing countries, for example, were much more likely to result in settler colonialism, while areas with non-hospitable temperatures were likely to be ruled indirectly. The struggle for independence has ever since been waged and won by what largely constitutes the Two-Thirds World countries. Many of the formerly colonized nations are, nonetheless, undergoing new forms of imperialism, neo-colonialism, or globalization (Ngungi, 1993:12–13; Lind: 26–43). Globalization here defines the "process which has led to the creation of a single, international (global) financial or capital market" (Lind: 31) and landed most Two-Thirds World economies in huge debts and worse situations than in colonial times. The latest form of imperialism is also evident in ecological control, military muscle, universal media, and economic domination by the former and new imperialist powers. Neo-colonization, in particular, underlines the differences that characterize imperialist movements, for unlike ancient and modern empires, globalization largely excludes geographical occupation, or colonization proper, and, to some extent, it excludes government as transnational corporations take the lead.[3] The dominated countries in the globalization era seemingly retain their own political leadership and appear to be under control. These mutations of empires make it difficult to posit imperialism as a transhistorical institution even with a series of their reoccurrences. Nonetheless, it is hardly debatable that imperialisms of different times, forms, and strategies have affected and continue to affect this world on a global scale. Imperial images and structures of domination continue to affect the lives of billions of men and women, both the subjugated and the subjugator. How the people of the First World and Two-Thirds World perceive each other, how their cultural, economic and political institutions are structured, for instance, is

---

3 Williams and Chrisman: 273. Appadurai has suggested five landscapes that help to highlight the different levels and departments of modern and current imperialisms: "ethnoscape (people, especially groups in movements), 'technoscape' (institutions of technology and its informational flows), 'finanscape' (the disposition of global capital), 'mediascape' (both images produced and the mode of production), 'ideoscape' (ideologies)."

inseparably tied to the imperial movements and the strategies that have been employed to control foreign geographical spaces and its inhabitants.

Thus, cultural texts were central to the strategies of modern imperialism. Elleke Boehmer's study on *Colonial and Postcolonial Literature* indicates that modern imperial agents employed older and familiar narratives to read and to tame the "new" and strange spaces. As in Quint's findings on *Epic and Empire*, writing in the modern empires became an art of tapping

> the energy of metaphoric borrowings and reproductions within the wider tradition of colonial romance and adventure writing. Motifs of shipwreck, resourceful settlement and cultivation, treasure, slaves, and fear of cannibalism resurfaced time and again in boys' stories. . . . the pairing of white master and black slave/servant became an unquestioned commonplace. (Boehmer: 47)

Boehmer's analysis demonstrates that this web of intertextual reproductions was accompanied by a reproduction of certain cultural symbols and structures in different areas (51–59). Architecture, plantations, magic lanterns, foods, clothes, and names of European origin were transferred to various parts of the world.[4] Through this uniform transference of a few cultural structures and the reproduction of the same textual representations, different geographical spaces of the world and its inhabitants are homogenized, or colonized.

Imperializing texts are largely written during the peak periods of imperial movements mostly for and by the colonizing nations. The latter are exemplified by the likes of *The Aeneid, The Heart of Darkness, The Tempest,* and Kipling's classic poem "The White Man's Burden." They also include literary works that imperial powers bring and give to the colonized. Good examples of these are the so-called humanist tradition, which, as Ngungi aptly argues, was a powerful form of colonizing the minds of African students for "bourgeois Europe was always the center of the universe" (1986:17). Importing such texts functions to displace local cultures and colonize minds. Imperializing texts take many forms and are written by a variety of people, sometimes, even by the colonized, either collaborating with the dominant forces or yearning for the same power.[5] Regardless of who writes imperializing texts,

---

[4] See Mudimbe, 1994:105–53, for an exposition on the missionary strategies of domesticating both the physical space and minds of people, by setting up cultural structures such as houses, gardens, and schools that serve as beacons of colonial cultures.

[5] As I will show, New Testament texts are a good case in point. They were indeed produced by the colonized, yet they subscribe to the ideology of expansion to foreign land based on relationships of unequal power inclusion (Matt 28:16–20; Jn 4:1–42). Commenting on the tendency of the colonized to assume the strategies that befriend the colonizer's methods, Quint says, "The losers who attract our sympathies today would be—had they only the power—the victors of tomorrow" (18).

they are characterized by literary constructions, representations, and uses that authorize taking possession of foreign geographical spaces and people.

One of the strategies of imperializing texts is the employment of female gender to validate relationships of subordination and domination.[6] Quint's study on the genealogy of the epic and its role in the empires, for instance, finds a sustained recall, rewriting, and reproduction of the figure of a fleeing Cleopatra on Aeneas' shield in *The Aeneid* and its association with eastern nations (31–41). Manuier's sociological study of colonial processes and literature shows that "native women have often been the first agents of contact," providing what he calls a "classic literary motif of the tragic romance between the European man and native women" (70). Thus, Sigmund Freud, speaking within the imperial perspective of his time, could describe a "woman as the dark continent" (Williams and Chrisman: 194). The use of female gender to describe the colonized serves the agendas of constructing hierarchical geographical spaces, races, and cultures,[7] but it also comes to legitimate the oppression of women in societies where these narratives are used.

In sum, texts that legitimate and authorize imperialism include most canonized classics of ancient and contemporary times, of different disciplines and genres. Classical texts such as the Bible, *The Iliad*, *The Odyssey*, and *The Aeneid* have inspired and participated in different historical processes of imperialism (Quint). Contemporary texts range from modern English and French novels (Said), travel narratives, anthropological documentation, and world maps to missionary reports, paintings, tourist photography, museum collections, and intelligence satellite photography. The ensemble of these texts authorize imperialism through various values and strategies: by glorifying military might and conquest, by promoting travel that characterizes the travelers as authoritatively superior to foreign lands and their inhabitants, and by constructing foreign people and spaces in particular forms. These imperializing textual representations depend on sharply contrasting the colonizer's lands and people with those of the colonized. Foreign people are often characterized as inferior, dangerous, diseased, ungodly, kind, lazy, and helpless in these texts, while their lands are constructed as empty, feminine, available, harsh, full of evil, and profitable for the colonizing powers. The colonized spaces and inhabitants are basically subjected to the standard of the colonizer and difference is equated to deficiency.

Given the centrality of cultural texts to imperialist projects, the struggle for liberation is not limited to military, economic, and political arenas. It nec-

---

[6] On gender roles, representations, and politics of reading in imperializing texts and contexts, see Blunt; Blunt and Rose; Donaldson; Mohanty; and Strobel.

[7] See Blaut: 1–124 for the construction of hierarchical geography that legitimated the hierarchical racial construction which accompanied contemporary empire.

essarily requires and includes a cultural battle of reader-writers who attempt to arrest the violence of imperializing texts. The centrality of literary texts in imperialism has, therefore, stimulated a literary response from the subjugated at different places and periods of imperialism (Ashcroft et al.: 1–109; Harlow: 1–75; Said: 1–150). The colonized reread the imperializing texts[8] and write new narratives that assert the adequacy of their humanity, the reality of global diversity, and their right to independence. They write in search for liberating ways of interdependence between nations, races, genders, and economies, ways which do not depend on oppressive and exploitative relationships.[9] The formerly colonized, who approximate the majority of the Two-Thirds World countries, therefore, constitute communities of reader-writers who struggle to decolonize. Their practice challenges the Western or the so-called First World academic schools of cultural texts to expose and to reject the literary forms of imperialism, or to admit their acceptance of it. As Said points out, a neutral position is not possible: to read or write for or against imperial domination is an unavoidable position—one that is already taken (68).

Biblical Texts and Empire-building

The African saying cited at the beginning of the essay highlights that the Bible is one of the imperializing texts. For many African nations the success of colonization is inseparably linked with the use of the Bible. Ngungi wa Thiongo, a Kenyan writer, underscores this experience when he asserts that the "English, French, and the Portuguese came to the Third World to announce the arrival of the Bible and the sword" (1993:31). Ngungi insists that in the modern colonization of Africa, "both William Shakespeare and Jesus Christ had brought light" (1986:91). Such a view does not belong to the colonized people alone. David Livingstone, the renowned colonial hero who championed the colonization of Africa, made it an open secret that in colonization, "civilization—Christianity and commerce—should ever be inseparable" (Thomas: 68). In 1820 missionary Pringle could proudly say,

> Let us enter upon a new and nobler career of conquest. Let us subdue Savage Africa by justice, by kindness, by the talisman of Christian truth. Let

---

[8] See Achebe: 1–20 and Ngungi, 1993:12–25 for readings of *Heart of Darkness* as an imperializing text.

[9] See Said: 3–43, 303–36 on the concept of interdependence, interconnectedness, and the overlapping of territories, histories, cultures, and identities. Said holds that interdependence is unavoidable: it is a necessary form of survival sought by both the colonizer and the colonized. The question, therefore, is to seek liberating forms of interdependence, since survival is about "connections of things," people, nations, genders, and economies rather than independence from one another (336).

us thus go forth, in the name and under the blessing of God, gradually to extend the territorial boundary also of our colony, until is shall become an empire. (Mudimbe, 1988:47)

Both Livingstone and Pringle found no contradiction, no secrecy, or any reason to separate the Christian mission from the imperialist agenda of their countries. The likes of Livingstone can be easily dismissed by some as an arena of church history which has little or nothing to do with biblical studies. Yet the question remains as to whether their travels were also sanctioned by Christian texts and whether the mission texts advocate liberating ways of interdependence or suppression of difference. The question of what and where is "the talisman of Christian truth" remains.

If Livingstone and Pringle can be dismissed as zealous church missionaries, yet figures like Albert Schweitzer, who influenced academic biblical studies substantially (Borg: 3–4, 18), cannot be. Their profession as biblical scholars did not hinder them from acting as colonial envoys, nor exempts academic biblical studies, scholars, their interpretations, and, indeed, the texts themselves from the violence of imperialism. Modern European and American colonizing powers openly defined their task as a Puritan "errand to the wilderness," "a duty to the natives," or "a mission to civilize" (Said: 63, 69, 103–8; Delavignette: 29–30), moral claims closely derived from Christian texts, and which beg to be investigated.[10]

Reading the Bible and other cultural texts for decolonization is, therefore, imperative for those who are committed to the struggle for liberation. Why the Bible is a usable text in imperial projects and how it should be read in the light of its role are central questions to the process of decolonization and the struggle for liberation. As a Motswana woman of Southern Africa, my reading for decolonization arises from the historical encounter of Christian texts functioning compatibly with colonialism; of the Bible functioning as the "talisman" in imperial possession of foreign places and people. My reading seeks to investigate if the use is supported by the ideology of Christian mission texts. It seeks to interrogate the travel/mission texts of the Bible and the power relations they advocate between different cultural lands and people.

In reading a mission text for decolonization, I am not denying cross-cultural exchange between races and nations that has gone on, that still goes on, and that must continue outside imperialist tendencies. Neither am I equating every attempt to spread one's influence to other cultures and lands with imperialism. Rather, my reading seeks to confront the overwhelming at-

---

[10] Rudyard Kipling's "The White Man's Burden" is dependent on biblical images: The colonizing travelers are portrayed as the light to the heathen and half-devil people. Like Moses, the colonizer is confronted with the complaints of the colonized who cry to return to the night and bondage of Egypt. In short, colonizers' projects are equated to the Christian mission.

testation of biblical texts and readers functioning compatibly with imperialist projects and to investigate the grounds of their partnership.[11] I have chosen the story of the Samaritan woman for obvious reasons: it is a mission narrative, one that authorizes its reader-believer to "go forth," so to speak. My reading will interrogate and highlight the power relations John 4 proposes for international cultural relations and exchange.

READING FOR DECOLONIZATION: JOHN 4:1–42

My reading attributes the construction of this story to the Johannine community and their missionary vision rather than to the historical Jesus and his disciples. In reading for decolonization, I will deal with the imperial setting, hidden interests, travelers, geography/lands, expansion, and the construction of the Samaritan woman/people/land. I will conclude by looking at one Two-Thirds World woman's attempt to decolonize the story. Throughout the explication of these factors, I will use particular quotations from the story as subtitles to highlight some of the main imperial ideological constructions of the narrative. Despite my attempt to treat each point independently, the reader will find them closely intertwined.

"The Pharisees had heard Jesus is making and baptizing more disciples than John . . . !" (John 4:1)

The mention of Pharisees, Jesus, and John the Baptist highlights an intense struggle for power directly related to imperialist occupation. Historically, the Gospel is written several decades after the Roman Empire had destroyed Jerusalem and the Temple in CE 70. The destruction of the central Jewish symbols has contributed to intense intergroup competition for power, characterized by negotiation, collaboration, and revolt against the Roman Empire by various national groups. Evidently, in Jn 4:1, three movements/interests groups are vying for power in Palestine: The Pharisees, Jesus and his disciples, and John the Baptist and his disciples. As the first verse clearly indicates Jesus is fleeing from the Pharisees, who have heard he "is making and baptizing more disciples than John" (v. 1). I will now briefly explicate these competitions and how they are related to imperialist presence.

---

[11] Elsewhere, I have proposed the following questions as a criteria for identifying imperializing texts. 1. Does this text have a clear stance against the political imperialism of its time? 2. Does this text encourage travel to distant lands and how does it justify itself? 3. How does this text construct difference: Is there dialogue and liberating interdependence, or is there condemnation and replacement of all that is foreign? 4. Does this text employ gender and divine representations to construct relationships of subordination and domination? See my dissertation, "Toward a Post-colonial Feminist Interpretation of the Bible: A Study of Matt 15:21–28 and Jn 4:1–42," forthcoming.

First, there is competition for power between the disciples of John the Baptist, a representative of one interest group, and the disciples of Jesus. Many scholars argue that there is good reason to suggest that John and his disciples were an independent movement. Thus the text of John rhetorically subordinates John to Jesus. In the prologue, the narrator states that John the Baptist "was not the light, but he came to testify to the light" (1:6–9). On two other occasions the Baptist is characterized as devaluing himself to underline the superiority of Jesus. First, he says, "This is he whom I said, 'After me comes a man who ranks ahead of me because he was before me'" (1:27). Later, he says Jesus "must increase, but I must decrease" (3:30). This textual subordination of John to Jesus simplifies the conflicts as one between the Pharisees and Jesus and his disciples, who are, no doubt, the biggest rivals within the Gospel of John.

Second, there is competition between the disciples of Jesus and the disciples of Moses, the Pharisees. In the post–CE 70 period the Pharisees were not only another interest group, but were also an officially recognized power in Palestine (3:1, 7:48, 12:42). Therefore, the Pharisees and the Sadducees appear as a united authoritative power in John's Gospel (7:32, 45; 11:47, 57), a construction which tries to be faithful to Jesus' times and the author's times. As the Gospel attests (7–12:50), competition for power and enmity between the disciples of Jesus and the disciples of Moses (Pharisees) has reached its peak with dire consequences. The disciples of Jesus have lost their influence and have been thrown out of the synagogue (9:22, 35; 12:42). Some may have died (16:2).

Third, when we enter the story of John 4:1–42, we witness the consequences of imperial disruption and intergroup competition at two levels. First, the disciples of Jesus are extending their influence to Samaria because they are losing the national competition to the Pharisees. Second, we enter into centuries of imperial subtexts of disruption, alienation, and resistance that strained the relationships of the Samaritans and Jews (4:9, 20–23). This tension goes back to the Assyrian Empire. Through intermarriage and the adoption of some of the religions of their Assyrian colonial masters, Samaritans became what some have termed "despised heretics" and "despised half-breeds." As a result, the Samaritan Jewish descendants distanced themselves from Samaritans on the grounds of religious impurity. Their strained relationship illustrates the extent to which imperial domination has affected and influenced the relationship of different people at different centuries in the world.

In sum, imperial domination is central to the story of the Samaritan woman and John's Gospel as a whole. The local leaders who plan the death of Jesus, for instance, are characterized as fearing that his fame will bring a Roman attack on the nation (11:48–53). At his trial, faithfulness to Roman imperial power is evoked to justify the guilt of Jesus (19:12, 15), and Pilate insists on crucifying Jesus as the awaited political liberator, a Jewish king, despite the chief priests' resistance to the inscription "Jesus of Nazareth, the King of the Jews" (19:19–22). The Roman imperial expansionist agendas and the imposition of its own cultural symbols and power stimulated a response and led to intergroup competition within the Jewish society.[12]

Likewise, Jesus and his disciples' turn to the land of despised Samaritans is linked to the competition for power between the Pharisees and Christian Jews. Both Pharisees and Christian Jews are trying to define Jewish identity during the Roman occupation of Palestine; in particular, after the destruction of their religious symbols, Jerusalem and the Temple. Their competition for power should not be divorced from the real enemy, from its root cause, the Roman empire. The story of the Samaritan woman illustrates how imperialism affects people in general: it leads the colonized to fight back, to collaborate with the enemy, or to fight among themselves.

It seems safe to say that Jesus' disciples are losing (6:66; 12:42–43), not making many disciples (4: 1), and hence they are turning to proselytize the Samaritans. Ironically, the alternative vision of the Johannine community embraces an ideology of expansion, despite the fact that they are themselves victims of imperial expansion and struggling for their liberation.[13] As is common in imperial ideologies of expansion, the search for expanded influence is not openly expressed. The lack of explicit admission brings me to the point of hidden interests in the ideology of imperialism.

"Look . . . See how the fields are ripe for harvesting . . . !" (Jn 4:35)

The ideology of imperialism typically conceals its interests and presents its project in such rhetorical terms as the "duty to the natives," who "require and beseech domination" (Said: 9). Similarly, the Johannine community conceals its interests through the literary characterization of Jesus and his disciples in John 4. First, the narrator states that Jesus is in transit through Samaria; but his real destination is Galilee. Thus at Sychar, we meet Jesus sitting by the well; notably, outside the village because "he is tired out by his journey" (vv. 5–6) to Galilee. The refusal to admit any intentions to enter and missionize is further underscored by the fact that he only enters the village when the Samaritans themselves "asked him to stay with them" (v. 40). The narration of Jesus journey resists an open acknowledgement of any intention to evangelize Samaria. The story prefers to hold that the Samaritans needed

---

[12] See Overman: 1–71 for an illuminating discussion on the impact of imperial forces on first-century Palestine. It led to conflict, competition, and the fragmentation of Jewish society as each interest group attempted to define the cultural boundaries and collaborated with the imperial powers.

[13] See Koester: 665–80 who highlights the direct borrowing of imperial ideology, to express the Christian faith in John 4.

Jesus' missionary work (v. 22); they followed Jesus (v. 30); and they asked for Jesus' message (v. 40).

The hidden interests are also evident in the characterization of the disciples in the story. First, they appear as a faint background of the story. They have gone to buy food in the city, *not* to missionize (v. 9). The dialogue between Jesus and the Samaritan woman takes place in their absence. When they return, she departs, and Jesus begins to speak to them about his food, that is, "to do the will of him who sent me and to complete his work" (v. 34). In this discussion, they are notably puzzled by Jesus' talk, which turns into a monologue. In general, his disciples remain silent, and they never openly question or seem to understand. All these literary constructions distance the disciples from any intention to missionize the Samaritans. The evangelization of Samaritans thus falls squarely on the Samaritans themselves: it is the woman and the villagers who beg Jesus to enter the village and stay with them.

Jesus' response to the disciples in this short scene (vv. 31–38), however, is central to the whole story of the Samaritan woman. The scene provides the disciples with an interpretive grid through which they must understand their food, that is, like Jesus who is sent, they are sent, (vv. 34, 38). They are authorized to go, to enter, and to teach other nations. In this scene the rhetoric of interests and power is aggressively articulated; yet it remains concealed by an ideology of disinterest. Jesus says to them: "Look around you, and see how the fields are ripe for harvesting. . . . One sows, another reaps. I sent you to reap that for which you did not labor. Others have labored, and you have entered into their labor" (vv. 37–38). Many scholars have wrestled with these sayings.[14] Two factors are pertinent to my reading. First, the fields are ripe for harvest. The statement articulates an evident search for profit and a desire to take possession of something. Whether the possession is spiritual or material, it involves a will to power which is invested in real people and affects real people. Second, the legitimation of the disciples' power entails frightening values: the disciples are *sent to reap that for which they did not labor*. Such a statement reflects the intensity of competition and struggle for control and, of necessity, depends on unequal relationships.

Consequently, the Samaritans are construed as passive fields to be entered and harvested.[15] Yet, these fields are not limited to Samaria, they

---

[14] The main problem lies in the contradictory statements about the sowers. At first, it seems there is equal division of labor and rewards (vv. 36–37), but the concluding verse suggests otherwise (v. 38). While the reapers are disciples, the identity of sowers remains ambiguous. Jesus has been suggested, but since the verse speaks of "many other sowers," former prophets, Hellenists evangelicals, and the Samaritan woman have been posited.

[15] According to Brown's interpretation, "the disciples must learn to harvest the crop of believers even though they have not sowed the seed." He points out that, "In Acts 8:4–25 Philip the Hellenist evangelizes Samaria, and then the Jerusalem apostles send Peter and John to con-

include the whole world (v. 42). But, once more, this global vision is placed in the mouth of the Samaritans, who must proclaim him "the Savior of the World." This characterization distances the disciples from any self-interest and propounds an imperial ideology that portrays the colonized as people who "require and beseech for domination" and the colonizers as people with a moral "duty to the natives."

We must remember that historically the story represents a much later vision of the mission (v. 38) arising, as I said, from the Johannine community, rather than the historical Jesus and his disciples. It is therefore striking how the disciples (or the Johannine community) who are most probably the proponents of the missionary vision and authors of the story, present themselves as mute and puzzled by Jesus' talk of ripe fields. Through this literary presentation, the disciples/Johannine community rhetorically distance themselves from their own vision precisely to conceal their interests to the very end. For instance, if they are going to take all credit for the Samaritan woman's work, at least the Samaritan people themselves will discredit her importance (v. 42).

Although the rhetoric of concealment pervades the narrative, the story authorizes the Christian disciples/readers/believers to travel, to enter, to educate, and to harvest other foreign lands for the Christian nations in a literary fashion that is openly modelled on imperialist values. This evident in both the saying, "I have sent you to reap that which you did not labor. Others labored, and you have entered into their labor" and the title "Savior of the World," designated to Jesus. The saying notably evokes Josh 24:13, where the Lord God speaks to the Israelites through Joshua saying, "I gave you a land on which you had not labored, and towns that you had not built, and you live in them; you eat the fruit of vineyards and oliveyards that you did not plant." The book of Joshua is a highly dramatized and idealized capture of the Canaan. It is a narrative that glorifies conquest and openly advocates violent colonialism in the name of God. "Savior of the World," as noted above, was a title used to refer to the Roman Emperors in the first century (Talbert: 118; Koester: 665–80; Cassidy: 6–16). Surprise, surprise—the Johannine Jesus emerges fully clothed in the emperor's titles. Thus Jesus too lays claim to unlimited access to all geographical spaces and foreigners. In evoking Joshua's narrative and borrowing titles of emperors to articulate the Christian mission and to characterize Jesus, John 4 models its vision along imperial goals, strategies, and values. The mission is portrayed as a violent entry and domestication of foreign lands and people that involves reaping fields that one did not plant. This brings me to travelers themselves and their role in imperialist projects. This point will be elucidated through focusing on Jesus and his disciples as travelers.

---

firm the conversion" (18). Brown's reading leans towards validating hierarchical structures, even though he mentions that the sower and the reaper must rejoice together.

"My food is to do the will of him who sent me . . . . I send you. . !"(Jn 4:34, 38)

Imperialism as an ideology of expansion involves superior travelers who represent the superiority of their origin. Similarly, Jesus and his disciples are the authorized travelers from above (3:34, 8:26; 20:21–23). Their travel is linked with expansion, and it is both locally and globally oriented. First, they are traveling because their expansion has brought them trouble (v.1); but soon after, their departure results in further expansion (v. 30, 39). Jesus' commission to the disciples to harvest the ripe fields and the Samaritans' declaration that Jesus is the "Savior of the World" indicates that their expansion espouses global levels. The disciples of Jesus are global travellers. Like their master, they are authorized from above; hence, they are superior.

Jesus and his disciples are travelers invested with high authority far above their hosts. To begin with, Jesus is a very superior traveler. His superiority is communicated through the literary style used for his identification: a gradual unfolding which shows his superiority at every stage. The Samaritan woman, who first thought he was just a simple Jewish man, discovers that Jesus can give her living water which leads to eternal life (v. 10); he is greater than Jacob (v. 12–14); and he is not only a prophet (v. 19) or a Messiah (v. 26) but the "Savior of the World" (v. 42). This gradual unveiling of Jesus' identity characterizes him as an extremely superior traveler who surpasses all other local figures.

The characterization of Jesus is consistent with the whole Gospel of John. For instance, scholars of John have noted how Jesus is compared to other Christological figures such as the Word, Lamb of God, King of Israel, Moses, Messiah/Christ, a literary device designed to show that he is well above all these figures (Kysar: 22–46; Martyn: 9–54). The comparison is a rhetorical ladder for his elevation: it foregrounds his superiority and almost equates him with God (1:1, 20:28) while it derogates the validity of all others.

While in the story of the Samaritan woman the disciples are rhetorically obscured, they nevertheless travel with Jesus. The story serves to give them the right to travel with authority (v. 38). Their authority is derived from and is closely related to that of Jesus (v. 34, 20:21–23). It is authority from above, from God. However, such authority can only be justified by a negative portrayal of those nations and lands that must be entered, taught, and converted. This brings to me to the characterization of the Samaritan woman, or, as some have noted, the Samaritan land.

"If you knew . . . You worship what you do not know . . . We worship what we know!"
(Jn 4:10, 22)

Imperialism expounds an ideology of inferior knowledge and invalid religious faith of those who must be colonized. Authoritative travellers depend heavily upon constructions of ignorant natives. There is a sharp division between those who know, the colonizers, and those who know nothing, the colonized. Thus the Samaritan woman is characterized as an ignorant native (v. 10) and in need of help (v. 10). She is constructed as morally/religiously lacking, that is, she has had five husbands, and the one she has is not her own (vv. 17–18),[16] and she does not know what she worships (v. 22). On the contrary, Jesus, a superior traveller, is knowledgeable (vv. 10, 22); powerful (vv. 14, 25, 42); sees everything about her past (vv. 17–18, 29); knows and offers answers for her society (vv. 21–26); and teaches her and her people (vv. 21–23). The ignorance of the Samaritan woman is pathetic. Despite all these revelations (v. 26), she remains ignorant to the end (O'Day, 1986). That is, she is still uncertain and asks, "he cannot be the Messiah, can he? (v. 29). As O'Day (1987:48–49) correctly notes, her inability to understand is well above that of male disciples (vv. 27, 31–33).

Ignorance here is furthered by employing female gender. In a mission story, a narrative that authorizes traveling to and entering into foreign lands and places, that she becomes a first point of contact is significant. As in imperializing narratives, this pattern is a statement about the targeted land and its inhabitants. Like the woman who represents them, the foreign land must be entered, won, and domesticated. As such the next sub-title highlights the rhetoric of hierarchical geographical spaces.

"Are you greater than our ancestor Jacob, who gave us this well and . . . drunk from it?" (Jn 4:12)

Authoritative travelers also depend on an ideology of hierarchical geographical spaces. Jesus is the highest authority and the most authoritative traveler in John's gospel. Consequently, a specific geography had to be constructed. That is, he has descended from the Father and will ascend to the Father.[17] His origin allows him to become a 'World Savior' because he is not of the world. This also necessitates that the world should be constructed negatively (8:12, 23; 9:39; 12:31; 13:1).

Within the story of the Samaritan woman, hierarchical constructions of geographical spaces are also evident. There is Judea and Galilee, lands that are much holier than Samaria and Sychar, lands which are best avoided (v. 9). Concomitantly, the occupants of Samaria are also of questionable

---

16 Whether she is a real woman or a symbolic representation of Samaria is debated. What is important, however, is her function. Whether readers interpret the five husbands as Samaria's religious unfaithfulness or just the real woman's low standards, the question of why a woman remains pertinent.

17 See Segovia: 23–54 for an extensive treatment of journeys and origins embedded in the plot of the Gospel. For the concept of descending and ascending and its sociological function, see Meeks: 44–72.

value. The negative characterization of Samaritans allows Jesus to assert his religious superiority (v. 22), even when he is discrediting both Gerizim and Jerusalem (v. 21). Jacob's well in Samaria (v. 12) pales besides Jesus' spring of superior waters (v. 13). Ripe fields must be entered and harvested by those who did not sow them (v. 35–38); and, lastly, the world must be saved (v. 42). These hierarchical geographical constructions authorize travelers of superior origins and values (Jesus and his disciples) to expand, to enter, and to control, at both local and global levels, those geographical areas that are depicted as inferior in their systems of values (Samaria and the world).

"You will worship the Father neither on this mountain nor in Jerusalem. . . . ! (Jn 4:22)

Imperialist ideology of expansion uses the promotion of its own cultural values to devalue, replace, and suppress diversity. Its strategy is characterized by a massive inclusivity but not equality. Similarly, in John 4:1–42 the mission expands from the well to the world (Neyrey: 419–37). The expansion notably declares the cultural centers of Jerusalem and Gerizim as inadequate and replaces them with Spirit and truth.[18] The seemingly inclusive replacement maintains the religious/racial superiority of Jesus (v. 22), a characterization that clearly shows that imperialism's universal standards never intend to create relationships of equals but to win devotees. Therefore, the transcendence of both Jewish and Samaritan cultural spaces by the realm of Spirit and truth (vv. 23–24) is, in fact, an installation of the superiority of Christianity—which, as we now know, proceeds by discrediting all other religious cultures for its own interests. We perceive this unequal inclusion through the discursive use and final dismissal of a person with female gender in the story.

"They said to the woman, "It is no longer because of what you said that we believe. . . ." (Jn 4:42)

Imperialist ideology of subjugation constructs extremely gendered discourse. The lands that must be subjugated are equated to a woman, and narratives about the penetration of distant lands feature a woman. Ancient epic texts feature numerous Goddesses and women at many foreign shores and lands. Biblical examples are the stories of the Jericho prostitute (Josh 2) and the Canaanite woman (Matt 15:21–28). Like a woman, the target of colonialism is entered, conquered, and domesticated. Many scholars have also noted that the Samaritan woman represents her land. She is the point of entrance, but finally she is domesticated (v. 41); while those who did not sow,

---

[18] See Swansom who describes how the devaluation of cultural spaces in John was party to legitimating Western colonization and why it will always be resisted.

male disciples, are invited to move in to reap the harvest, while she is dismissed (37–38).[19]

As previously mentioned, imperialist expansion suggests a massive inclusion of races, lands, genders, and religions, but not equality. The inclusion is intended to legitimate control, and control depends on unequal relationships. The unequal inclusivity of this narrative is grounded in the very literary device employed. Esther Fuchs' research on the betrothal type-scene is instructive here. Fuchs notes that betrothal type-scenes are literary motifs employed to mark the launching of a young patriarch's career. The type-scene story begins with a young man's journey to the outside world where he meets his future bride at the well. As the scene proceeds, the status of the woman decreases into obscurity. Men take over to discuss her future and wealth. She marries and departs with her husband. As Fuchs notes, betrothal type-scenes, therefore, are not about the woman but about the launching of a patriarch's career.

The story of the Samaritan woman is built on the same literary foundation. At first, the narrative leads the reader to celebrate her role (and other relationships involving worship, sowers, and reapers). Yet when she finishes announcing Jesus Christ in the town, she never speaks out again. The discussion of her work and its product is transferred into the hands of Jesus, male disciples, and the village converts, who after meeting with Jesus relegate her work to a secondary status (v. 42). Here we perceive the launching of Jesus' career outside his home, that is, the birth of his bride (the church or Johannine community). Jesus's relationship, and by extension Christianity's relationship, to foreign people and lands is, unfortunately, grounded on a very unequal foundation, as attested by these portrayals of race, gender, and geography. Accordingly, what seems to be an inclusive gospel of Spirit and Truth is the installation of Christianity as a universal religion: an installation that proceeds by disavowing all geographical boundaries in order to claim power over the "world" and to relegate all other religions and cultures to inadequacy.

Given the global experience of imperial domination, its persistence, and the real suffering and exploitation of those who are at its receiving end, how can one read the story of the Samaritan woman for decolonization? How can

---

[19] Although many readers compare the woman's role to John the Baptist or the disciples as one who point others to Christ, her story is quite different. John the Baptist is at least given a chance to speak for himself and say that his honor is to decrease while Christ increases (Jn 3:28–30). The disciples continue to follow Christ and are finally commissioned (20:21–23). The Samaritan woman, however, is never given a chance to say a word after returning from the city. Instead, there is an open dismissal or devaluation of her work, v. 42. If her story represents a later time, when the church began to consider seriously the mission to the Gentiles, then her dismissal is a serious statement on the role of women, rather than just a Johannine pattern of discipleship.

one arrest its imperial violence and foster a new narrative of liberating interdependence that recognizes and nurtures diversity? In search for the answers to some of these questions, I now turn to one Two-Thirds World woman's attempt to rewrite the story for decolonization.

ONE WOMAN'S DECOLONIZING READING OF JOHN 4:1–42.

The Victims' setting is the pre-independent to post-independent Botswana and apartheid South Africa. Mositi Torontle's major concerns are the settler colonial practices of the white apartheid regime and their effects on the whole region of Southern Africa; in particular, the breakdown of family life due to structurally coerced mine labor immigration. As one of the characters describes it, it "is a sick land and a broken people" in need of healing, for the "whole society has been shaken, shattered and scattered" (Torontle: 122). Within this setting of brokenness, Torontle re-writes the story of the Samaritan woman as follows:

> Mmapula. . . . went down the river to fetch water for her plants. Beside the well sat a still woman dressed in white clothing. Her head was bowed and focused in her open hands. Mmapula trod slowly, wondering who she was and what she was doing at this place and time. Mmapula sat down by the well and began to fill her container with water. Just when she was about to leave, the woman in white looked up and said, "Samaritan woman, give me a drink." Mmapula gave her a drink. "Samaritan woman, go and call your husband," she said retaining Mmapula's gourd without drinking the water. "I am not a Samaritan woman and I have no husband." The woman in white closed her eyes for some seconds and said, "You have spoken well, Samaritan woman. You have no husband. In fact, the husband that you have does not belong to you but to the mines. I have come to give you a drink of living water," she said handing Mmapula the same gourd of water. "Go back to your village and announce that a prophetess has come bringing healing to the broken-hearted." "A prophet has come bringing healing to Borolong." The news spread at the speed of a veld fire through the small village. (57–58)

Torontle's decolonizing reading of John 4:1–42 recognizes and makes attempts to arrest the imperializing aspects of the story. I will now discuss how she arrests the oppressive constructions of gender, race, geography, and religion. Last, I will discuss the author's use of the Samaritan identity as the ideal space to emphasize interconnections in a world constructed by imperialism.

Central to Torontle's rereading is an attempt to decolonize hierarchical gender and race. First, she arrests gender superiority by featuring a female character in the place of Jesus.[20] Second, the Samaritan woman is explicitly "sent" and so has the status conferred on the male disciples in John 4:38. Concerning racial superiority, an attempt to decolonize its construction is also evident. When asked for water, Mmapula responds positively without any questions. Mmapula's response challenges and dispenses with any claims of cultural purity or impurity, and hence it undercuts the ideology of superiority and inferiority of races that heavily depends on such dichotomies. Her response is subversive to the imperial ideology that heavily depends on the claims of superiority of race and chosenness, as attested by the histories of the North American and South African colonization. Yet Mmapula denies her Samaritan identity while the prophetess insists on it. Her insistence is a point I shall revisit later.

Torontle's reading also decolonizes geographical hierarchy by offering the Samaritan woman living water from her own well in her land. The geographical affirmation of her land serves to affirm its occupants and the adequacy of their cultural values. To accentuate this point, nothing is said about Mmapula's possession of many husbands although we are informed that she has no husband. Furthermore, prophecy, that is, social criticism and the search for new visions of reconstruction, is preferred over universal salvation. Therefore, the woman in white is notably a prophetess and not a Savior of the World. She has come to bring healing to the village, and her style of healing affirms that the villagers already have strength and abilities in and among themselves.

Concerning religion, Torontle's decolonizing reading avoids any replacement or rejection of other faith orientations. In fact, the prophetess, who is later identified as Mother Mary Magdalene, is also a preacher and a faith-healer. In her preaching, she retells biblical stories from her memory, and in her healing she calls on the African Ancestral Spirits and Jesus to heal the land and bind its wounds (Torontle: 60, 73–76). In short, she does not privilege the Christian stories over the religious stories of Africans; she uses them both as she finds them useful. Thus the characterization of Mary Magdalene as a decolonizing interpreter serves to underline and to embrace the identity of Mmapula as despised heretic and promotes it as the ideal model for a truly post-colonial and inclusive world![21] The latter point brings me to the

---

[20] See Tolbert: 18–19 who suggests "imagining Jesus and the twelve as women and a man anointing her head with oil (Mark 14:3–9)" and how such reversal of characters can give a different way of seeing some of these biblical stories.

[21] Torontle's description of Mother Mary Magdalene's depicts her remarkable diversity. She "was wearing a white turban, a red cape, a rosary, white and red beads on her wrists and held a Zion hymn book in her hands. Dineo tried to place her various lines of faith and found that her dress pronounced her a mixture of various things and follower of none" (71).

category/identity of the Samaritan as the ideal space for acknowledging cultural interconnections and as well as nurturing differences.

Despite Mmapula's denial of her Samaritan identity, Mother Mary Magdalene's insistence implies emphasis on the imperialist setting. Like the biblical Samaritan woman, Mmapula is a despised heretic, a despised halfbreed; she cannot claim any purity of race or religion, and she has lived through several types of imperialist domination. Various forms of imperialism have affected and constructed Mmapula as well as the Pharisees, John the Baptist, and Jesus and his disciples. The Samaritan identity is, therefore, highlighted as the reality of both the biblical characters of John 4 and Mmapula. Torontle's decolonizing reading shows that imperialism is the reality for those nations and races who claim purity and those who cannot, for those who are consciously aware of imperialism as a pervasive reality in the world and for those who are not aware. It is indeed a reality for First World biblical readers and for Two-Thirds World biblical readers as well. Mmapula's final response underscores the pervasiveness of imperialism: she does not deny her Samaritan race any further. In short, she comes to the reality of who she is—a mixture of many different things: a despised heretic, a despised halfbreed so to speak.

Conclusion

Many biblical narratives are imperializing texts, through their use in history and through the power relations they propound. The mission passages, which can be fairly termed the central Christian narratives that authorize traveling and entering into foreign cultures and lands, exemplified by John 4, hardly propose relations of liberating interdependence between races, cultures, and genders. Both the prefatory African saying and the words of missionary-colonial agents attest to the participation of biblical texts in colonial projects; they bind the Bible to the history of subjugation and exploitation. This obligates First World and Two-Thirds World communities of readers-writers to interrogate the biblical ideology of travel, expansion, representations of differences, and their function.

Because of the historical reoccurrences and the contemporary persistence and mutations of imperialisms, imperialism will not be easily bracketed from academic biblical critical practice of interpretation without validating the unjust international relations of exploitation. It is, therefore, imperative to take cognizance of a world that is wedged between imperial domination, collaboration, and resistance; of texts that, more often than not, offer models of international relationships which are less than liberating; of texts born from and that have served in different imperialist projects; and of writing-reading communities who are calling for decolonization. Torontle's decolonizing reading of John 4 challenges biblical readers, hearers, believers, and writers to acknowledge and to embrace their Samaritan social spaces of heretics and half-breeds. Similarly, biblical critical practice must be dedicated to an ethical task of promoting decolonization, fostering diversity, and imagining liberating ways of interdependence.

WORKS CONSULTED

Achebe, Chinua
    1989   *Hopes and Impediments: Selected Essays*. New York: Doubleday.

Ashcroft Bill, Gareth Griffiths, and Helen Tiffin
    1989   *The Empire Writes Back: Theory and Practice in Post-colonial Literatures*. New York: Routledge.

Balch, David L. and John E. Stambaugh
    1986   *The New Testament in Its Social Enviroment*. Philadelphia: Westminster.

Blaut, James M.
    1993   *The Colonizer's Model of the World: Geographical Diffusionism and Eurocentric History*. New York: Guildford.

Blunt, Alison
    1994   *Travel, Gender, and Imperialism: Mary Kingsley and West Africa*. New York: Guildford.

Blunt, Alison and Gillian Rose
    1994   *Writing, Women, and Space: Colonial and Postcolonial Geographies*. New York: Guildford.

Boehmer, Elleke
    1995   *Colonial and Post-colonial Literature*. New York: Oxford University Press.

Borg, Marcus J.
    1992   *Jesus in Contemporary Scholarship*. Valley Forge: Trinity.

Brown, Raymond E.
    1988   *The Gospel and Epistles of John*. Minnesota: Liturgical.

Cassidy, Richard J.
    1992   *John's Gospel in New Perspective*. New York: Orbis.

Delavignette, Robert
    1964   *Christianity and Colonialism*. New York: Hawthorn.

Donaldson, Laura
    1992   *Decolonizing Feminisms: Race, Gender, & Empire-building*. Chapel Hill: The University of North Carolina Press.

Fuchs, Esther
    1987   "Structure and Patriarchal Functions in Biblical Betrothal Type-Scenes: Some Preliminary Notes." In *JFSR* 3:7–13.

Harlow, Barbara
   1987   *Resistance Literature.* New York: Methuen.

Kipling, Rudyard
   1962   "The White Man's Burden," In *The Imperialism Reader.* Ed. L. Synder. New York: D. Van Nostrand.

Koester, Craig
   1990   "The Savior of the World (John 4:42)." *JBL* 109:665–80.

Kysar, Robert
   1976   *John: The Maverick Gospel.* Louisville: John Knox.

Lind, Christopher
   1995   *Something Is Wrong Somewhere: Globalization, Community and the Moral Economy of Farm Crisis.* Halifax: Fernwood.

Martyn, J. L.
   1978   *The Gospel of John in Christian History: Essays for Interpretation.* New York: Paulist.

Maunier, Rene
   1949   *The Sociology of Colonies: An Introduction to the Study of Colonies. Vol. 1.* London: Routledge.

Meeks, Wayne
   1972   "A Man From Heaven in Johannine Sectarianism." In *JBL* 91:44–72.

Mohanty, Chandra T.
   1991   "Under Western: Feminist Scholarship and Colonial Discourses." In *Third World Women and the Politics of Feminism.* Ed. Chandra Mohanty, Ann Russo, and Lourdes Torres. Bloomington: Indiana University Press.

Mudimbe, V. Y.
   1988   *The Invention of Africa: Gnosis, Philosophy, and the Order of Knowledge.* Bloomington: Indiana University Press.

   1994   *The Idea of Africa.* Bloomington: Indiana University Press.

Ngungi wa Thiongo
   1986   *Decolonizing the Mind: The Politics of Language in African Literature.* London: James Curry.

   1993   *Moving the Centre: The Struggle for Cultural Freedoms.* London: James Curry.

Neyrey, Jerome
   1979   "Jacob Traditions and the Interpretation of John 4:10–10:26." *CBQ* 41:419–37.

O'Day, Gail R.
   1986   *Revelation in the Fourth Gospel: Narrative Mode and Theological Claim.* Philadelphia: Fortress.

   1987   *The Word Disclosed: John's Story and Narrative Preaching.* St. Louis: CBP.

Overman, Andrew J.
    1990   *Matthew's Gospel and Formative Judaism: The Social World of the Matthean Community.* Minneapolis: Fortress.

Quint, David
    1993   *Epic and Empire.* Princeton: Princeton University Press.

Roettzel, Calvin J.
    1985   *The World That Shaped the New Testament.* Atlanta: John Knox.

Said, Edward
    1993   *Culture and Imperialism.* New York: Alfred A. Knopf.

Segovia, Fernando F.
    1991   "Journey(s) of the Word: A Reading of the Plot of the Forth Gospel." *Semeia* 53: 23–54.

Schneiders, Sandra
    1991   *The Revelatory Text: Interpreting the New Testament as Sacred Scripture.* San Francisco: Harper Collins.

Strobel, Margaret
    1991   *European Women and the Second British Empire.* Bloomington: Indiana University Press.

Snyder, Louis
    1962   *The Imperialism Reader: Documents and Readings on Modern Expansionism.* New York: D. Van Nostrand.

Swansom, Tod D.
    1995   "To Prepare a Place: Johannine Christianity and the Collapse of Ethnic Territory." *JAAR* 62:241–63.

Szymanski, Albert
    1981   *The Logic of Imperialism.* New York: Praeger.

Talbert, Charles
    1994   *Reading John: A Literary and Theological Commentary on the Fourth Gospel and the Johannine Epistles.* New York: Crossroad.

Thomas, Norman E.
    1995   *Classic Texts in Mission & World Christianity.* Maryknoll, NY: Orbis.

Tolbert, Mary Ann
    1990   "Protestant Feminists and the Bible: On the Horns of a Dilemma." Pp. 5–23 in *The Pleasure of Her Text: Feminist Readings of Biblical and Historical Texts.* Ed. Alice Bach. Philadelphia: Trinity.

Torontle, Mositi
    1993   *The Victims.* Gaborone: Botsalo.

Williams, Patrick and Laura Chrisman
    1994   *Colonial Discourse and Post-colonial Theory: A Reader.* New York: Columbia University Press.

A CANAANITIC WORD IN THE LOGOS OF CHRIST; OR THE DIFFERENCE THE SYRO-PHOENICIAN WOMAN MAKES TO JESUS

Jim Perkinson
University of Chicago

ABSTRACT

The pericope focused on the Syro-Phoenican woman in Mk 7:23–30 stages a rhetorical encounter with Jesus that briefly bifurcates the *logos* of God between two human subjects. In her repetition of Jesus' brief *parabole*, but with a twist, the woman secures her request and is sent on her way for her "saying" (*logos*). The motive is unprecedented in Mark. It seems to emphasize that her word is not to be gathered into the folds of Jesus' own speaking, but "stands out," literally, as a counter-word, a reiteration of his own discourse that repeats-with-a-difference. To the degree the text is embraced as "incipient christology"—normative discourse about the Christ in the moment of its making—that counter-word reveals a trace of colonial heterogeneity in christology's origins. *Contra* dominant "christocentric" readings, I will argue that the story offers a minute disruption in the witness of the gospel to Jesus as the entire locus of salvation. In particular, I will make use of insights from feminist and post-colonial discourse theory to exhibit this slight self-difference or non-coincidence within the *christo-logos* as a trace of messianic power operating for a brief moment *against* Jesus himself from a subject-position represented as non-Jewish, female, and pagan. In postcolonial reading, it opens the discourse of Jesus to the possibility of the word of salvation issuing *from* an other who is "not Christ."

> Let the children first be fed, for it is not right to take the children's bread and throw it to the dogs.
> —Jesus

> Yes, Lord; yet even the dogs under the table eat the children's crumbs.
> —the woman

Robert Allen Warrior highlighted the need to put Canaanites at "the center of Christian theological reflection and political action . . . [as] the last remaining ignored voice in the [biblical] text, except perhaps for the land itself" (264). He cautioned Native Americans, as "contemporary Canaanites," against any facile collaboration with recent Christian liberationist impulses, given the latter's reliance upon the Exodus and Conquest traditions for its notion of liberation.

In the liberationist project, scholarly interventions have concentrated on retrievals of what may have been the actual history of various internal Canaanite revolts against their own oppressive city-state structures and their absorption into the new politico-religious experiement that became known as Israel. Warrior argues that however warranted such retrievals may be, the actual text we are left with nonetheless depicts a conqueror-God ordering the complete suppression and annihilation of everything "Canaanite" (262). The historical effect of that text has been a long hermeneutic tradition equating Canaanite *indigenes* with religious pollution and perversion. As he further emphasizes, it is the tradition that eventually supplied the spiritual rationale for five hundred years of European conquest and domination of indigenous "American Canaanites."

I in no way want to gainsay his caution in what follows. What I do want to do in this essay is to take up Warrior's *ab-original* concern for the sake of a postcolonial reading of the one Canaanite trace (Matt 15:21–28)[1] that strangely emerges inside of Christian discourse itself.

Reading the gospels in the situation of postcolonialism invites a hermeneutical strategy that recognizes a form of colonialism as also having had an effect in shaping the Christian scriptures. In this essay, I will bring the insights of postcolonial discourse theory[2] to bear on the pericopes in Mark and Matthew about the Syro-Phoenician (Canaanite) woman in a way that raises a theological question about "the other" of biblical authority. I am particularly concerned to develop a reading strategy that opens the biblical text itself to the power of difference that inevitably troubles situations of colonial and postcolonial cultural contact.

---

[1] Linking Warrior's use of the term "Canaanite" with Matthew's covers over a real difference. The Syro-Phoenician woman, as we shall see, cannot be understood as subject to the same kinds of oppressions as modern-day Native Americans or other indigenous peoples who have suffered the ravages of colonialism. Rather, I am concerned to read the Syro-Phoenician passage, and Matthew's gloss of the woman as "Canaanite," in such a manner that contemporary Christianity and christology is opened to "other" oppressed voices today in ways that respect their heterogeneity.

[2] Cf. especially Gayatri Spivak, "Can the Subaltern Speak" and "The Politics of Translation"; Said; Bhabha; and critiques of the same which simultaneously underscore their theoretical achievements and limitations in Parry and Donaldson. While each of these represents a theoretical position arising out of a distinctively modern, colonial or post-colonial "moment," here I use the perspective opened up by them to ask questions of a text of antiquity. Whether such a retrojection of contemporary methodology and perspective can be theoretically justified is an argument that can not be pursued here. That argument is perhaps analogous to arguments for the use of modern sociological or even Marxist theory in relationship to biblical exegesis, such as found in Theissen or Gottwald.

Of initial moment in such a project is a recent "turn to rhetorics." Various feminist theoreticians of biblical interpretation (Schüssler Fiorenza, Wire, Kinukawa) have opted in recent years for a shift from literary-hermeneutical strategies to a critical rhetorical paradigm in which, authorship is understood to encompass both the writer and the audience. Interpretation elaborates a discourse already scored by competing voices and material conflicts. The texts so elaborated are thus neither data nor evidence, but sites of a perspectival and persuasive "will-to-speak" that also encodes its subjects of address. Interpretation of such texts is then likewise a venture in polyvocality.

Influenced by that shift, I approach the pericopes in question as part of an early form of "christology," of discursive rhetoric about the Christ,[3] and interrogate the way they center discursive power in the speaking subjectivity of Jesus. My own interest in doing so is not primarily that of retrieving the elided voices of women (Schüssler Fiorenza) or of the role of the signifier "woman" in Mark (Selvidge) or of the faith (Belo, Ringe) and courage (Brock) of this particular woman as an other. Nor is it primarily one of exhibiting the residual patriarchy operating in the historical Jesus or the colonialism and anti-Judaism in his Markan and Matthian redactors (Kwok) or exposing its mission ideology (Sugirtharajah). Rather, I am ultimately concerned to raise a soteriological question out of the text's evident heteroglossy (Bakhtin). How are we to interpret a word of saving deliverance when it is spoken against the Word of saving deliverance?

The analysis of this essay will move from the contemporary horizon to early christological text to earliest text and back out again. With Warrior's concern in mind, I will develop a brief analysis of Matthew's version of the story and then focus most of our attention on Mark's text. After elaborating a postcolonial reading of the Markan version of the Syro-Phoenician woman, I will then move back out of that primal text of christology to revisit Matthew's Canaanitic reference and, finally, offer a challenge to contemporary christology.

Matthew's Canaanitic Re-Reading of Mark's Syro-Phoenician Woman

Matthew Levi writes his Gospel with the creative product of Mark in hand and retells the story for his own audience. When he comes to the memory of Jesus' encounter with a woman from the region of Tyre—to whom in Mark's pericope, Jesus himself, astonishingly, loses an argument—he makes an unprecedented New Testament move (Mk 7:24–30; Matt 15:21–28). He names her "Canaanite." I am not concerned here systematically to deci-

---

3 Cf. Kwok Pui-lan, who describes the the Syrophoenician woman's speech as "clearly framed in a christocentric and androcentric discourse" (1995:73).

pher Matthew's redactional motive, but only to pause before the citation and let it signify. For the mind steeped in Israelite history, "Canaanite" glimmers summoning up a troubled image of polytheism, sacred prostitution, and ethnicity beyond the pale. The word opens an old memory, a rent in Matthew's text. It marks the woman herself as metaphor, as more (and less) than mere flesh and blood (Kwok, 1995:71–73). In the designation "Canaanite," the voice that emerges is cast as a cry from far back, asking mercy, confessing a genealogy of possession.[4] But it occasions from Matthew's Jesus not even a word in answer.

At first pass, here, the messianic voice remains mute. It is a moment, in the first written attempts to articulate the *logos* of the Christ, of a surprising "*a-logos*"—"a refusal to speak." We are here presented, I would argue, with a represented silence of Jesus that can be read as an attempt at silenc*ing*. She speaks; he is silent; she refuses the silence he imposes. His attempt to keep her word out of the flow of his own speech, out of his "text," as it were, fails. The silence outside the borders of the text—a silence that the silencing of Jesus fails to keep in place—erupts in a word that takes over his own. From a postcolonial perspective, it might be tempting to assert that here, for a moment, "the subaltern speaks" (as we shall examine in the last section).[5] But in any case it is a speaking that will demand much theoretical attention in what follows. Its valence is not immediately decidable. It is strangely written into this pericope by the tactic of what has been called "iteration," the interruption of a discourse from within its own terms by means of a repetition that is yet different (in this case by a voice that is at once non-Jewish, female, and pagan). As Matthew has recognized, more speaks in the Canaanite's speaking than a simple subject. She speaks "for." But what she speaks for remains to be determined.

This sudden but subtle irruption of a foreign word inside the Jewish-Christian Word will exercise our fascination in what follows. As the Matthean text has it, the word of deliverance for the daughter will have to be wrestled from the constrained silence of Jesus by both harried disciples and irrepressible woman. Eventually, the woman prevails and Jesus is "forced" to speak a word of resistance to her word ("It is not right . . .) that will end up, in one sense, resisting him. Not only is his silence here sullied, but his speech-response is effectively co-opted by hers—put at odds with itself and pushed back at him, in a brief riposte. Neither his silence nor his speaking are simply left to themselves.

---

[4] The woman speaks for her possessed daughter and thus already occupies the place of "concerned mother," rather than some place of her own in the male discourse of Matthew.

[5] The "subaltern" is an "other" who is "under," a class of those whose voice and agency are submerged in a hegemonic social formation. Cf. Spivak, "Can the Subaltern Speak?" and Parry's questioning of Spivak's thesis that hegemonic formations attain absolute powers of subject-formation that constitute and disarticulate the subaltern or non-elite woman (35).

Just this juncture in the text—a double articulation (of words and silences) that marks a major crossroads and turning point in the narrative of the Gospel—we could be tempted to say hope for the Canaanites emerges within Christian discourse. But it is really, as we shall see, only a disguised form of hope for Christians. The text is finally not about Canaanites.

But it is also just here that we must interrupt the editor and skip back to the Markan precedent, presumably still in Matthew's hand. For the strange silence of Jesus that Matthew conjures as a "refusal of the Canaanitic" will comport in Mark even more strangely. Matthew's introduction of the phrase, "But he did not answer her a word," in fact interrupts, edits, and renders readable what is in Mark left more implicit. There Jesus is represented as going into hiding, seeking to escape detection (Mk 7:24). He enters a house and "would not have anyone know it." He is represented as submerging his voice in a general silence, refusing further interrogation and scrutiny.

A quick glance at the end of Mark's rendering will set the stage for a more painstaking progression through his representation of the interaction in and out of this more generic silence. In Mark's version, the woman is finally sent away by Jesus with a very distinctive word of dismissal: "For this *word* [that is to say, "her" word, her "*logos*"], go! The demon has gone from your daughter." It is the only time in Mark that a demonstration of messianic power has been so won—wrested from the Christ by the word of the other. We seem to have here in Mark a "messianic word" that is not simply Jesus' own. Rather the *logos* of power is represented, ever so briefly, as having jumped track, crossed the divide between Jesus and this woman, reversed its valence and come back *at* him, re-iterated, revised, repeated with a difference. Said otherwise and more thematically, christology here, in its most primal text, is faced with the outside, the exterior, of its own logic. There is a split-ting apart (or doubling) of the saving word that renders suddenly undecidable the subjectivity of its authorship. Whose word has wrought deliverance? Indeed, who has spoken to whom? But we must stage this reading carefully—as carefully as it has been (unwittingly?) prepared for by Mark's own staging.

The Syro-Phoenician Encounter as "Point Farthest Out" in Mark's Gospel

Recent exegetical studies have displayed the richness of this passage from various narrative (Rhoads), socio-historical (Theissen), and ideological-critical (Myers) perspectives. Building on these more definitively exegetical perspectives, I offer a few theological comments.

First, to the degree Mark can be understood as a diptych, two basic display panels (roughly chapters 1–7 and 10–16) hinged by a short, but intense, transitional section (chapters 8–9), the Syro-Phoenician pericope falls at the beginning point of the transition. It is strategically placed near the epicenter of change in the narrative.

Even more significantly, the colonial geography of the encounter marks this moment as a kind of "point farthest out." Never does Mark—for whom geography is a key code—have Jesus venture at a greater remove from the center (Jerusalem) of the national region defining his area of mission. His trek north into the rural district surrounding the urban centers of Tyre and Sidon constitutes a kind of self-exile. He exits "the nation" proper, into a hybrid domain where three distinct cultures—Phoenician, Jewish and Hellenistic—intersect (Theissen: 68). And he does so seeking anonymity. He is at least "on retreat," although in view of the intensity of the opposition he has evoked (plots on his life begin in Mark as early as chapter 3), we might better think of his status as perhaps "underground."

Jon Sobrino interprets this gesture as one sign among many of a severe crisis in Jesus' ministry (91–92). In the chapters leading up to this encounter, Jesus has taken on the powers that be from his base in rural Galilee. After what seemed initially to be great popular success, he has come up against increasing surveillance, public attempts at entrapment, and defamation whose stakes are capital punishment. He has suffered the misunderstanding of the poor, the target group of his ministry, met the cynicism of his own Nazareth neighbors, endured the doubt of his own family about his sanity, and discovered the deep ideological blindness of his own disciples. Despite the healings and exorcisms, the kingdom has not arrived in overt power so much as in ambiguous trace.

After his furtive encounter with the woman, Jesus is depicted in a new mode. In the second half of his ministry, centered now not in Galilean villages and synagogues, but on the road in largely out of the way places, Jesus is no longer cast as the miracle man. He no longer astonishes the crowds with his power and perspicacity. Rather, he is shown increasingly heavily burdened and harried. The intensity of his passion comes into view only cryptically—in secretive "sidebars" with his disciples, or carefully chosen moments of public confrontation with his adversaries.

Once in Jerusalem, Jesus is represented as immediately taking over the Temple grounds for a day, "exorcising" it of predatory economic activity, and then slipping back outside the city at dusk. In his subsequent teach-in activity in the Temple precincts, parabolic irony sharpens, authority emerges as an explicit issue, apocalyptic pessimism shuts down the disciples' bedazzlement at the site's ostentation.

The text then takes us rapidly through Jesus' betrayal, arrest, over-night imprisonment, trial, torture, ritual delegitimation, and finally his execution as an insurrectionary in a public display of imperial sovereignty. And if Mark indeed ends, as now is commonly thought, at verse 8 of chapter 16, the last word is one that is not spoken. We are rather left with the flight of three "trembling and astonished" women into an uncanny silence.

Sobrino reads all of this as offering a markedly different venue of ministry, and indeed, of self-identification, from that underscored in Mark's first seven chapters. The christology in evidence in the second half of Jesus' career is one that is conflicted and surreptitious. He is faced not with clear signs of the kingdom's imminence but rather with the terrifying possibility of being a fool. He is represented as confident, now, not of success, but of catastrophe. For Sobrino, the "dark night" foreboding that irrupts in the hinge section (e.g., chapters 8–10 in Mark) between these two distinct itineraries can be grasped only by way of "crisis"—presumably something bordering on the severity of breakdown. For him, if the difference (of the second half from the first) is not thus imagined from the various hints given, the deep *pathos* and painful uncertainty of the over-all representation lose their forcefulness. Synoptic craft is overcome by a willful and forgetful sentimentality.

The Geopolitical Context in the Syro-Phoenician Story

In his focus on the sociology of the passage, Theissen offers a thick description of the texture of relations between Jews and Gentiles in the border regions of Tyre and Galilee. He elaborates his description under six different rubrics: ethnicity, culture, social status, economics, politics, and social-psychology. What emerges in connection with our pericope is a portrait of a female resident of a bilingual (Greek and Aramaic) region harboring a minority mix of Jewish folk. As a Syro-Phoenician who is also a Hellene, and one whose daughter sleeps on a "bed" rather than a "mattress" (a detail evocative of status), the woman is subtly indicated as a well-to-do citizen.

The thematic focus on food in the exchange of aphorisms between Jesus and the woman directs Theissen's attention to regional economic structures. Economically, Tyre and Sidon depended upon the surrounding rural farming community for sustenance and used their financial power to expropriate much of the local product (Theissen: 72–75). Theissen presents a typical picture of urban/rural relations in which the hinterland usually got the short end of things in the struggle over food. He argues that in such an economy, Jesus' little parable may have amounted to saying something like: "First let the poor people in the Jewish rural areas be satisfied. For it is not good to take the poor people's food and throw it to the rich Gentiles in the cities" (75).

The tone of suspicion and antagonism hinted at in the text also gains plausibility for Theissen when read against the backdrop of local political tensions. It is clear that regular expansionist moves on the part of Tyre—countered by various Herodian and Roman policy initiatives—left a legacy of mutual hostility between rural northern Galilee and the urban centers on the coast (Theissen: 76–77). On the Jewish side of things: in the Gospels themselves, Tyre and Sidon are demonized as the large urban anti-types of tiny Galilean towns, equivalent in their wealthy, pagan odiousness to Sodom and Gomorrah (Matt 11:21–24). On the Tyrean side: so virulent was the active animosity at the outset of the Roman Jewish War (presumably just prior to when Mark was writing) that many Jews in and around Tyre were imprisoned or killed.

For my purposes, this socio-cultural context is highly suggestive. The passage invokes a context of multi-layered contradictions. I do not want to try to homogenize a reading strategy across these different possibilities. Rather, I wish to open one small site of incipient polyvocality where the word emerges, as it were, "contrapuntally." In Said's sense of that term, such a word must be analyzed in relation to "a set of intertwined and overlapping histories," demanding a reading strategy "modelled not . . . on a symphony but rather on an atonal ensemble"[6] (18, 318). Rather than seek narrative coherence or try to unearth a univocal witness from the text, such an analysis "focus[es] on rhetoric, ideas, and language . . . [as] "symptoms of power" (51, 281, 259). In this view, the Syro-Phoenician's word marks a peculiar form of counter-logic.[7] It remains a provocative gesture of something that both is and is not the *logos* of Christ.

Theissen's work organizes the details of this pericope into a complex picture of colonial power relations. For instance, in her representation as a privileged Greek citizen of a city regularly oppressing the local Jewish populace, the Syro-Phoenician woman could be understood to be occupying the position of the dominant. In such a construal, her solicitation of Jesus would represent a somewhat typical case of high cultural "ambivalence": a desperate fetishizing of the spiritual power of the weak who are otherwise despised in everyday life (Taussig). She would be participating in and perpetuating an ambiguously oppressive structure that accords mythic healing potency to those positioned as the lowly or the less-than-civilized (specifically, in this case, "the less-than-Hellenized"). Quite apart from his own self-representation, Jesus here would take on some of the character of the folk-healer, a kind of Jewish wild-man/shaman.[8] And in such a reading, his initial refusal of the woman's request could be grasped as an act of resistance to yet one more appropriation of the resources of the oppressed by the powerful.

From the point of view of the text itself, the woman as "woman," "non-Jew" and presumptively "pagan" would have to be herself considered to be occupying the margins. She is, perhaps more than almost any other character

---

6 In which, Said goes on to say, "We must take into account all sorts of spatial or geographical and rhetorical practices—inflections, limits, constraints, intrusions, inclusions, prohibitions—all of them tending to elucidate a complex and uneven topography" (318).

7 To the degree the text is embraced as incipient "christology"—normative discourse about the Christ in the moment of its making—the woman's counter-word can be theorized as the tentative emergence of a necessary "anti-christology," or in Juan Luis Segundo's re-formulation, a christic "anti-logic" (Nietzsche: 150–51; Segundo: 13–21).

8 Cf. M. Smith for a comprehensive treatment of this theme, especially pp. 107, 116. For a treatment of the Markan Jesus as a biographical double-entendre, a multi-leveled meaning-structure, only the first level of which is magical, cf. J. Z. Smith: 193–94.

in Mark, Jesus' "other"—not only geographically, but sexually, racially and religiously, "on the outside." She stands largely exterior to his concern or experience. To the degree the text is taken seriously as a discourse of power convening its own field of normativity, the woman is clearly a disruptive figure, figured in the text itself as a disruption. And here lies my real interest in her significance.

I want to suggest that this pericope can be read as a moment when, in its very genesis, christology offers us a detail that questions its own powers of normativity as discourse. In a complex manner, by means of subtle nuances in the text that are presumably outside of conscious redactional intent, this story marks a lack of closure in the witness of the Gospel to Jesus as the entire locus of salvation. It constitutes a site where the canonical source of christology can be read against itself as a totalizing authority.

THE SYRO-PHOENICIAN WOMAN AND POSTCOLONIAL SPACE

If geography is allowed to determine the pericope's pivotal significance, then we can construct the text's christological significance as follows. Jesus crosses the border into Israel's outside and in so doing moves from speech to silence. But the domain of silence into which he has sought to disappear itself now breaks out into speech *in spite of* him, *against* his own resistance to that unanticipated eruption of "voice." His has indeed been a ministry of giving voice to the voiceless: the most palpable evidence of the movement of Jesus into a new geographic region has usually been the report of an instant increase of "noise" in that region (Mk 6:56). People heretofore hegemonically silenced begin to shout and cry out their need, grief, and struggle (1:24; 7:37; 10:46–52). The very rumour of Jesus' coming into an area is enough by itself to clear the social space of official strictures of silencing (1:45). History begins to find its popular subject; the public square is reconfigured in terms of a new boldness to voice transcripts previously hidden (11:27–33).[9] Pain and hope gain a hearing.

In the instance we are looking at, a unique reversal takes place. The word of power Jesus bears crosses a border from his own interior to his social, political, religious other. Here, Jesus does not speak for the woman; the woman speaks for him. The saying of the Syro-Phoenician woman is not just an interesting rejoinder—it is *logos*, the word. In Mark's text, it is not (as it is in Matthew's) her faith that has won power. It is her "saying." We could almost say her saying becomes part of the tradition of the sayings of Jesus. But

---

[9] Cf. Scott for an argument that the oppressed remain critically conscious of their situation even when seemingly cooperating in maintaining a public transcript of its legitimation. "Hidden transcripts," developed away from public space, become the source of various forms of covert resistance and sabotage, and not infrequently, give rise to overt attempts at rebellion.

doing so would capitulate to the homogenizing effect of christology (as a discourse of power) a unique word that first demands a hearing on its own terms. The Word here is first a contest of words, a moment when difference is revealed inside of the Word itself. It is a difference that must be plotted in relationship to both space and time.

We will deal first with space. Postcolonial analysis will suppy perspective. Almost unnoticed by the reader, the spatiality of the encounter between Jesus and the woman is mediated by rumor. The Syro-Phoenician woman has already "heard" (rumor) of his power before encountering him. Sensitized to the role of rumor in another story of bread mediating power in a situation of conflict, we can assert that the first word of this story is one that does not conform to the boundaries imagined by Jesus for his ministry.

The other story is found in the work of post-colonial critic Homi Bhabha, who has traced the power of rumor attending the mysterious circulation of *chapatis* (unleavened flat bread) in northern and central India in the 1850s and 60s in connection with mutiny (199). According to British historiography on that mutiny, no one among the native people or in the army or the colonial administration quite knew what to make of those little loaves as they were passed from one village to another with great solemnity (201). But their effect was one of spreading alarm and heightening an uncertain expectation. For Bhabha, the alarm had everything to do with the rebellion that eventually erupted. Rumor became the manic vehicle of fear "as an uncontrolled, yet strategic affect of political revolt" (199). Its content was "one common electric thrill" under the vague sign of "the archaic, the awesome, the terrifying" (205). It spread across the landscape with an "almost 'timeless' speed" (205). Its "indeterminate circulation of meaning . . . with its perverse, psychic affects of panic, constitute[d] the intersubjective realm of revolt and resistance" (200).

By way of comparison, in our biblical story, we are told only that "immediately a woman . . . heard of him and came." The hint is quite cryptic, the barest of indications that something has preceded. But the text has already made us abundantly aware that "reports" have circulated, spontaneously generating crowds wherever Jesus halts (Mk.6:56). And we have also been made aware of the affective content of this "regime of rumor": the astonishment (6:51), the awe and frenzy (3:7–12; 4: 41; 5:20; 6:6), the aura of expectation that is not entirely positive, but fraught with fear (5:15) and even ominous foreshadowings (Herod's paranoia that Jesus is John the Baptizer reincarnate, 6:16). Indeed, so rapidly does talk spread about this mysterious new teacher that it "evicts" Jesus from his earliest planned itinerary: the "news" about him takes up his space before he can occupy it himself, pushing him away from towns out into the countryside (1:27–28, 38, 45). In time, it will provoke the plot on his life (11:18), frame the trial proceedings against him (14:55–61), fuel the derision at his crucifixion (15:29–31). And to the degree the messianic expectations alluded to in chapter 13 characterize the political climate when Mark is presumably writing (during the Zealot upheavals around 65 CE), here too, rumor finally underwrites revolt. The postcolonial problematic is undoubtedly unique to modernity, but popular panic, it would seem, is a generic text in situations of unrest.

Bhabha's point bears pondering here also. In India, the fear and panic that was largely attributed to a 'pre-literate' native mind, subject to superstition and misapprehension, also showed its force in the very *genre* of British intelligence gathering (204). Rumor was contagious. It bound native people and bureaucratic master alike in a structure of affective, if antagonistic, group psychosis (203). Its role in revolt resulted in a "disjuctive structure between and within groups" that cannot be represented in a simple binary opposition (206). It leads Bhabha rather to theorize the "subject of insurgence," in the colonial situation, in terms of "cultural hybridity" and a certain form of "undecidable collectivity" (204, 206). How do we understand the action of revolt in a space of shared panic? His analysis yields a form of "ambivalent" or "interchangeable" agency that is constituted not solely through the "negative consciousness" of the peasant, but also "through partial incorporation of the fantasy and fear of the Master" (206). The subject of this discourse is "split and doubled between native informer and colonial 'enunciator'" (206). And "what" is enunciated is simultaneously "native panic" and the "spreading, uncontrolled fear and fantasy of the colonizer" (206).

The insight arguably applies also to biblical rumor and the subject of healing. While in the case at hand the parallel is not exact—the structure in question is one between healer and healed, not colonizer and colonized—the hybrid character of events is similar. In Mark the affectation of awe that is the effect of rumor is not only the condition of the crowds, but of the leaders (6:14, 20). It even rebounds upon Jesus himself, who "marvels" in a place like Nazareth, where rumor has not been sufficient to affect a climate of belief conducive to effective action (6:6). In one sense, rumor is the constituting medium of Jesus' war of interpretation with "those who are on the outside" (presumably those who are already conspiring against him), leading him to adopt the parable as a form of teaching (4:11–13). In sum, the word of messianic power is inextricable from the excesses of popular articulation. Thus we could say of our Syro-Phoenician story: the beginning of deliverance is not clearly assignable. The boundary of healing is not Israel alone, its force not simply that of Jesus. It materializes rather as the co-creation of a popular cultural form of agency that straddles national borders and transgresses individual authorship. The word is first heard outside of its own authorization. Its space is anywhere talk is taken up. Its subject is both Jesus and "the people."

The Syro-Phoenician Woman and Postcolonial Time

Bhabha also helps sensitize us to the politics of time in this pericope. The *dialogos* of the encounter—the argument between the woman and Jesus—takes place over a temporal fold in the text that is only minutely represented. Jesus' resistance to the woman's initial request appeals to time as its motive for refusal. He says, "First let the children be fed . . ." Implied in the word "first" is a particular temporal structure, a new messianic "now," privileging the Jews, that renders all else past and secondary. Theologically, it hints at an apocalyptic time-frame operating an absolute caesura: time/end-time. In this schema, the nation "Israel" is figured as the space of a fulfillment that is defined in part against other spaces harboring "old time." In the initial discourse of Jesus, the woman is positioned "behind" him, part of something that is being brought to a close. And he is "ahead" of her, something that has not yet come "for" her, still out in her future (in the form of a Gentile mission). Whether that messianic organizing structure of "new/old" will be allowed to determine their interaction becomes the subject of their argument.

Bhabha's work examines a similar narrative organization of old/new that structures relations between contemporary metropole and colony. Indeed, the role of time in constituting national spaces and identities is, in one sense, the major focus of Bhabha's entire postcolonial project. While concentrated exclusively within the problematic of modernity, his explorations nonetheless raise questions of the relation between identity and temporality that are productive to think with even in relation to an ancient "colonial" text.

In exploring "forms of cultural identity and political solidarity that emerge from the disjunctive temporalities of the national culture," Bhabha is concerned to reveal the "temporal caesura" that founds the modern myth of progress (151, 237). For him, modernity is constituted by a time-lag that occurs as a disjuncture between the image of authority and its practice. It shows up everywhere in the way the various discourses of modernity ("civic and liberal humanism," "nationalisms," "racisms," etc.) invariably create an ambivalent narrative of modernity as the "ideology of the new" that is yet dependent for its meaning on the projection of the old (246). For Bhabha, such a narrative is subtly "split." Its authority can be established only in the gap between the "pedagogical symbol" and its "performative sign," between the "epochal events" in which modernity is grounded (e.g. the French Revolution) and the "empirical enunciations" of those events in practical life (e.g. everyday reiterations of the value of "freedom") (Bhabha: 242–43, 245–47). The split is everywhere but shows up with greatest effect in the colonial margins of modernity (244).

For instance, in relationship to the epochal event of the French Revolution, Bhabha asks what happens "if we take our stand, in the immediate postrevolutionary period, in San Domingo with the Black Jacobins, rather than in Paris"? (244). The distance, then, "that constitutes the meaning of the Revolution as sign, the *signifying lag* between event and enunciation, stretches not across the Place de la Bastille or the rue des Blancs-Monteaux, but spans the temporal difference of the colonial space" (244). Here, in the geopolitical space of the colony, the temporal structure of modernity is revealed in all of its contradictoriness.

> In [San Domingo]," Bhabha says, "the symbol of the Revolution [becomes] partially visible as an unforgettable, tantalizing promise—a *pedagogy* of the values of modernity—while the 'present efficacy' of the sign of everyday life—its *political performativity*—repeats the archaic aristocratic racism of the *ancien regime*. (244)

That is to say, in San Domingo, we can hear Toussaint L'Ouverture invoking "the moral, modern disposition of mankind" enshrined in "the sign of the Revolution" as if it applies to him as a black (244). He is a colonial subject "for whom the signs of modernity, 'liberty, equality, fraternity' (the signficance of the French Revolution), are a constant source of preoccupation and aspiration" (244). But we also hear him in the tragic moment when he grasps that this very disposition "only fuels the archaic racial factor in the society of slavery" (244). The pedagogy of a new freedom is repeated in a performative context of old oppressions.

In the space of the colony, Bhabha goes on to say, this "time" of repetition "ensures that what seems [merely] the same within cultures is [in fact politically] negotiated" (153, 247). It breaks up the teleological linkage of past and present that undergirds the republican fantasy of the People-as-One (249). In the example above, in the revolt of L'Ouverture and the slaves, San Domingo suddenly no longer plays as the (primitive) "past" for revolutionary France as the "modern present." But (obviously) neither is the former colony now suddenly the same as France. What emerges rather is an intersubjective domain articulating an "excess" or "disturbing alterity," a marginal discourse concurrently circulating "modern, colonial, postcolonial, 'native' ... time[s] in the same cultural space" (152–53, 247). The result is a certain "undecidability" in the temporal structure of identity (154). What "speaks" (in L'Overture) is "agonistically articulated" between "the pedagogical and the performative." The subject appears here suspended between a clear narrative structure of past/present (the pedagogy) and a disorienting repetition of that structure in the "place" of the past (its performance by the likes of L'Overture) (154). While the language is difficult, the meaning is patent: a split articulation, at the borders of the nation, that resists binary representation (154, 251).

When we move to the borders of the biblical text—indeed, to the complex colonial space around Tyre and Sidon—Bhabha's constructions offer provocative hints. We have seemingly clear subjects, but also a clearly split word, a *logos* that is really a *dialogos*. Jesus cites time and a proverb; the woman, in effect, repeats the proverb, but with a difference that collapses the time-structure. Her word opens a gap in his word: the past catches up to the present. Suddenly there are discontinuous times contentiously present in one discursive space. But just as quickly, the gap is closed by Jesus, recuperated in a messianic discourse hastily reconstituted as his own—but now including her difference in the repetition. The opening is only a flicker, a brief flash—there... then gone.

But in that moment, what has appeared? We have a complex dialogue of domination and resistance. Each of the two figures is simultaneously superior and subordinate in different registers. Jesus as "Jew" is under the colonial thumb of Rome, the comprador thumb of priest and scribe, the native-elite thumb of Herod, the economic thumb of Tyre. He is suspect, from "Galilee," hotbed of Zealot revolt. But he is also male and master of the discourse in this encounter. The woman is likewise dominated—as woman, as perhaps a single female without a male representative, as confessing a "gendered affliction" in her house that presumptively renders her likewise suspect as "mother-of-the-afflicted" (Kinukawa: 55). She is further suspect vis-a-vis Jesus as non-Jew and pagan. But she is also apparently well-to-do and Greek. The space of their dialogue is already filled with a particular discourse of domination. It is not neutral space, but a domain already figured in symbols of control cut by signs of resistance: Tyre as principality disturbed by Jewish dis-possession, local regnancy in conflict with alien refugee.

In this fraught space, however, the story is told from a geopolitical position that is centered in Israel, embedded in a discourse that carries (messianically) nationalist overtones. While the colonial borderland of Tyre and Sidon is not an adjunct region of "political" Israel, in the text it is a marginal space to the great events taking place to the south. At the borders of the nation, the rumor of Jesus enunciates the symbol of an epochal event: the healing of "the Messianic Endtime" ("the Kingdom Come," "the Apocalyptic Advent of the Son of Man," etc.).

Ultimately, in Mark's telling, the apocalyptic symbol of Resurrection stands as the epicenter from which the pedagogical discourse of "the New Age" emanates. But in Jesus' first words to the woman, she is positioned as still in the past, not yet eligible for the event of breakthrough, part of a domain that by definition remains outside the powers of the new. The "at hand" of the kingdom's irruption in Israel (Mk 1:15) remains a "not yet" in the borderland. Indeed, the very language of messianic abundance ("the children's bread") structures its meaning as a form of binary exclusion (against "the dogs" whose time of feeding will come only after "the humans" are done). The present People of God does not yet include Syro-Phoenician *ethnoi*. But the woman's word does strange "judo"[10] on Jesus' refusal. In her

---

[10] Judo is a form of defense that, rather than meeting force with opposing force, instead uses the opponent's own energy and momentum against the opponent.

repetition and re-valorization of the (messianic) possibility of healing embedded in his discourse, Jewish time and Gentile time are made to co-habit the same space. The "Now" of apocalypse becomes the "now then!" of its other. She re-presents "his" word—in a different performance.

The Syro-Phoenician Woman and Postcolonial Reiteration

It is worth imagining—with the text—how she accomplishes this. But in thus attributing the agency of this shift in some sense to her, I do not wish to underwrite a reading that locates that agency entirely in her subjective consciousness (nor do I want entirely to disavow such a reading). Rather, I want to remain attentive to the text as text, to let it do its inscriptive work of shuttling agency back and forth between character and discourse as well as between author and reader (and indeed, between theology and its critics and in the end, between Christian and Canaanite).

Theissen begins to uncover the tactic of the reversal we observe in suggesting that the Syro-Phoenician woman reconfigures the stereotypic distance structuring her encounter with Jesus (79). She does so by way of a repetition that contests Jesus's word in the name of his own iterated values. Jesus leverages his refusal of her approach by invoking the "little ones": it is not right to take what children need and—while they are still hungry—give it to "dogs." She capitalizes on the positive valuation given children in this refusal by "playing off the image against the content" (80). She is, after all, herself speaking on behalf of a child. What he proposes in general, she takes up concretely.

Rhoads gives full scope to the textual play here (356–58, 366–67). What emerges is a kind of "politics of diminutives." In the text as we have it, Jesus casts what appears to be a "dispersion" in using the diminutive word for "dogs." Literally, he speaks of puppies. The connotation may well be that he is refusing not just adult Gentiles (such as her), but Gentile progeny—"little Gentiles" who grow up into big ones and who represent, for Jews, the reproduction of Galilean oppression. In any case, her rejoinder tropes his refusal. She does not oppose the reduction he has introduced into the interaction, but she finds in its diminution the opening for her own countermove. The word for puppy introduces a second meaning of "littleness" alongside the pejorative sense (of unclean "dogness") which he presumably intends. It allows her response subtly to contest his own from within. By repeating the diminutive form, "puppy," and qualifying its placement as down "under the table," she shifts the implication from predatory scavenging outside the house to an internal domestic scene of begging for scraps (357).[11]

---

[11] Kinukawa emphasizes the renegotiation of space involved here. The outside of Jesus' image is suddenly recast as interior in the woman's (59).

At the same time, she reiterates the reference to smallness by also using the diminutive forms of the words for crumbs and children (a different word from the one Jesus used in his saying). In so doing, she creates a kind of "solidarity in littleness" (linking "puppies" with "crumbs" and "little kids"). Its effect is dual. She valorizes Jesus' own "politics of the least" (Mk 9:33–37) in her discourse. But she also thereby opens up room for her own daughter in the privileged position he accords the most vulnerable.

To recapitulate: in the battle of wits, Jesus' discourse offers the Syro-Phoenician woman only one subject-position: that of "little dogness." She is represented as taking up this space-of-the-small in the name of her own child's need and expanding it by her reinscription of its referentiality. In net effect, however, it includes not only her daughter, but also herself. Rhoads notes that she becomes "'least' on behalf of her daughter" (366). She kneels, begs, gives honor as an inferior, "diminishes herself by being willing to be identified as a little scavenger dog—in order to get her daughter freed" (367). "In so doing," Rhoads remarks, she "anticipates Jesus' teaching about the greatness of being least" (367).[12]

But it is critical to note that she does so precisely by beating Jesus at his own speech game. Her littleness is a "posture," a negotiation, a canny playing of herself in the discursive nexus she foists upon Jesus, that effects, as we have seen, a covert displacement of his exclusionary manuever. She "brokers" the possibilities of shame and honor into a transcript that doubles his word back upon himself. He refuses in the name of children; she "repeats" ("accepts") his refusal, but in a deft phrase that links human little ones and canine little ones in a common valuing of littleness. It allows him an honorable way out only through a tacit acknowledgment that she has rewritten the boundaries of his discourse in a manner that includes her request, by definition. Continued refusal on his part—in that reconfigured discursive space—could only show up as shameful dissimulation. Or said another way, she *does* (covertly) shame him—into honoring her appeal by re-presenting it as the concrete implication of his own reason for refusal.

What thus appears as a relatively powerless posture on the part of this Hellene—a show of submission on the part of a humble least one—can actually be read as a *powerful* redeployment of the terms of talk. She is "little" only by way of self-definition, and even then, only in this moment. Or more accurately, in the politics of a double difference, she adroitly doubles her own self-presentation. A diminutive "put-down" becomes the occasion for a savy "put-on" by a big woman holding and claiming her own. As Bhabha and other theorists have noted in examinations of postcolonial politics, reiteration is an effective tactic where domination is dilatory.

---

12 According to Kinukawa, in challenging Jesus to cross the barrier of uncleanness between Jew and Gentile, the Syro-Phoenician invites him to submit to defilement and "to become least [himself] in order to break through the exclusively group-oriented faith of his fellow Jews" (61).

There is a last hint that remains to be highlighted. Jesus' response does not quite claim responsibility for the outcome. In the laconic bluntness of the Greek (according to Rhoads), he is represented as saying simply: "Because of this saying—Go on off! Gone off is the demon from your daughter!" And we are left to ask, without answer: Which word actually effected the exorcism? Or at an even deeper level: From whence did the word of deliverance ultimately come and whose space of subjectivity was finally cleared out and opened up?

The Syro-Phoenician Woman's Tactic in The Rest of Jesus' Markan Career

Having queried the passage at its various crossing-over points, we now must work our way back out of the text towards some larger christological questions. There is a way of reading this encounter as a moment of initiation for Jesus.[13] Positioned as such, the pericope yields a picture of him moving through a crisis of ministry, if not of identity, and—upon coming out the other side—reversing his direction and center of reference geographically and tactically. The geographic about-face would seem to be particularly telling. It points to this encounter as perhaps critical for all that happens afterwards. Rhoads picks up on the fact that the woman's response immediately opens up a new Jesus-initiative among the Gentiles of the Decapolis region (Rhoads: 362). He reads the episode as Mark's way of foreshadowing the coming world-mission, thus consoling readers in the time of Mark's writing that their inclusion in the community of the redeemed is rooted in the practice of Jesus himself, not in some aberrant after-thought.[14] My own interests, however, stay a bit closer to the question of generic strategy. I read the rhythm of riddle and riposte as pedagogic for Jesus himself.

It is possible to understand the effect of the woman's "work" upon Jesus as one of *mentoring*, preparing him (in the fore-knowledge of the text—not of her, personally) for the increase in confrontation he will face in his march on Jerusalem.[15] She has taken the "no" he has thrown up and split it into a

---

[13] Cf. Victor Turner's notion of "liminality" as characteristic of the initiatory movement from one stage of life to another across a ritualized threshold that serves to deconstruct one identity for the sake of the emergence of a new identification (1969:94–130).

[14] Sugirtharajah emphasizes that this episode cannot be understood as a missionary initiative on Jesus' part in spite of its subsequent ideological deployments for that purpose by the Christian church (14). Kwok points out the incipient anti-Judaism operative in a salvation history model of understanding the text (1995:77–79).

[15] According to Ringe, "Here Jesus himself must learn about being that sort of Christ [one who offends the privileged while occasioning joy for the poor] from one of the poorest of the poor and most despised of the outcast—a Gentile woman on her own before God and humankind" (72). Cf. also Kinukawa's characterization that "she frees Jesus to be fully himself . . . She has set the stage for him to act out his mission" (60).

simultaneity of "yes" and "no," refusing its refusal by using its negative power to secure her own positive purposes. Such will become the essence of his own strategy—a continual redeployment of the specific terms of the rejection he provokes from the authorities. He will constantly probe hegemonic religiosity for the contradictory points which can be opened out into a creative affirmation without ceasing to oppose its negations. The chief priests, scribes, and elders will challenge his "authority" in clearing the Temple; Jesus will take up that precise term in response, but displace it (into a question about John the Baptist) in such a way that it becomes a questioning of the leaders themselves (Mk 12:27–33). The Pharisees and Herodians will seek to trap him on the issue of paying taxes to Caesar; but the very image they seek to impugn is deftly made the source of a counter-trap: why are they carrying the coin, if they refuse the jurisdiction? (12:13–17). The Sadduccees will solicit Moses to challenge the idea of resurrection; Jesus will invert the solicitation so that it rebounds as an affirmation of exactly what they thought to discredit (12:18–27).

We could perhaps even say the saavy revision of the Syro-Phoenician's riposte prefigures the style of Jesus' own coming passion. His encounter with her confronts him with the very form of the word he must henceforth bear and become.[16] For a singularly graced moment, in her response, he is put discursively "beside himself": he gets to see and feel the irony "from without," working its erosions over against his own negativity. Thereafter, it will be his to carry in a suffering increasingly disclosed out loud to his followers. More and more often, in the latter half of the gospel, the disciples themselves become the objects of riposte (e.g. 8:33). They are "schooled" by Jesus in the same schooling the woman began with him. Thus in the movement of the text, the "initiation" begun with the Syro-Phoenician does not stop with Jesus.

Matthew's Canaanite Reading Again

Indeed, I argue that the pedagogy does not even stop with the text, but finally seeks out "us," its readers on the text's outside, in our own approach to the word of salvation, wherever it may arise. In one sense, the message of that pedagogy "is" the outside—the instability of the line any of us draws in trying to secure salvation discursively. It is finally our own (albeit very differently positioned) powers, discourses, and sufferings of exclusion that are brought into question. We are returned whence we began.

It is a stroke of genius that Matthew marks this moment in his reading of Mark as somehow peculiarly "Canaanitic."[17] It reveals his own particular

---

[16] Ringe says, "Her gifts and her ministry become the vehicle of the gospel to Jesus and to us" (72).

[17] Albeit his innovation remains patriarchal at the same time. It is thus a genius that offers a simultaneity of effect: it both raises a critical question about past exclusions, and at the same

readerly "map," his coordinates of the known and the unknown. For him, exteriority (the outside of his own community of Jewish Christians) implies not just "the Gentile," his other, but also something that he recognizes as harkening back to the very *origin* of his own genealogy. For one writing in a self-consciously Jewish stylistics, pushing the gospel form towards midrash, the "Canaanite" is the quintessential other of both space *and* time, haunting memory as well as vision. With a single stroke, Matthew presses the incident into service of a whole culture, a whole era. He writes the woman back into the beginning, the founding discourse of his entire tradition. Or more accurately, he writes the tradition forward into a crisis of his present—a kind of return of the repressed. She re-presents primally unfinished business. What had been staged by Mark as an encounter outside the field of Jewish messianic responsibility is re-positioned by Matthew as a sign of uncertainty evoking its interior. The erasure of the Canaanite presence in Israelite history was part of the mode of constructing the national identity. But here, the erased begins to reappear like a palimpsest.

What of the present moment? How does the Syro-Phoenician's gesture read in the various and varied contexts of the late twentieth century postcolony or metropole? By Matthew's leave, the reader can at least ask after the beginning of his or her own temporality—in my case: the dominant North American myth of origins. For me, as a white male, the word of the woman as "Canaanite" begs juxtaposition to voices either "black" or "Indian." I am not just repeating Matthew's innovation by simply plugging in my own "others" in cavalier fashion. I am not for a moment suggesting that the text can be transposed by mere substitutionary fiat.

Canannites on the Contemporary Horizon of Christology

But I am concerned to specify a more generic implication. I want to offer a kind of third order trope upon Matthew's secondary troping of the original Syro-Phoenician trope on Jesus—one that is finally aimed at christology as such. I am arguing that the dominant Western traditions of Christianity can (and indeed must, if they take the text seriously as a source of theology) translate the meaning of this pericope's gesture of displacement into their modes of christology. (Or what amounts to a slightly less active posture, they must at least allow for such a translation. As Robert Warrior has suggested, it is finally not up to those in the position of dominance to write such, however liberatory their intent.) I am arguing that mainstream Eurocentric christologies must attend to the *formal possibility* of such a displacement, whatever its actual historical content, as part of the on-going reiteration of the word of sal-

---

time, "uses" the place of the woman to carry out that critical question, thus one more time submerging her voice in another project.

vation in various local contexts and discourses. Such an attention would constantly seek to anticipate what finally cannot be fully anticipated: new interruptions of christology as discourse that repeat a word of its text from a place that cannot be recuperated entirely into its meaning.

Said another way, the text we have been examining inscribes a hybridity within the word of deliverance that eludes the control of even Jesus himself.[18] The text installs the Syro-Phoenician woman on the outside of his messianic mission and then through her stages a reiteration of "his" messianic word that speaks outside of its normative subject position. In that moment, the word is represented as speaking in her voice in a very peculiar difference. She speaks as "the other" not only of Israel (as non-Jewish, pagan, female), not only of early Christianity (as Gentile), but indeed of Jesus *himself*, as the normal subject of messianic discourse. For a brief moment, she speaks in his place.

And it is tempting to read this moment under the rubric of postcolonial critic Gayatri Spivak's claim that "the subaltern cannot speak." "Subalterity," in Spivak's designation, refers particularly to non-elite women in the Indian colonial context, whose consciousness and voice remain unrepresented (and indeed, unrepresentable) in either British or native historiographies of the time. While Spivak perhaps overvalorizes the power of hegemonic discourse to co-opt and re-constitute subaltern consciousness, her caution regarding representation is well taken. The burden of her argument is that critical theory errs when it presumes to "speak for" the subaltern subject. At best, it can "speak to" the possible place of such a subjectivity, but only by embracing and representing its own limitations as discourse. In connection with the discipline of christology, Spivak's formulations raise the question of the limits and outside of christology as discourse. In light of the Syro-Phoenician passage, they provoke the question of whether the subjectivity of salvific discourse can be centered entirely within the speaking of Jesus alone.

In general, the christological text could be said to constitute a space of speech empowering the possibility of other speech: salvation is, in part, a liberation of oppressed voices, a freeing of subjects to speak their own creative words. (And it would then also be necessary to say that, in general, if the same christological discourse is used to shut down "other speech," to close off dialogue and creativity, it is functioning "non-salvifically" or even "demonically.") The effect of salvation would be understood to issue not so much from Jesus himself, as from the open place between his words and the words of his others—at times, even as the power effected largely by the way

---

[18] Although concerned to maintain more of a christocentric reading than is being offered here, Kinukawa recognizes a similar sort of thing when she says, the Syrophoenician woman's "intuition about who Jesus should be and Jesus' sensitivity to the marginalized are drawn into one vortex and create a mutual transformation" (61).

their word contests his own. It emerges, as Rita Nakashima Brock has argued, as a power of relationship, a power operating through mutual vulnerability and interdependence (52). As such, it is arguable that, in the text at hand, the Syro-Phoenician woman becomes the place from which the word of power issues. She briefly occupies the space (even the subject-position) of "Christ" in her speaking to and against Jesus, speaking briefly "in his place" without entirely giving up her own.

But if so read, the Syro-Phoenican herself would also have to be taken as simply one more patriarchal figuring of "Woman" whose effect is one more erasure of the actual woman who is speaking. While this is perhaps interesting as a momentary dislocation of the messianic voice, the woman's own voice is nonetheless lost She would remain "subaltern": an "other" who is "under" the text, given representation in its discourse only in the fact of being "spoken for." She speaks "for Christ," which is also to say Christ speaks through and for her. She is made to carry out his agenda, enrich his presentation, submerge her difference in his sameness. She indeed speaks the messianic word, but her voice is valued *only* because it speaks such. "Christ" remains a hegemonically totalizing figure. And ultimately, the woman becomes merely a place of ventriloquism.

Bhabha's emphasis on hybridity opens up a more troubling and productive perspective It is worth noting in the Markan passage that the Syro-Phoenician woman does not ever acknowledge Jesus as the "Christ," nor does he ask for such acknowledgement. Her concern is practical: deliverance for her daughter. His concern is proprietary: staying within the bounds of his task. Nothing overtly religious transacts. He is indeed presented as "lord" of the discourse that structures their interaction, but in a surprise epiphany, she is revealed, in this particular instant, as master of its performance.[19] It is arguable that the deliverance won is effected as much by her reconfigurement of the time and space of messianic healing as by anything he does. He seems merely "to confirm"—the demon has *already* gone before he opens his mouth a second time! She is perhaps not so subaltern after all. But in any case, the "effective word" appears composite, of uncertain authorship.

And at the generic christological level I am attempting to address, the question then arises: Is it possible to understand the discourse on Christ, the *christo-logos*, as harboring a certain possibility of "difference" *within* itself? Can we as readers let it provide, at one and the same time, a framework for interpreting the world that is yet capable of being mobilized in a practical word challenging the very boundaries of that frame? Can we who are Christians allow for a word that speaks a saving value from a different time and space, an irrecuperable place that serves christological discourse precisely by

---

[19] Both Bhabha (1994:241–46) and Butler (26–29) have been helpful in thinking through issues of performativity.

thwarting its inevitable drive (the drive of any "logy"[20]) towards the mastery of totality?[21] Does christology here face its own necessary self-limitation, its incarnational finitude, as a human word? If so, then I would argue it can only be by way of honoring that irrecuperability.

I would argue that ancient and contemporary Syro-Phoenicians and Canaanites must be allowed to remain such, even in the moment of speaking a messianic (or saving) word to those identified with Christ. Their word is not to be facilely gathered into the fold of *the* Word. Rather, such a speaking represents a peculiar undecidability. On the one hand, it represents a word of the "not-Christ" that begs to be embraced by Christians as a "christic" word. But it does so solely on the basis of its *performance* and not in its credentials or claim of identification with Christianity. On the other, to the degree such an intervention effects a "real" moment of deliverance or healing, it cannot be entirely screened off discursively as somehow absolutely different from the salvation associated with Christ. Its value may be soteriological even though its author is not clearly "Jesus." Here, christology must anticipate an irreducible hybridity of the discourse and even the "subject" of its own good news. The introduction of a saving word "from without" cannot simply be "colonized" or appropriated as a form of anonymous Christianity. Neither can it be entirely differentiated as "other." The Syro-Phoenician pericope, I would suggest, authorizes a reading of the word of salvation as itself heterogeneous. Not only can the latter come from an other who speaks "in the place" of Christ. But it also may be spoken "instead of Christ"—in interruption of his word—from a subject-position not his. The difference "from without" may remain different, even on the inside. Obviously, claiming such does *not* clarify soteriological politics for Christians in relationship to contemporary others and their religious beliefs. It merely authorizes the struggle to read and act alongside of those others in pursuit of words of hope and healing wherever such are spoken.

Works Consulted

Bakhtin, Mikhail
    1981   *The Dialogic Imagination: Four Essays.* Ed. M. Holquist. Trans. C. Emerson and M. Holquist. Austin: University of Texas Press.

---

[20] Cf. Jacques Derrida, "Structure, Sign, and Play in the Discourse of the Human Sciences," in *Writing and Difference.*

[21] Invoking Spivak, Kwok characterizes the Markan and Matthean pericopes as instances of a "master discourse" serving to legitimate a Gentile mission (1995:76). Even in the moment of its own early formulation as a type of anti-colonial discourse, christology yet articulates elements of anti-Judaism, sexism, and colonialism that demand postcolonial deconstruction.

1984   *Rabelais and His World*. Trans. H. Iswolsky. Bloomington: Indiana University Press.

Belo, Fernando
1981   *A Materialist Reading of the Gospel of Mark*. Trans. M. J. O'Connell. Maryknoll: Orbis.

Bhabha, Homi K.
1994   *The Location of Culture*. New York: Routledge.

Brock, Rita Nakashima
1988   *Journeys by Heart: A Christology of Erotic Power*. New York: Crossroad.

Burkill, T. A.
1966   "The Syrophoenician Woman: The Congruence Of Mark 7:24–31." *Zeitschrift fur die neutestamentliche Wissenschaft* 57:23–37.

1967   "The Historical Development of the Story of the Syrophoenician Woman (Mark 7:24–31)." *NovTest* 9:161–77.

Butler, Judith
1993   *Inside/Out: Lesbian Theories, Gay Theories*. Bloomington: Indiana University Press.

Derrett, J. Duncan
1973   "Law in the New Testament: The Syrophoenician Woman and the Centurion of Capernaum." *NovTest* 15:161–86.

Derrida, Jacques
1978   *Writing and Difference*. Trans. A. Bass. Chicago: University of Chicago Press.

Donaldson, Laura
1992   *Decolonizing Feminisms: Race, Gender, and Empire-building*. Chapel Hill and London: The University of North Carolina Press.

Kinukawa, Hisako
1994   *Women and Jesus in Mark: A Japanese Feminist Perspective*. Maryknoll: Orbis.

Kwok, Pui-lan
1993   "Racism and Ethnocentrism in Feminist Biblical Interpretation." In *Searching the Scriptures: A Feminist Introduction*. New York: Crossroad.

1995   *Discovering the Bible in the Non-Biblical World*. Maryknoll: Orbis.

Myers, Ched
1988   *Binding the Strong Man: A Political Reading of Mark's Story of Jesus*. Maryknoll: Orbis.

Nietzsche, Friedrich
1968   *The Anti-Christ*. Trans. R. J. Hollingdale. New York: Penguin.

Parry, Benita
1987   "Problems in Current Theories of Colonial Discourse." *Oxford Literary Review* 9:27–58.

Rhoads, David
    1994   "Jesus and the Syro-Phoenician Woman in Mark: A Narrative-Critical Study." *JAAR* 62:343-76.

Ringe, Sharon H.
    1985   "A Gentile Woman's Story." Pp. 65–72 in *Feminist Interpretation of the Bible*. Ed. Letty Russell. Philadelphia: Westminster.

Said, Edward W.
    1993   *Culture and Imperialism*. New York: Alfred A. Knopf.

Schüssler Fiorenza, Elisabeth
    1983   *In Memory of Her: A Feminist Theological Reconstruction of Christian Origins*. New York: Crossroad.

    1992   *But She Said: Feminist Practices of Biblical Interpretation*. Boston: Beacon.

Segundo, Juan Louis
    1985   *The Historical Jesus of the Synoptics*. Trans. and Ed. J. Drury. Maryknoll: Orbis.

Selvidge, Marla
    1990   *Woman, Cult, and Miracle Recital: A Redactional Critical Investigation on Mark 5:24–34*. Lewisburg: Bucknell University Press.

Smith, Jonathan Z.
    1978   *Map Is Not Territory: Studies in the History of Religions*. Leiden: E. J. Brill.

Smith, Morton
    1978   *Jesus the Magician*. New York: Harper & Row.

Sobrino, Jon
    1978   *Christology at the Crossroads: A Latin American Approach*. Trans. and Ed. J. Drury. Maryknoll: Orbis.

Spivak, Gayatri C.
    1988   "Can the Subaltern Speak." Pp. 271–313 in *Marxism and the Interpretation of Culture*. Ed. C. Nelson and L. Grossberg. Chicago: University of Illinois Press.

    1992   "The Politics of Translation." Pp. 177–200 in *Destabilizing Theory: Contemporary Feminist Debates*. Ed. M. Barrett and A. Phillips. Stanford: Stanford University Press.

Sugirtharajah, R. S.
    1986   "The Syrophoenician Woman." *ExpTimes* 98:13–15.

Taussig, Michael
    1987   *Shamanism, Colonialism and the Wild Man: A Study in Terror and Healing*. Chicago: The University of Chicago Press.

Theissen, Gerd
    1991   *The Gospels in Context: Social and Political History in the Synoptic Tradition*. Trans. Linda M. Maloney. Minneapolis: Fortress.

Turner, Victor
    1969   *The Ritual Process: Structure and Anti-Structure.* New York: Cornell University Press.
Warrior, Robert Allen
    1989   "Canaanites, Cowboys, and Indians: Deliverance, Conquest, and Liberation Theology Today." *Christianity and Crisis* 49:261–65.
Witherington, Ben, III
    1984   *Women in the Ministry of Jesus.* London: Cambridge University Press.

THE GOSPEL OF LUCAS GAVILÁN
AS POSTCOLONIAL BIBLICAL EXEGESIS

Hector Avalos
Iowa State University

ABSTRACT

Postcolonial biblical interpretation in Latin America has been reflected in various literary genres ranging from theological essays to modern paraphrases of biblical texts. *The Gospel of Lucas Gavilán* is a paraphrase of the Gospel of Luke published in Spanish in 1979 by Vicente Leñero, a Mexican advocate of liberation theology. Leñero follows closely the formal structure of the Gospel of Luke while at the same time replacing and adding new characters and events that foreground parallels with the politics of modern Latin America, especially Mexico. Jesucristo Gómez (Luke's Jesus), the hero of Leñero's version, becomes a vehicle for the critique of traditional Catholicism and an advocate of Rudolf Bultmann's program of demythologization. This essay will discuss how Leñero modifies the biblical texts and traditional interpretations to accomplish his goals and the implications of Leñero's efforts within the larger theoretical context of postcolonial literature and biblical interpretation in Latin America.

INTRODUCTION[1]

Despite its relatively recent advent, postcolonial literature is already a diverse phenomenon. If by postcolonialism one refers to the socio-political situation that obtains after the achievement of formal independence by nations, then the postcolonial experience of countries around the globe has not been uniform, and the achievement of freedom itself spans a variety of historical contexts.[2] As Ashcroft, Griffiths, and Tiffin (6–7) suggest, many "postcolonial" writers might argue that the economic dependency in otherwise politically independent nations is a form of colonialism, and so the term "postcolonial" is a misnomer altogether. Rather the modern world is more akin to the relations between an economically hegemonic core and an

---

[1] The abbreviations we shall use are: ELG = *Evangelio de Lucas Gavilán* (original Spanish edition); GLG = *Gospel of Lucas Gavilán* (English translation); JG = Jesucristo Gómez.

[2] Paz (14–15), for example, argues that New Spain "was never a colony" in the same sense as the American colonies; American colonists came here to escape religious orthodoxy, while in New Spain colonists came to expand orthodoxy.

economically exploited and dependent periphery outlined by Immanuel Wallerstein (1974, 1979).

As it pertains to Latin America, we may define postcolonial literature as writings that scrutinize critically the colonial experience, whether past or present.[3] Thus postcolonialism here refers to a state of consciousness that does not accept colonialism as the proper political arrangement. Under this definition the writer may or may not be living in a colonial situation. Colonialism may be seen as any form of social, political, or economic subjugation undertaken by a state and its allied institutions.

Postcolonial biblical interpretation in Latin America has been reflected in various literary genres ranging from theological essays to paraphrases of biblical texts. Examples of such postcolonial literature include the foundational works of liberation theology produced by Gustavo Gutierrez and Juan Segundo, as well as the paraphrases of biblical Psalms by Ernesto Cardenal, the controversial Nicaraguan priest.[4]

The Gospel of Lucas Gavilán is a paraphrase of the Gospel of Luke that was originally published in Spanish in 1979 by Vicente Leñero, a Mexican advocate of liberation theology. Leñero follows closely the formal structure of the Gospel of Luke while at the same time replacing and adding new characters and events that foreground parallels with the politics of modern Latin America, especially Mexico.

Jesucristo Gómez (Luke's Jesus), the hero of Leñero's version, is an advocate of Rudolf Bultmann's program of demythologization, which becomes a vehicle for the critique of capitalism and traditional Catholicism. This study will discuss how Leñero modifies the biblical texts and traditional interpretations to accomplish his goals and the implications of Leñero's efforts within the larger theoretical context of postcolonial biblical interpretation in Latin America.

Vicente Leñero

Vicente Leñero was born in Guadalajara, Mexico, in 1933. He has followed a dual career as a journalist and a writer of fiction. His best known works include *Los albañiles* (1964), *Redil de Ovejas* (1972), *Los Hijos de Sanchez* (1972), and *Alicia, tal vez* (1980). Most recently he has been an assistant director for the periodical called *Proceso*.

Although analysis of *The Gospel of Lucas Gavilán* is only beginning, Leñero's work has been the subject of various studies.[5] One of the main stud-

---

[3] Our definition is a variant of Elleke Boehmer's (3), who defines postcolonial literature as literature which "critically scrutinizes the colonial relationship."

[4] The foundational books on liberation theology by Gustavo Gutierrez (1972) and Juan Segundo (1975) have been considered primary documents of postcolonial literature in Latin America by Gallagher (25). For a study of Cardenal's paraphrases, see DeHay.

[5] These studies include those of Langford; Lipski; and Robles.

ies of *GLG* is included in a survey of a number of Latin American authors by Wolf Lustig. Lustig provides an excellent overview of Leñero's work, and he identifies the search for justice and modernizing the Gospel as some of the main themes of *GLG*. But Lustig does not concern himself much with how Leñero reinterprets specific Lucan texts to accomplish his goals.

Basic Approach of *The Gospel of Lucas Gavilán*

The demythologization program of Rudolf Bultmann provides the basis for the approach that Leñero uses in *The Gospel of Lucas Gavilán*. This dependence on Bultmann is acknowledged in the Foreword of the English edition (*GLG*, xiii), which characterizes Leñero's book as a "Bultmannian demythologizing of the Gospel of St. Luke."

Rudolf Bultmann's "demythologization" attempts to reinterpret or eliminate the supernatural aspects of the Gospel, viewing them as expressions of socio-psychological phenomena (1951–55; 1958). For Bultmann, the essential message of the Gospels did not reside in their historicity or scientific accuracy. References to demon possession, for example, may be seen as expressions of psychological disorders which the ancient writers interpreted within the pre-scientific language of their day. The essential message, even in pre-scientific language, of demon possession can be extracted and interpreted to mean that Jesus was concerned with persons in distress.

Accordingly, Leñero feels free to change any historical contexts in order to extract the essential messages of each of the episodes of the Gospels that he paraphrases.[6] At the same time, Leñero describes modern historical contexts that are recognizable and relevant for the modern reader.

Setting and Time of *The Gospel of Lucas Gavilán*

Validating the geographical spaces of the "Third World" or the "periphery" is one of the principal features of postcolonial literature (Huggan; Ashcroft, Griffiths and Tiffin, 24–29). In the case of *GLG*, the setting is modern Mexico, and more particularly the capital city of Mexico and its outlying areas such as Michoacan and Campeche. These Mexican settings parallel the settings of Jerusalem and outlying areas of Galilee in the Gospels. In turn, such geographical symmetry is paralleled by the core and periphery in the economic geography expounded by Immanuel Wallerstein and Marxist economists.

Leñero is relatively explicit about the time of the ministry of Juan Bautista and Jesucristo Gómez in his paraphrase of the inception of the preaching of John the Baptist (Lk 3:1–18):

---

[6] For a recent commentary on Luke, see Fitzmyer (1981, 1985).

> The dates are not all precise. In the final years of Luis Echeverria Alvarez's presidency or in the first years of José Lopez Portillo's . . . Juan Bautista, the son of Zacarias Bautista, the sexton, returned to his birthplace and begun stirring up the people of the region and in the outlying districts of the capital.[7]

The administrations of Luis Echeverria Alvarez (1970–1976) and José Lopez Portillo (1976–1982) were marked by great change and turmoil in Mexico. In 1975, for example, underemployment affected some 45% of the population (Camín and Mayer: 203). Inflation became so great that it was cheaper to import crops such as corn, of which Mexico had a surplus a few years before.

Despite new discoveries of oil, the riches expected from those discoveries never were sufficient to pay for the national debt. The problem of servicing the national debt ($80 billion in 1982) and other problems eventually culminated in the dramatic devaluation of the Mexican currency by some 70% in 1982. Corruption, which has always been a problem in Mexico, was also rampant during the seventies. Equally significant, during the seventies there was labor unrest which was precipitated not only by lower income groups, but, as Camín and Mayer (205) note, by "highly stratified, privileged, and technical sectors of the industrial proletariat . . . Examples of this were the extended agitation of the electricians and railroad workers in 1971 and 1972."

The setting of *GLG* in Mexico may reflect more than an attempt to modernize the Gospel of Luke. For Leñero, the economic and social oppression of the Jewish people by the Roman empire and traditional Jewish authorities has its parallels in the social and economic oppression of the poor in Mexico by international corporations and the traditional Catholic Church. In many ways, Mexico is still a colony of foreign capitalists and their Mexican allies just as the Jews were a colony of Rome administered by their royal surrogates (e.g. the Herodians). Accordingly, the setting and time of *GLG* is quite consistent with the critique of colonialism and imperialism found in postcolonial literature.

Name Changes

The imposition of the names and language of the imperialist is an important theme in postcolonial literature (Srivastava). In addition, native persons often change their own names to conform to the nomenclatural pat-

---

[7] *GLG*, 29 ; *ELG*, 49: "No se tienen bien precisadas las fechas. En los últimos años del sexenio presidencial del licenciado Luis Echeverria Alvarez o en los primeros del licenciado José Lopez Portillo . . . Juan Bautista, hijo de Zacarías Bautista el sacristán, regresó a su comarca y andaba alborotando por los pueblos de la región y los alrededores de la zona metropolitana."

terns of the imperialist. Awareness of this nomenclatural imposition by superior powers on their vassals can already be observed in the Bible (e.g. Dan 3). Leñero shows his awareness of how subjugating labels can replace personal names in the story of the demon-possessed son (Lk 9:37–43). The corresponding character in *GLG* is a gay young man. In Leñero's version the young man was tormented, not by a spirit, but by a society which had "virtually replaced his given name of Mario Benitez with the nickname 'Sissy!'" (*GLG*, 106).[8]

For the most part, the names of the characters in *GLG* are transparent and closely related to those in the Gospels. The characters are, however, "Latin Americanized" as much as possible. Thus, Jesus is now Jesucristo Gómez, Joseph is Jose Gómez, a bricklayer, and Mary is now Maria David, a seamstress (*GLG*, 17). Other names receive novel twists. Thus, the Satan of the Gospels receives a cognomen, Samperio, which is reminiscent of the Latin word for "always" (*semper*). In *GLG*, a former prostitute, corresponding to Mary Magdalene in Luke 8:2, is named Magdalena Santoyo, the latter which can mean literally in Spanish "Saint (am) I."

Likewise, many biblical places are often replaced with locales that bear Mexican Indian names. For example, the paraphrase of the episode of the walk to Emmaus (Lk 24:13–53) selects Cuautla, Iztapalapa, and Yecapitxtla for the corresponding biblical locales. Leñero could be using Latin American names to transfer biblical stories to a Latin American setting, yet the use of Latin American cognomens and Native American place names serves to identify Latin Americans with the oppressed classes of the Gospels. As we shall see below, anonymous female characters in the Gospels receive names in *GLG*, something that may reflect the act of naming as an act of empowerment.

Jesus

The main character of the Gospels, of course, is Jesus. Luke portrays him as the son of God who comes to bring salvation to Israel and the world. Jesucristo Gómez is Jesus's counterpart in Leñero's version. Leñero's paraphrase of the episode about Jesus' circumcision (Lk 2:21) provides the following account of his birth "with only a word or two changed here and there": "Jesucristo Gómez David . . . was born at 22:45 on the twentieth day of December, in the year 1942, at fifty-six Topacio Street in this city."[9] Luke 2:39–40

---

[8] *GLG*, 104; *ELG*, 135: "Marica, Marica, . . . el insulto se fue convirtiendo en un apodo, mas bien en el nombre de pila de Mario Benitez." On the use of names in other works of Leñero, see Lipski.

[9] *GLG*, 17; *ELG*, 34: "Jesucristo Gómez . . . nació a las veintidos cuarenta y cinco horas del veinte de diciembre de mil novecientos cuarenta y dos en la calle Topacio cincuenta y seis de esta ciudad."

portrays Jesus as a precocious youth who asks many questions about biblical interpretation. Leñero also portrays JG as a precocious youth, but his questions are directed at the wealth of the Church. Thus, JG asks: "Why is the priest so rich?" (*GLG*, 22).[10] In the paraphrase of the story where Jesus finds himself among the scribes (Lk 2:41–50), the narrator of *GLG* tells us that JG would argue with modern priests concerning the wealth of the Church. This concern continues into adulthood.

As to JG's appearance as an adult, Leñero informs us that he is "dressed as always in an open shirt, old tweed trousers and leather sandals" (*GLG*, 146).[11] This precision concerning JG's life and appearance contrasts markedly with the Gospels. The Gospels generally are not very precise about the timing of Jesus' birth or his other vital statistics, and Mark does not even have an account of Jesus' birth. Leñero thus insists on placing Jesus's modern counterpart within a concrete *Sitz-im-Leben* which maximizes the relevance of contemporary events.

Leñero's portrayal of JG departs markedly from what most traditional Christians might expect of Jesus. Gómez uses foul language, smokes cigars, vandalizes the sacred objects of a church (*GLG*, 202), has frequent temper tantrums, and will engage in fist-fights. The Lucan Jesus recruits fishermen as his first disciples, but Jesus does not really engage in fishing (Lk 5:1–11). Jesucristo Gómez recruits garbage-dump scavengers as his first disciples, and he does scavenge the garbage dumps alongside of them.

Thus Leñero's version of Jesus exemplifies and extends the notion of the incarnation, even if demythologized, to a more human level than in the Gospels. In the Gospels the incarnation of Jesus reflected a divine willingness to share the human experience. Nonetheless, the Jesus of the Gospels is still a being of a higher order that does not always share all human experiences. Jesucristo Gómez wallows in the most repugnant human activities alongside his disciples. JG is totally engrossed in the affairs of this world, and talk of heaven or some other supernatural utopia is non-existent.

Jesus vs. Modern Colonialists/Imperialists

In the biblical Gospels the main human adversaries of Jesus are the traditional Jewish religious authorities, namely the Pharisees, scribes, and Saducees. In *GLG* the main opponents of Jesucristo Gómez are the institutional Catholic Church and the secular power structures such as the health care system. For Leñero, the rich also are destined to be the enemies of JG from the womb. In the paraphrase of the visitation (Lk 1:39–56), Maria David

---

10 *ELG*, 39: "Por qué el señor cura es tan rico?"
11 *ELG*, 181: "vestido como andaba siempre: camisa abierta, su viejo pantalon de mezclilla, huaraches."

says concerning the biblical Jesus: "He condemned the rich. He fought the oppressors. He gave his life to change the world . . . that's why I want my son to be named Jesucristo."[12]

The Gospel portrays the Pharisees as obsessed with material gains, and Leñero portrays modern priests as more concerned with making money than with the spiritual needs of the flock. This is evident already in the complaints of JG's father concerning the fees expected by the local priest to baptize his child. Jose Gómez says of the priest: "He's as rich as any of the fat cats in town" (*GLG*, 19).[13] Instead of cash, Jose Gómez could only afford to give the priest a turkey and two pigeons. The narrator adds that the priest "would have preferred cash, since he wanted to complete the payment on a little lot of land in the Colina Dorada [= golden hill] subdivision" (*GLG*, 19).[14] In the episode of the cleansing of the temple (Lk 19:45–48), JG complains that "priests and faithful alike [have turned] the churches into God's tombs, into fashion salons, into branches of the banks."[15]

For Leñero, the Church encourages the oppressed to accept their lot, thus perpetuating socio-economic oppression. This is illustrated in the paraphrase of Luke 4:16–30. In the biblical version, Jesus goes to the synagogue on the Sabbath and reads a passage from Isaiah 61:1–2. That passage includes a proclamation of "Good news to the poor . . . release to the captives." Jesus then implies that he is the fulfillment of the prophecy, something that arouses the ire of his listeners. Jesus complains that a prophet is without honor in his hometown, and further proclaims that the passage in Isaiah applies to the gentiles. The congregation then tries to kill Jesus, but he manages to flee, offering no apparent physical resistance.

In Leñero's version, JG is much more aggressive. The equivalent portion of the conflict begins when Father Marcelino Farias begins a sermon as follows:

> God came to earth, dear brethren, to teach us to bear up under the afflictions of life and to tell us that we will receive the rewards of his love up in heaven . . . We must accept our misfortunes and accept our sufferings, ever confident in the divine promise of everlasting life which he came to make known to us.[16]

---

[12] *GLG*, 9; *ELG*, 24: "Maldijo a los ricos. Combatió a los explotadores. Dio su vida para cambiar este mundo . . . Por eso quiero que mi hijo se llame Jesucristo."

[13] *ELG*, 35–36: "El es tan rico como cualquier rico."

[14] *ELG*, 36: "hubiera preferido efectivo, porque necesitabla completar el enganche para un terrenito en el fraccionamiento Colina Dorada."

[15] *GLG*, 202; *ELG*, 246: "sacerdotes y fieles de haber convertido los templos en tumbas de Dios, en salones de modas, en sucursales bancarias."

[16] *GLG*, 41; *ELG*, 65: "Dios vino al mundo, queridos hermanos, para enseñarnos a soportar las penas de la vida y para decirnos que allá en el cielo recibiremos la recompensa de su amor . . . debemos aceptar las desgracias y tolerar nuestro sufrimientos confiados siempre en la promesa divina de esa vida perdurable que él nos vino a anunciar."

JG interrupts the sermon by shouting "That is a lie!" He then paraphrases Luke's quotation of Isaiah 61:1–2 as his prooftext. When one of the members of the congregation attempts to strike him, JG punches back. Nonetheless, members of the church beat and expel him from the church, at which point he remarks to one of the beggarwomen sitting outside the church, "Nobody can be a prophet in his hometown" (*GLG*, 43).[17]

The message of Leñero's version seems clear. Any theology which urges the oppressed to accept their lot in exchange for future heavenly rewards is simply a vehicle by which the ecclesiastical elite perpetuate oppression. Moreover, pacifism is not a virtue. Fighting back, including with physical violence, is permissible and even preferable.

In Luke, the Devil, is the principal supernatural archenemy of Jesus. In the temptation in the wilderness (Lk 4:1–13) the Devil challenges Jesus to a series of tests meant to question whether Jesus is the son of God or to fracture Jesus' self-confidence. The encounter with the Devil is an extraordinary event in Luke, and Jesus has no intention of being friendly with Satan.

In *GLG* (36), by contrast, Jesucristo Gómez "always went around with Satan Samperio," who corresponds to Luke's Devil.[18] JG, in fact, shared the same profession, bricklayer, with Satan Samperio. Samperio seems intent on boosting JG's self-confidence rather than destroying it. As depicted by Leñero, the temptation of JG consists of coaxing Jesus to become a politician, priest, or bishop. According to Samperio these are the professions that are most effective in producing change.[19] Jesus's rejection of Samperio's advice assumes the tone of incredulity about his chances of becoming a politician or bishop rather than outright rejection of such advice as evil. Nonetheless, JG does reject the idea of becoming part of the traditional ecclesiastical and political institutions, which is where the parallel to Jesus' resistance of the Devil's advice in Luke is most apparent.

The selection of the traditional Catholic Church and capitalist power structures as the adversaries of JG corresponds well to the general complaints of liberation theology and postcolonialist authors. The traditional Church is viewed by Leñero as an ally of capitalist structures. The traditional Church is the equivalent of the traditional religious authorities that Jesus saw as oppressive in the Gospels.

Healing as Socio-Political Liberation

Consistent with his Bultmannian position, Leñero demythologizes all narratives of miracles in his paraphrase. This is particularly evident in the

---

[17] *ELG*, 66: "Nadie es profeta en su pueblo."
[18] *ELG*, 57: "Con Jesucristo Gómez andaba siempre el Diablo Samperio."
[19] For an interpretation of the temptation of Jesus as a class struggle in Luke, see Fuliga.

case of the miracle healings in the Gospels. Biblical illnesses are not attributed to demons or other supernatural causes, but are reinterpreted as socio-political ills. The cure is not prayer or some supernaturally-based ritual, but non-supernatural solutions to the corresponding problems.

A good example of Leñero's approach is the paraphrase of the healing of Peter's mother-in-law (Lk 4:38–39). In Luke's version the whole story is confined to two verses. In *GLG*, Simon's mother-in-law has been suffering from colic, but her therapeutic options are limited by the Mexican health care system. For example, Gómez asks Simon, "Did you take her to the clinic?" Simon replies, "We don't have the dough for a private doctor, and at the Health Service they won't do it because we don't have a card. They only handle people with a card."[20]

Unlike the Gospel version, Gómez's solution is not prayer. His solution is to confront the administrators of the clinic. Gómez goes to the private clinic and asks why they will not operate on Simon's mother-in-law. A doctor replies: "We only treat insured people" (*GLG*, 49).[21] The administrators of the clinic suggest that she go to the General Hospital, which is the publicly subsidized provider of health care. But JG objects that "The General Hospital is a dump" (*GLG*, 49).[22] JG then vows that he will not leave the clinic until they perform surgery free of charge. Finally, the administrators relent and offer to make an exception. The story ends with a party celebrating the recovery of Simon's mother-in-law.

The healing of the blind man in Luke 18:35–43 provides another opportunity for Leñero to transform a Lucan story into a discourse about socio-political problems. In the Lucan version, Jesus is surrounded by a crowd as he approaches Jericho. A blind man by the roadside attempts to attract Jesus' attention by shouting at him, but the crowd tells the blind man to be quiet. The crowd's admonitions, however, do not discourage the blind man, who shouts even louder. Jesus finally asks someone to bring the blind man to him. The blind man asks that his sight be restored, and Jesus cures him immediately.

In *GLG* the corresponding character, named Jerico Montaña (Jericho Mountain) is not physically blind. The episode begins with Jerico stating, "I don't see it clearly" (*GLG*, 181).[23] But Jerico is speaking about the best plan to change the political system in Mexico. Jerico engages in a lengthy monologue which proposes that to change Mexico "you've got to start thinking

---

[20] *GLG*, 47; *ELG*, 72: "Para doctor particular no hay de dónde, y ahi no quieren porque no tenemos tarjeta. Nomás curan a los de tarjeta."

[21] *ELG*, 74, "sólo atendemos a los asegurados."

[22] *ELG*, 74: "El Hospital General es una lata." Mowry's translation is not the best here. "Lata" is best translated colloquially as "hassle" or "bother."

[23] *ELG*, 221: "No veo claro."

about an organization" (*GLG*, 181).[24] As his monologue progresses, he begins to realize that the new system that he advocates will not remain static because "systems are continually modifying and improving each other" (*GLG*, 183).[25] The needs of the people dictate whether systems need change. The episode ends with Jerico saying "I am still not fathoming it fully, but I am beginning to see clearly, little by little" (*GLG*, 183).[26]

Leñero's version, thus, transforms Luke's story in at least two fundamental ways. First, the supernatural is replaced by a totally natural interpretation. Second, while in Luke the patient takes an active role in seeking help from Jesus, in *GLG* the patient betters himself through critical thinking. Gómez really plays a very minor, if non-existent, role in producing Jerico's growing awareness of the political process. So again, Leñero emphasizes a people's ability to take control of their own lives and come to self-realization. As such, the story provides an illustration of the celebrated notion of "conscientization" expounded by Paolo Freire (1974).

Gay liberation forms yet another theme that is illustrated in the context of the healing of a demon-possessed youngster in Luke 9:37–43. Instead of torment by a demon, however, *GLG* identifies the tormentors of the youngster as a society which targets homosexuals. In this case Mario Benitez, the gay young man who corresponds to Luke's demoniac, refuses to fight or engage in other stereotypical masculine activities. His father beats him in an effort "to make a man out of him" (*GLG*, 105).[27]

Eventually Mario declares his true inclinations at age eighteen, and engages in his first homosexually intimate experience. When his father learns of his encounter, he beats Mario. Mario, however, only becomes emboldened by the beating, and declares that "God had made him that way" (*GLG*, 106).[28]

Unlike the case in Luke, healing really applies to the father rather than the son. Gómez tells (*GLG*, 109) the father that "the one who has to straighten out is you."[29] JG, in fact, says (*GLG*, 108), concerning Mario's homosexuality, "It's no sin to be the way he is."[30] Eventually, Mario escapes the male tormentors of his hometown and pursues a musical career with a male lover in other towns.

Aside from illustrating Leñero's modernist view of the supernatural, his reinterpretation of Luke's miracle stories is quite consistent with the themes

---

[24] *ELG*, 221: "hace falta ir pensando en una organización."
[25] *ELG*, 223: "Se van modificando y mejorando los sistemas."
[26] *ELG*, 223: "Todavia no pesco bien la onda pero empiezo a ver claro pian pianito." More literally, we may translate: "I have not yet quite caught the wave, but I am beginning to see clearly bit by bit."
[27] *ELG*, 136: "para que se hiciera hombre."
[28] *ELG*, 137: "Asi lo había hecho Dios."
[29] *ELG*, 141: "El que necesita enderezarse es usted."
[30] *ELG*, 140: "No es ningún pecado ser así."

of postcolonialist literature. He uses these stories as opportunities to critically scrutinize the Mexican health care system, the traditional Catholic Church, and other social institutions. He also adds new categories of oppressed groups (e.g. homosexuals) into his call for liberation.

Death and Resurrection

The Resurrection of Jesus is often hailed as the single most important miracle in Christianity. Its importance is expressed in 1 Cor 15:14: "And if Christ has not been raised, then our proclamation has been in vain and your faith has been in vain." JG's general beliefs about resurrection are expressed in the paraphrase of the story about the captious question posed by the Sadducees concerning the marital status of the dead in heaven (Lk 20:27–40).

In *GLG* the question about the reality of resurrection is not captious but rather reflects the simple curiosity on the part of some students. Jesucristo affirms that he believes in the resurrection (*GLG*, 210). When pressed about whether his belief is literal and whether he believes in the resurrection from a scientific point of view, JG admits that his definition is not the same as in the Gospels. He then says: "I've never been dead to find out . . . I believe in resurrection as life" (*GLG*, 210).[31]

As to the resurrection of Gómez himself, *GLG* traces the belief to a reinterpretation or misinterpretation of the statements of a simple undertaker. Such an ambiguity begins with the location of the burial site of Gómez. In *GLG* government officials bury the body, whereas in Luke it is Joseph of Arimathea, one of Jesus's disciples, who persuades government officials to allow him to bury his leader. In the paraphrase of Luke 24:1–12, *GLG* locates the tomb of Gómez in "a common grave without any record of identification."[32]

In Luke 24:5 the women who accompanied Jesus saw his tomb and his burial. In *GLG* the three women (Maria Magdalena, Juana Morales, and Maria de Santiago) really do not know where Gómez is buried, but they decide to go to the cemetery and attempt to determine which "common grave" belongs to their leader. They engage in a conversation with the undertaker who knows of JG's reputation as a courageous social reformer. The undertaker states that "As far as I am concerned those guys never die . . . They can kill them, but they don't die" (*GLG*, 250).[33] When Maria Magdalena sobs, the undertaker adds "Remember the things he used to say . . . The road goes on, and he hasn't stopped walking" (*GLG*, 251).[34]

---

31 *ELG*, 256: "Nunca he estado muerto para saberlo . . . creo en la resurrección como vida."
32 *ELG*, 299: "fosa común sin registro ni señas."
33 *ELG*, 301: "Para mi esos hombres no mueren nunca . . . Pueden matarlos pero no se mueren."
34 *ELG*, 301: "Acuérdese de lo que él decía . . . El Camino es para adelante y él no ha dejado de caminar."

These statements by the undertaker, which were simply figurative and metaphorical, are then interpreted literally by Maria in her report to the rest of the disciples. "They told us the chief was alive . . . That he was walking around."[35] Luke's episode concerning the road to Emmaus (24:13–53) is perhaps less ambiguous about what is meant by "resurrection." In Luke's version, it is Jesus who comes back, though his disciples do not recognize him.

In *GLG*, a man who carries on Gómez's agenda and rhetoric encounters the disciples. He is so similar in his ideology to Gómez that the disciples "even began to imagine that they were hearing Jesucristo Gómez himself when he was at his best" (*GLG*, 256).[36] The man says: "The only way to prevent Jesucristo from dying is to carry on his work" (*GLG*, 256).[37] The disciples seem ready to anoint him as their leader, when he divulges that he is a priest. Tomas Carrillo, one of the disciples, then begins to insult the priest, complaining that what happened to JG was the fault of the priests. The priest is escorted out of their midst, though Simon pleads for understanding from the priest. Simon adds that "we've understood that our leader isn't dead and that's the important thing" (*GLG*, 257).[38] *GLG* ends with the priest walking out into the night.

The ending of *GLG* is a bit ironic and ambiguous. First, it seems to confirm Satan Samperio's claim, expounded in the paraphrase of Satan's temptation of Christ, that the best way to help the poor was to become a priest. But the fact that the priest was rejected by the disciples seems to indicate that JG's work need not be continued by a priest. In any, event for Leñero, Jesus lives in the sense that his ideas and work are embodied in his followers.

As is the case with the other miracles of the Gospels, *GLG* has demythologized the resurrection. Leñero's version of the resurrection is consistent with much of postcolonial literature's rejection of traditional Christian interpretations of the Bible. Leñero wishes to maintain the reader's attention on solutions within a concrete world. A resurrected heavenly Christ of the Gospels is not present in the world in a concrete manner for Leñero. For Leñero a supernatural version of the resurrection only seems to divert attention from every Christian's obligation to embody the work of Christ in their lives.

Women

Postcolonialism features the ascendance of female voices in literature (Lionnet). We may note Ellen Kuzwayo's *Call Me Woman* (1985), Michelle

---

[35] *GLG*, 251; *ELG*, 301: "Nos dijeron que el maestro estaba vivo. Que seguía caminando."
[36] *ELG*, 306: "Hasta se les figuraba estar oyendo al mismísimo Jesucristo Gómez en sus mejores tiempos."
[37] *ELG*, 306: "El unico modo de hacer que Jesucristo no se muera es continuando su obra."
[38] *ELG*, 308: "Entendemos que el maestro no esta muerto. Y esto es lo importante."

Cliff's *Abeng* (1984), and Ananda Devi's *Rue de la Poudriere* (1988) as just a few of the works which reflect this ascendance. *GLG* appears very concerned about empowering women and enhancing their prominence in the work of Jesucristo Gómez.

Part of the empowerment is the naming of women who are often anonymous in the Gospels. Indeed, in the Gospel of Luke one finds many stories in which a man is named, but a woman, who might have a close relationship with that man, remains anonymous. For example, Jairus, the head of the synagogue, is named but his daughter is not in Lk 8:40–56. The corresponding version in *GLG*, however, names the daughter (Clarita Jordan). Gómez further encourages her to become educated. Likewise, the anonymous widow of Nain in Lk 7:11–17 becomes Genoveva Galindo. We cannot extend this pattern of providing names too far, as many other women of Luke still remain without a name in Leñero's Gospel (e.g. Simon's mother-in-law) and many men also receive names. Nonetheless, *GLG* has, whether intentionally or not, provided names to women who did not have much of an identity in the Gospels.

Unlike the biblical Gospels, *GLG* is explicitly concerned with exposing the oppression of women by men. Leñero uses some episodes in Luke involving women as opportunities to speak about this oppression. One example is found in the pericope of the prostitute who bathes Jesus' feet with her own tears (Lk 7:36–50), arousing the indignation of the Pharisees, who do not deem it proper for Jesus to associate with prostitutes. Jesus then launches into a discourse about how one loves most those who have incurred the greatest debts. He finally announces that her sins are forgiven.[39]

Luke's story is not really about the oppression of women, but rather the woman is used as an instrument by which the biblical author wishes to assert Jesus' authority to forgive sins. Leñero, though, uses the biblical episode as an instrument to expose the oppression of women rather than to highlight Jesus's authority. In particular, Leñero uses the episode to assert that there are "Thousand injustices suffered daily by the women of the region: wives beaten by their husbands and forced to breed children like rabbits; girls raped by poor wretches and later sold to white slave traffickers.[40]

Leñero also transforms the episode of the raising of the widow's son (Lk 7:11–17) into a story of a woman's liberation. In Luke's version there was a widow in a city named Nain. When Jesus approached the gate of the city, he saw a funeral procession for the only son of that widow. Jesus was moved by her weeping and then proceeds to resurrect her son. Verse 15 emphasizes

---

[39] For further comments on the Lucan story, see Cavalcanti.

[40] *GLG*, 78; *ELG*, 107: "Mil injusticias sufridas diariamente por las mujeres de a tener chamacos como conejas, jovencitas violadas por infelices y vendidas luego a los tratantes de blancas.

the reunion of mother and son by stating that "he gave him to his mother" (καὶ ἔδωκεν αὐτὸν τῇ μητρὶ αὐτου).

Leñero's version is quite different. In *GLG* the widow has been distraught about the death of her son for months, and is now looking like a skeleton herself. Her neighbors are beginning to think that her grief is unnecessarily long and she is even the subject of ridicule. JG first encounters the woman when a doctor takes him to meet her. The widow begins to tell JG of her problems. "What am I going to do without children, without money, and burdened with grief and debts?"[41] Gómez's reply is not really an offer of monetary help or even a compassionate word. Instead, JG replies: "Work!" he shouted again. "Work!"[42]

The son is not resurrected at all, and the compassionate Jesus of Luke is replaced by an impatient and scolding Jesucristo Gómez, who says, "Your son isn't dead, you stupid woman! The dead person is you—always clinging to your dead husband, to your father, to your son. Weak woman! Use-less, cowardly, good-for-nothing—dead!"[43] Thus, there is no reunion between mother and son. In fact, JG insists that the woman accept the separation between her and the males to whom she seems attached. The scolding apparently prompts her to overcome her grief and continue with *her* life.

The paraphrase of the story of the healing of the crippled woman in Lk 13:10–17 is yet one more instance where Leñero reinterprets Luke to promote the liberation of women. In Luke's story Jesus happens to see a crippled woman while he is teaching in a synagogue. The woman has been crippled for eighteen years by some "spirit." Upon seeing her, he says, "Woman, you are set free from your ailment" (Lk 13:12). This healing incurs the wrath of the men of the synagogue who deem it improper to perform a healing on the Sabbath. The moral of the story is that it is proper for Jesus to disregard calendrical restrictions when caring for the ill.

In *GLG* the woman, who is given the name *Remedios* ("Remedies"), is not physically crippled. Rather she is a sixty-year old nun who had "spent eighteen years serving the priest like a slave" (*GLG*, 139).[44] Remedios first sees JG, not in a church, but in a warehouse where he is organizing workers. She subsequently invites him for supper at the parish house. At that gathering, Remedios complains about her travails, whereupon Jesus instructs her to divest herself of her "habit" if it interferes with God's service. He adds:

---

41 *GLG*, 73; *ELG*, 101: "Que puede hacer una mujer viuda, sin hijos, sin dinero, cargada de penas y deudas."

42 *GLG*, 73; *ELG*, "'Trabajar!'"—gritó de nuevo—'Trabajar'"

43 *GLG*, 73; *ELG*, 101: "Tu hijo no esta muerto estúpida! La que ha estado muerta eres tú. Siempre atenida a tu esposo, a tu padre, a tu hijo. Floja! inútil, miedosa, inservible, muerta!"

44 *ELG*, 174: "dieciocho de servir al señor cura como una esclava."

"To follow God you don't need a habit" (*GLG*, 141).[45] A week later she and two other nuns leave the convent and found a "community" of their own.

The education of women is usually not a priority in the Gospels. Jesus never encourages any woman to become a scholar or to have a career, something which is, of course, not surprising given the culture of the time. In *GLG*, however, Leñero portrays JG as encouraging the education of women. This is reflected in the paraphrase of the story about Jairus's daughter (Lk 8:40–56). The daughter, named Clarita, has been despondent and ingests a bottle of nembutal. JG keeps a vigil until she recovers. Upon her recovery, he counseled her and finally "convinced her to begin studies for entering the university" (*GLG*, 96).[46]

The purpose of these types of episodes in *GLG* then are quite the opposite of the purpose of the Gospels. For the Gospel writers, the focus of most stories involving women (and men) is on showing Jesus' glory and authority. For Leñero the stories involving women are opportunities to promote their liberation. Leñero shifts the focus from the promotion of Jesus' authority and glory to the dignity and authority deserved by women who are oppressed.

Race Relations

The complex race relations of the modern world are in large part the result of the colonial experience (Klein; Russell). Africans, for instance, were brought to the New World as part of an imperialist economic policy. New racial mixtures resulted from the encounter between imperialist newcomer and native Americans.[47]

The Gospels do not lack an awareness of ethnic relations. The story of the Samaritan and the extension of Jesus' ministry to the Syro-Phoenicians and other non-Jewish ethnic groups is part of the agenda of Luke and other evangelists. Yet, color differences and their social consequences are not really emphasized in the Gospels.

Postcolonial literature validates and celebrates the non-white races (Fanon). Leñero's Jesus is "earth colored" in the episode paraphrasing the transfiguration (Lk 9:28–36). The Gerasene Demoniac (Lk 8:26–38) is portrayed as a "mulatto." The episode of the sinful woman in Luke 7:36–50 does not mention anything about her skin color, but Leñero's version describes her as a "dark-skinned" (*morena*) woman. While Leñero's critique of racism is not as extensive as that found in some postcolonial works, Leñero is part of a postocolonial literary tradition which affirms that non-white races deserve the dignity and respect afforded to their European counterparts.

---

[45] *ELG*, 177: "Para seguir a Dios no necesitas de un hábito."
[46] *ELG*, 126: "La convenció de que entrara a estudiar en la prepa."
[47] For the cultural implications of these racial mixtures, see Hyatt and Nettlesford.

Conclusions

Insofar as Leñero believes that he can extract the essential meaning of Lucan stories while transferring them to modern settings and situations, he is engaging in biblical exegesis. If by postcolonial literature we refer to writings which scrutinize critically the imperialist-colonial relationship, then *The Gospel of Lucas Gavilán* may be considered part of the postcolonial literary tradition, and so his paraphrase of Luke may be viewed as postcolonial biblical exegesis. As such, *GLG* is the complete opposite of the compilation and inteprepretation of biblical texts of a paradigmatically imperialist work such as Columbus' *Libro de las profecías*, which uses biblical texts to justify the subjugation of Native Americans.[48]

The type of colonialism that *GLG* criticizes is more than the colonialism imposed by Spain upon Mexico. Rather, it is a type of social and economic colonialism imposed upon the lower-income classes of Mexico by capitalist structures, the traditional Catholic church, and other allied institutions. Setting the Gospel in the "Third World" is certainly one sign of the postcolonial current in *GLG*. The effort to empower and have those in lower socioeconomic levels become aware of their oppression is another sign of a postcolonial perspective.

Some of the oppressors have relatively transparent parallels. Traditional religious authorities still feature prominently in both Luke and *GLG*. Yet, the specific types of oppression that *GLG* critiques have been expanded. Thus, one finds mention of the oppression of women and gays, groups which were not explicitly treated as oppressed groups in the Gospels.

Leñero has also integrated a number of themes of liberation theology into his paraphrase. Liberation theology argues that the Church must ally itself with the poor, and that is certainly the case in *GLG*. The sympathy towards Marxism, and the anti-capitalist stance of Gómez is another feature shared with liberation theology and many postcolonialist writers.

The elimination of the supernatural is characteristic of modernity; thus *GLG* is also part of a modernist literary tradition. Indeed, Leñero no longer accepts miracles, the efficacy of prayer as a solution, the resurrection of Jesus, and other literal biblical claims. For Leñero problems and solutions, if any, originate in the present socio-political realm, not in the supernatural realm. Religion is not necessarily to be found in traditional organizations, but in praxis. Perhaps the main conclusion of Leñero's postcolonial biblical exegesis is that the Jesus of the Gospels lives only insofar as his teachings are continually embodied by those working for the liberation of the oppressed from capitalism, corrupt ecclesiastical organizations, a heartless health care system, and other imperialist institutions.

---

48 For a study of Columbus' *Libro de las profecías*, see Avalos.

Works Consulted

Adam, Ian and Helen Tiffin, eds.
    1991   *Past the Last Post: Theorizing Post-Colonialism and Post-Modernism.* New York: Harvester/Wheatsheaf.

Ashcroft, Bill, Gareth Griffiths and Helen Tiffin, eds.
    1989   *The Empire Writes Back: Theory and Practice in Postcolonial Literatures.* London: Routledge.

Avalos, Hector
    1996   "Columbus as Biblical Exegete: A Study of the *Libro de las profecías.*" Pp. 59–80 in *Religion in the Age of Exploration: The Case of Spain and New Spain.* Ed. Bryan Le Beau and Menahem Mor. Omaha: Creighton University Press.

Boehmer, Elleke
    1995   *Colonial and Postcolonial Literature: Migrant Metaphors.* New York: Oxford University Press.

Bultmann, Rudolf
    1951–55   *Theology of the New Testament.* Trans. Kedrick Grobel. New York: Scribners.

    1958   *Christ and Mythology.* New York: Scribners.

Camín, Hector Aguilar and Lorenzo Meyer
    1993   *In the Shadow of the Mexican Revolution: Contemporary Mexican History 1910–1989.* Austin: University of Texas.

Cavalcanti, Tereza
    1994   "Jesus, the Penitent Woman and the Pharisee." *Journal of Hispanic/Latino Theology* 2:28–40.

DeHay, Terry
    1994   "Ernesto Cardenal's *Salmos.*" Pp. 48–60 in Gallagher.

Devi, Ananda
    1988   *Rue de la Pudriere.* Abidjan: Nouvelles Editions Africaines.

Dussel, Enrique
    1995   *The Invention of the Americas: Eclipse of "the Other" and the Myth of Modernity.* Trans. Michael D. Barber. New York: Continuum.

Fanon, Frantz
    1967   *Black Skin, White Masks.* New York: Grove Weidenfeld.

Fitzmyer, Joseph
    1981   *The Gospel According to Luke I–IX.* AB 28: Garden City, NY: Doubleday.

    1985   *The Gospel According to Luke X–XXIV.* AB 28A; Garden City, NY: Doubleday.

Freire, Paolo
    1974   *Conscientización.* Buenos Aires: Burqueda.

Fuliga, J. B.
1994   "The Temptation of Jesus as a Class Struggle." *Asian Journal of Theology* 8:172–85.

Gallagher, Susan VanZanten, ed.
1994   *Postcolonial Literature and the Biblical Call for Justice*. Jackson: University Press of Mississippi.

Gutierrez, Gustavo
1972   *Teología de la liberación*. Salamanca: Sigueme.

1973   *Theology of Liberation*. Maryknoll: Orbis.

Huggan, Graham
1991   "Decolonizing the Map: Postcolonialism, Post-Structuralism and the Cartographic Connection." Pp. 125–138 in Adam and Tiffin.

Hyatt, Lawrence and Rex Nettleford
1996   *Race, Discourse, and the Origin of the Americas: A New World View*. Washington, DC: Smithsonian.

Kadir, Djelal
1993   *The Other Writing: Postcolonial Essays in Latin America's Writing Culture*. West Lafayette, Indiana: Purdue University Press.

Klein, Herbert
1986   *African Slavery in Latin America*. New York: Oxford University Press.

Langford, Walter M.
1975   "Vicente Leñero: ¿Un Graham Greene Mexicano?" Pp. 187–205 in *La novela mexicana. Realidad y valores* Ed. Walter M. Langford. Mexico.

Leñero, Vicente
1979   *El Evangelio de Lucas Gavilán*. Barcelona: Seix Barral.

1991   *The Gospel of Lucas Gavilán*. Trans. Robert Mowry. Lanham, MD: University Press of America.

Lionnet, Françoise
1995   *Postcolonial Representations: Women, Literature, Identity*. Ithaca: Cornell University Press.

Lipski, John M.
1982   "Vicente Leñero: Narrative Evolution as a Religious Search." *Hispanic Journal* 3:41–59.

Lustig, Wolf
1989   *Christliche Symbolik und Christentum im spanischamerikanischen Roman des 20. Jahrhunderts*. Main: Peter Lang.

Manning, Patrick
1990   *Slavery and the African Life: Occidental, Oriental and African Slave Trades*. Cambridge: Cambridge University Press.

Mendieta, Eduardo
    1996   "From Christendom to Polycentric Oikunumé: Modernity, Postmodernity, and Liberation Theology." *Journal of Hispanic/Latino Theology* 3:57–76.

Miller, Joseph
    1988   *Way of Death: Merchant Capitalism and the Angolan Slave Trade, 1730–1830.* Madison: University of Wisconsin Press.

Mishra, Vijay and Bob Hodge
    1991   "What is Post(-)colonialism?" *Textual Practice* 5:399–414.

Paz, Octavio
    1988   *Sor Juana.* Cambridge, MA: Harvard University Press.

Robles, Humberto E.
    1970   "Aproximaciones a Los albañiles de Vicente Leñero." *Revista Iberoamericana* 36:579–99.

Russell, James W.
    1994   *After the Fifth Sun: Class and Race in North America.* Englewood Cliffs, NJ: Prentice Hall.

Segundo, Juan
    1975   *The Liberation of Theology.* Maryknoll: Orbis.

    1976   *La liberación de la teología.* Buenos Aires: C. Lohlé.

Slemon, Stephen
    1991   "Modernism's Last Post." Pp. 1–11 in Adam and Tiffin.

Srivastava, Aruna
    1991   "'The Empire Writes Back': Language and History in *Shame* and *Midnight's Children.*" Pp. 65–78 in Adam and Tiffin.

Stern, Steve J.
    1988   "Feudalism, Capitalism, and the World System in the Perspective of Latin America and the Caribbean." *American Historical Review* 93:829–74.

Wallerstein, Immanuel
    1974   *The Modern World System: Capitalist Agriculture and the Origin of the European World-Economy in the Sixteenth Century.* New York: Academic.

    1979   *The Capitalist World Economy.* Cambridge: Cambridge University Press.

"Everybody Talking about Heaven Ain't Going There": The Biblical Call for Justice and the Postcolonial Response of the Spirituals

Kimberly Rae Connor
San Francisco, California

ABSTRACT

The creators of the spirituals were practicing a postcolonial biblical discourse long before it was ever identified as such. Setting forth their resistance in song, the creators challenged the prevailing biblical doctrines of its professed adherents that presumed to justify slavery. At the same time they honored the liberating elements of the Bible by employing African and African-American adaptations that simultaneously stripped the Bible of its hegemonic colonial power while restoring its intended liberating power. In the spirituals enslaved people critically analyzed their colonial conditions, fashioned a creative theological response, indicted their oppressors without overtly denigrating them, re-asserted the influence of an African sensibility, and empowered themselves by exercising a form of resistance that would endure longer than the conditions to which they were subject.

I.

"I got a robe, you got a robe,
All God's children got a robe
When I get to heaven I'm gonna put on my robe,
I'm gonna shout all over God's Heaven, Heaven, Heaven,
Everybody talking about heaven ain't going there, Heaven, Heaven,
I'm gonna shout all over God's heaven."

These lines from the Negro spiritual "All God's Children Got Wings" reveal features foundational to the form as it functions to advance a postcolonial discourse. The community who sang this song saw themselves as a group of talented individuals trapped in an oppressive colonial structure that did not call on them to use their talents. The donning of a robe (or wings, or shoes, or harp as described in additional verses) does not suggest one aspires to acquisition; rather the lyrics place an emphasis on the fulfillment of unfulfilled talents, the desire to be of "creative service" (Lovell: 351). When enslaved people sang this song they were using the garments as metaphors for transformation, proposing that when they got the chance to wear them, in heaven or in heaven on earth (in emancipation), they would be able to express their aspirations toward creativity. They may also have been recalling imagery reminiscent of Jesus's parable of the prodigal son in which the father—usually understood as signifying God—said "Bring forth the best robe, and put it on him" (Lk 15:22). Yet as John Lovell explains, the Bible to which enslaved singers alluded was viewed less "as religious doctrine" and more as "the kind of pithy story the African had been used to for centuries" (150–51). Thus the song both calls for the human freedom to create in a new setting that provided the Bible as a spiritual resource and demonstrates the human ability to create that had long been part of the singers' African cultural tradition. Furthermore, the heaven to which the singers aimed was recognized as a place of justice, where the twisted talents of slaveholders who manipulated theological discourse—who talked about heaven in exclusively colonial terms—would not be displayed. In this one simple spiritual (as in all others) enslaved people critically analyzed their colonial conditions, fashioned a creative theological response, indicted their oppressors without overtly denigrating them, re-asserted the influence of an African sensibility, and empowered themselves by exercising a form of resistance that would endure longer than the conditions to which they were subject.

At the beginning of the twentieth-century, the poet James Weldon Johnson and his brother and frequent collaborator, J. Rosemond, began collecting and editing Negro spirituals like "All God's Children Got Wings," eventually bringing them out in two volumes. In the first volume, *The Book of American Negro Spirituals* (1925), Johnson introduces the spirituals to the public with a prefatory poem, "O Black and Unknown Bards," in which he characterizes the creators of the spirituals as people who "sang a race from wood and stone to Christ" (12). Johnson's metaphor, which animates the creators as people possessed by creative self-determination, demonstrates how the spirituals operated functionally to mediate the distinction between African religion and Christianity. However, the singing that eased the enslaved Africans's painful transition from one culture to another also, as Anthony Pinn (24) asserts, "answered hard religious questions," particularly those that applied to the biblical justifications for slavery. Setting forth their resistance in song, the creators of the spirituals challenged the prevailing biblical doctrines of its professed adherents that presumed to justify slavery. At the same time they honored the liberating elements of the Bible by employing African and African-American adaptations that simultaneously stripped the Bible of its hegemonic colonial power while restoring its intended liberating power; which is to say that the creators of the spirituals were practicing a postcolonial biblical discourse long before it was ever identified as such. They engaged in a sophisticated postcolonial interpretation of the Bible not from the abstract perspective of a contemporary academic, but from the concrete perspective of those who, oppressed by a colonial legacy, used the Bible as a basis for developing an aesthetic mode of resistance.

A postcolonial analysis like the one performed by the creators of the spirituals begins with the recognition that to be colonized is to be removed from history. As James Cone has observed, "when white people enslaved Africans, their intention was to dehistoricize black existence, to foreclose the possibility of a future defined by the African heritage" (24). What the spirituals record, therefore, is a difficult and highly complex means of working one's way back into history. How one reinserts oneself back into history is as important as the history one wishes to re-write; thus the postcolonial analytical process proposed by the spirituals is directed by "the African heritage" of call and response. It proceeds by means of a dialogic process to initiate and perpetuate the necessary correction of colonialism's legacy of monologically narrated history. The creators of the spirituals metaphorically wrote themselves into biblical history while at the same time they were composing their own representational history of enslavement. Holding together the many tensions that resulted from the colonial imposition of slavery on Africans, the creators of the spirituals aroused "the dialectic that undergirds African-American life" (Kirk-Duggan: 151) and established the foundation for an ongoing postcolonial analysis of and response to the internal colonization experienced by African-Americans.

This dialectic that undergirds African-American life was first identified by W. E. B. Du Bois, a contemporary of Johnson's who, like him, was one of several prominent African-Americans of his time to appreciate the postcolonial discourse embodied in spirituals. Du Bois and Johnson were both initiators and products of the Harlem Renaissance which mandated the responsibility to identify and extol black contributions to American cultural life. Their recognition of the importance of the spirituals was an integral contribution to their participation in the spirit of the movement. Du Bois's examinations into African-American culture led him to the spirituals or "sorrow songs" because in them he heard how "the soul of the black slave spoke to men." In *The Souls of Black Folk* (1903) Du Bois devotes considerable space to a discussion of the music and message of Negro spirituals as related to the history of black people striving for humanity in a society of oppression. Identifying them as the "singular spiritual heritage of the nation and the greatest gift of the Negro people," the spirituals fascinated Du Bois because of their tension between polarities of joy and sorrow. Rather than dismissing this tension as the frustrated expression of a people overcome by oppression, Du Bois came to see it as a progressive dialectic. The spirituals embodied this dialectic in functional terms, as a reflection of the African-American struggle to merge a double self into "a better and truer self" that held out "a faith in the ultimate justice of things . . . that sometime, somewhere, men will judge men by their souls and not by their skins" (189).

Because of the way in which the spirituals embodied resistance, Du Bois concluded that the spirituals provide a model for survival that bequeaths to us an interpretive framework for understanding African-American culture.

In so doing he also anticipated how the history of the reception and appreciation of the spirituals would reveal aspects of broader cultural currents, including the positions African Americans assumed in relation to their enslaved past and the roles played by representatives of the dominant culture who either aided in the preservation and promotion of the spirituals or exploited and appropriated them. But it is Du Bois's assessment of the functional role the spirituals performed that has had lasting impact, borne out by the significant role they have played in providing a foundation for the development of a distinctive African-American postcolonial aesthetic. Key distinguishing terms by which we have come to evaluate this tradition have derived from the spirituals, including the pattern of call and response and the act of signifying. Because they give compelling testimony to the presence and influence of African retentions in the development of African-American culture, the spirituals also underscore the important role non-canonical oral traditions play in accomplishing what Gayatri Chakravorty Spivak intends for post-colonial discourse: an interrogation of "our ideological acceptance of error as truth" (109).

Judged by many as the pre-eminent interpreter of spirituals, Du Bois's analysis laid the foundation for what we now describe as a postcolonial understanding of African-American cultural production. Yet Du Bois's description of the spirituals as "sorrow songs" led to an unfortunate association of the spirituals with lamentation. The error to which Spivak alludes is the history set forth by colonizers and by denoting the spirituals in terms of sorrow, Du Bois unwittingly contributed to the colonizers's version of history. Because his term veiled the resistance that undergirds the form, subsequent interpreters often located only other-worldly deliverance as a source of solace expressed in the music. But to focus on the spirituals as sorrow songs is to miss an appreciation of the full postcolonial context—social and religious—in which they were performed and the insight they lend into the extraordinary power of cultural production to shape the experience and conscious identity of a people. The spirituals are a unique demonstration of one way in which an oppressed people empowered themselves through an aesthetic achievement that challenged the colonial condition to which they were subject. Viewed holistically, the spirituals represent both postcolonial reading and writing practices of the highest order.

James Cone's *The Spirituals and the Blues* was among the first contemporary studies to link the power of song in the struggle for black survival with a theology of liberation focused on resistance. Critical of the ways in which previous theologians (Howard Thurman and Benjamin Mays) had stressed a compensatory religious function of the spirituals, Cone examined the spirituals and their secular counterpart the blues as cultural expressions of black people, delineating the functional techniques employed for cultural survival that the songs embody. In Cone's estimation, the spirituals created by enslaved people became a unique means to "keep on keeping on" under the physical and psychological pressures of daily life because they testified to the belief that the supernatural interacted with the natural and that humanity had a distinctive role to play in God's efforts to deliver them from oppression.

That the spirituals were archetypes of protest for actual and spiritual liberation is reaffirmed by Jon Michael Spencer who in *Protest and Praise* sees the spirituals as embodying what he terms a "theomusicology." John Lovell agrees and in his comprehensive study of the spirituals in context of enslaved life demonstrates how the spirituals assisted in resistance to slavery.

> They were not religious songs in the sense of a compartment of life, nor religious in the sense of the theology of the camp meeting, nor religious because they often used Biblical symbols, nor religious because the hope of heaven was substituted to solve the problems of earth, nor religious for any other such reason. They were religious and spiritual because they tried, with inspired artistry, to pose the root questions of life, of before life, and of beyond life, and to react to these questions as the aroused human being and the bestirred folk have done since the rosy dawn of literature. (17)

In *Black Song: The Forge and the Flame*, Lovell insists that the songs project not just religious and otherworldly visions but were enslaved peoples' description and criticism of their environment and an index to their revolutionary sentiments and desire to be free.

In *Black Culture and Black Consciousness*, Lawrence Levine also argues persuasively for an appreciation of the profound connection between the other world and this world in slave consciousness that the spirituals describe. Like Cone and Lovell, Levine underscores the roots of resistance behind the spirituals and rehistoricizes the experience of enslaved people for whom religion was wrought out of an encounter with the divine in the midst of social realities. These scholars share a belief that the spirituals provide one clear instance in American cultural production when the colonized were creators, when the creations themselves were part of an ongoing challenge to the oppressive dominant structure, and where the performance of these cultural texts did more than advocate resistance: they were resistance.

Although the creators remain anonymous, the spirituals were "hammered out" in the forge of oppression and have had vast subsequent social implications when, over time, their "flame" cast a liberative spirit far and wide (Lovell). As "the liberating offspring born of a communal 'inspiring fire,'" the spirituals "recreate the enslaving experience" fueled by "African and Eurocentric theological, anthropological, sociopolitical, and literary perspectives" (Kirk-Duggan: 151). The "fuel" that feeds the spirituals is distinguished in large part by the ways in which the spirituals provide an overwhelmingly successful critical engagement between postcolonial and biblical criticism. Synthesizing sacred and secular meaning, creators of the spirituals drew images from the Bible "to interpret their own experience, measuring it against a wider system of theological and historical meaning. Simultaneously, the biblical symbols were translated in the light of the slaves' own day-to-day experiences" (Raboteau: 264). For "what they had found true in their experience lived for them in the sacred Book" (Thurman: 15).

The ways in which enslaved people adapted the Bible to become representative of their situation, the ways in which they "othered" it by blending African and folk elements with conventional Christian categories, establish the spirituals as a unique demonstration of signifying levels of resistance. The intertextual play in which the creators of the spirituals engaged is a hallmark of African-American aesthetics which often demonstrates contradictory dependence on and independence from what the dominant culture offers. The creators of the spirituals validated and made acceptable their resistance to slavery by couching it in familiar and non-threatening biblical language. In the process they also protected themselves from the reprisals of slaveholders who missed the coded messages embedded in their texts. Employing what Henry Louis Gates Jr. and others identify as the "signifying" levels of discourse, the full meaning of the spirituals "was known to the [slave] community not so much because of the elaboration within the specifics of the music itself, but because of the commonly held assumptions generated by a common life-situation" (Bergesen: 338). That the spirituals were capable of communicating on more than one level is noted as early as 1845 by Frederick Douglass in his autobiography. Here Douglass insists that references to Caanan implied the North. Formally and thematically spirituals were open to change and improvisation as a spiritual in one situation might mean something else in another, yet in nearly every instance there is reflected an intertwining of theological and social messages, borne out in Douglass's description of how "every tone was a testimony against slavery, and a prayer to God for deliverance from chains" (57–58).

The kind of artistic "othering" practiced on the Bible by the creators of the spirituals Nathaniel Mackey views as typical for those who are subjected to social othering by the dominant culture. Employing rhetoric common to postcolonial analysis, Mackey elaborates how "artistic othering" like that practiced by the creators of the spirituals "has to do with innovation, invention, and change, on which cultural health and diversity depend and thrive" while "social othering" such as practiced by the slaveholders has to do with power, exclusion, and privilege, the centralizing of a norm against which otherness is measured, meted out, marginalized." "Other," Mackey insists, is "something people do, more importantly a verb than an adjective or noun" (76). The spirituals, however, embody more than an artistic othering. They constitute both a postcolonial analysis of the role the Bible played in slavery and a creative response fashioned out of that analysis.

James Cone affirms the presence of an analytical process behind the creative process when he draws attention to the fact that it was slave thought—the theological and biblical reflections of enslaved people—that gave rise to spirituals in the first place (14). Cone's observation is supported by one of the earliest published articles by a credentialed black theologian. In 1907, Henry Hugh Proctor asserted that enslaved people formulated a system of "theologico-religious conceptions" in the spirituals. Moreover, Proctor notes that the kind of theology advanced in the spirituals is more faithfully biblical than other more contemporary forms of theological discourse. As he explains: "The Bible itself is not a theological treatise. The writers of that sacred Book would not be considered theologians in the commonly accepted sense. The Bible is a collection of deliverances, addresses, sermons, discourses, songs, letters, and narratives. From these a student constructs a theology of the Books of the Bible—Biblical Theology" (52).

Proctor's observation of the multi-genre literary dimensions of the Bible also supports the contention that out of their postcolonial biblical criticism the creators of the spirituals developed a way in which to use the Bible to shape aesthetic production. Indeed, in his book *Negro Folk Music, U.S.A.*, Harold Courlander notes that if the spirituals "are arranged in a somewhat chronological order, they are equivalent to an oral version of the Bible. Each song presents in a capsulized or dramatic form a significant Biblical moment" (36–43). In creating the spirituals, therefore, enslaved people amplified the biblical implications of a postcolonial challenge by relying on the Bible as a primary model for shaping their analysis of and response to oppression. As the greatest "conjure book" of all (Hurston, 1978:194), the Bible was an important source for the slave's postcolonial critique, their creative empowerment, and their actual liberation.

Although slavery is ubiquitous throughout most of human history, including biblical history, it is unique to the American nation because from its beginning, when twenty blacks were brought to the Jamestown settlement in 1619, "America was heavily dependent on coerced labor" and "by the early eighteenth century, slavery, legal in all of British America, was the dominant labor system of the Southern colonies" (Kolchin: 3). As slavery grew, so too did the spread of Christianity among slave populations so that "by the eve of the Civil War, Christianity had pervaded the slave community" (Raboteau: 212). Understanding the postcolonial biblical challenge offered by the creators of the spirituals, therefore, requires one appreciate not just the effects of slavery but the influence of Christianity. The cultural context in which Christianity in general and the Bible in particular were presented to enslaved people provided the Bible as the chief hegemonic text.

In America the Bible, as Giles Gunn has observed, was "expressive of the Word that commissioned [colonists's] 'errand into the wilderness,'" and it was also "a repository of the norms in relation to which that errand was judged" (2). Even though it stood to represent the hegemonic text for their European colonizers, the Bible became a primary source for supplying enslaved people with historical, spiritual, and textual modes of resistance. It was in this paradoxical context of slavery and Christian conversion that the spirituals were created. The introduction of the Bible to the consciousness of enslaved people came by way of their slaveholder's attempts to convert them to Christianity. Christian conversion of enslaved Africans was seen by some slaveholders as a practical way to unify the diverse people who represented different cultural groups but also as an ideology that would reconcile them into accepting their new culturally imposed status as slaves. Although Peter Kolchin's study on American slavery reveals slaveholders as divided on the efficacy of conversion to achieve these ends—and wary that the slaves and others may come to equate baptism with freedom—the common conception that prevailed, as James Byrd explains, held that "biblical injunctions demanded no re-alignments in social structure. People who hear the gospel are converted and content with their present circumstance" (200).

Southern versions of Christianity that became apologetics for the system of slavery were among the most egregious examples of what postcolonial theorists might see as the synonymous relationship between colonialism and Christianity. Using all the available agencies of Christianity to aid and abet one of the worst instances of colonial oppression, Southern slaveholders were convinced (or convinced themselves) that they were carrying out God's purposes. What Kolchin describes as a "pervasive conservatism" (184) accompanied the growing identification of slavery as central to Southern life. During the revolutionary era, liberal Southern statesmen had often been at the forefront of enlightened thought by questioning the morality of slavery. But during the antebellum decades, even as Northern states abolished the last remnants of slavery, Southerners turned rigid and challenged the proliferation of a huge variety of reform movements, and even more vigorously defended slavery as the bedrock of social order. In their challenge to Northern reformers, Southerners like D. R. Hundley lectured that immorality did not reside in institutions like slavery but in humanity itself which suffers the conditions of original sin. Religion cannot, Hundley believed, improve the human condition because "the true and only mission of Christianity is, not to abolish institutions . . . but to make every individual man, where bound or free, rich or poor, high or low, a new creature in Jesus Christ" (Kolchin: 189).

Thus slavery became allied with Christianity to such a degree that religious principles became the warrant for the Atlantic slave trade. Elizabeth Fox-Genovese and Eugene D. Genovese demonstrate in their essay, "The Divine Sanction of Social Order: Religious Foundations of the Southern Slaveholders' World View," that the Southern Christian defense of slavery was in essence a defense of not just the South but an argument that purposely raised a defense of slavery "to an abstract model of necessary social order" (211). Slavery became not just necessary evil but a positive good and the "best possible bulwark against the corrosive and un-Christian impact of industrial capitalism and its cruel and morally irresponsible market in human labor-power" (211–12). Religious arguments became the discourse that bridged their practical justifications based on slavery's necessity and more far-reaching theories predicated on its desirability. Religious idioms pervaded pro-slavery literature and ministers played a leading role in defending slavery. Because scriptural defenses of slavery probably accounted for a majority of all published defenses (Fox-Genovese and Genovese: 220), historian Drew Gilpin Faust has suggested that "the Bible served as the core" of the "proslavery mainstream" (10).

But as Fox-Genovese and Genovese elaborate, "From the start, Christianity as a discourse had been obliged to find its accommodations with other discourses that contravened its central purposes. The history of those accommodations, which constitutes the history of Christianity itself, took a distinct turn in the United States during the first half of the nineteenth century, when internal transformation of the Christian discourse took numerable forms from extreme utopianism to extreme authoritarianism" (214). Utopian abolitionists who countered Southern authoritarian scriptural arguments by emphasizing the overall liberative spirit of the Bible rather than its specific prescriptions left themselves vulnerable to Southern charges of trivializing the Bible. Because of America's long-standing "veneration of the Bible" (Gunn: 2), the South "stood as God's bastion against all the isms that were threatening Christian civilization" (Fox-Genovese and Genovese: 218) and its sacred text, the Bible.

Peter Kolchin cites three kinds of religious arguments on behalf of slavery that were most common to Southerners steeped in the Bible and predisposed to look to precedent for guidance: the fact that ancient Hebrews (God's chosen people) owned slaves; that Jesus, who was not hesitant to condemn behavior that he considered immoral never criticized slavery or reproached anyone for owning slaves; and the biblical antecedent provided by Noah's curse of his son Ham, and through him his grandson Caanan, for Ham's indiscreet gaze on his father as he lay drunk and naked in his tent: "Cursed be Caanan; a slave of slaves shall he be to his brothers" (Gen 9:18–29). Of this last defense, Southerners saw God's condemnation of black—or Hamitic—peoples to eternal slavery (Kolchin: 192). But the most widespread and effective religious argument (that was supported by colonial historical and sociological theory) was not entirely scriptural but based on the projected assumption that slavery was part of God's plan to expose a heathen and inferior people to the blessings of Christianity. These combined defenses appealed to the whole colonial analysis of race, class, religion and economy, allowing slaveholders to take what they saw as high moral ground to express slavery defense in terms of principle rather than interests.

It was in this "Manichean world"—which Frantz Fanon views as characterized by an unequal relationship between oppressor and oppressed, a relationship in which the oppressor dominates not only physically and economically but also culturally and morally—that the spirituals were created. Despite the forces of colonialism and the religious discourse that supported them, what enslaved people understood was that the slaveholder's "feelings of moral superiority, although frequently couched in religious rhetoric, were not always explicitly informed by Christianity" (Gallagher: 20–21). Frederick Douglass spoke for many voiceless slaves when he wrote "between the Christianity of this land, and the Christianity of Christ, I recognized the widest possible difference" (153). As the views of the dominant Southern culture became more entrenched, so too did the postcolonial response of enslaved people gather force in the creation of the spirituals, the "people's response to the social contradiction" (Cone: 32–33). It is the "American-biblical-Christian mythology" that "nurtures racism" that the spirituals "combat and transcend" (Kirk-Duggan: 158).

II.

Despite the fact that we are unable to date precisely the composition of the first spirituals, we can project that the spirituals constitute a direct engagement with an internal form of colonial oppression for at least a century. Spirituals were viewed by the first whites who encountered them as highly developed forms that enjoyed widespread familiarity among disparate slave communities. Oral folklore traditions often link the spirituals with slave uprisings led by Denmark Vesey, Nat Turner, and Gabriel Prosser. The earliest known reports of distinctive black religious singing date from the early nineteenth century, but many of these reports are vague and the musical notation practiced at the time was inadequate to capture distinctive features of music as performed. Before the Civil War descriptions of black music are scattered and intermittent. But when the war shattered the closed society to which enslaved Africans were confined and brought them in to large-scale contact with the world outside the plantation, Northerners, often agents of the federal government or missionaries, came to appreciate their distinctive music. As with ex-slave narratives, the African-American authorship of the spirituals was challenged at first. But in an 1867 article published in *The Atlantic Monthly*, Thomas Wentworth Higginson, a militant New England abolitionist who commanded the first freed slave regiment to fight against the Confederacy, was among the first to describe how he heard "the choked voice of a race at last unloosed" (Sernett: 111) as he took down the songs sung by the First South Carolina Volunteers around evening campfires. Although Higginson failed to recognize all the cultural components of the slave songs, he did appreciate the forms of resistance articulated in their performance, describing them as a "stimulus to courage and a tie to heaven" (Sernett: 131).

The spirituals underscore that, despite their apparent tie to the colonizers's heaven, how enslaved people became Christian took no simple and direct path. As Kolchin explains, "Antebellum slaves increasingly experienced a number of overlapping—sometimes competing—religious influences, from paternalistic masters who prayed and read the Bible with their 'people,' from white religious denominations that mounted a 'mission to the slaves,' and from the 'invisible church' that operated quasi-secretly among the slaves themselves" (143). Enslaved Africans did not simply accept Christianity as it was given to them; "they creatively fashioned a Christian tradition to fit their own particular existence of enslavement in America" (Raboteau: 209). As Zora Neale Hurston explains in the essay "Spirituals and Neo-spirituals," Christianity as understood and practiced by enslaved people was unique. Although it had all the intellectual force we customarily attribute to a theological enterprise, slave religion was not characterized by abstract, meditative practices but by highly reactive and experiential responses, like the spirituals, that were shaped as much by aesthetic principles as they were by religious principles (Hurston, 1984:81).

Despite the intentions of the slaveholders to erase the history of the enslaved people by converting them to Christianity, "Christianity provided some aspects of spirituality that were continuous with African experience" (Wilmore: 24). That the slaveholders could underestimate the power of the "others'" culture does not surprise Amiri Baraka (Le Roi Jones). He sees their ignorance and dismissal of ongoing African influences and their potential to generate resistance in the lives of enslaved people as typical of the mentality of colonial oppressors. To explain, Baraka returns to the pioneering observations of Melville Herskovits who "points out that most of the 'myths' about the Negro past were formed by the new masters' refusal to understand that the Africans were not governed by the same mores and culture references as Western man, that they had come from an alien land and culture. But one of the most persistent traits of the Western white man has always been his fanatical and almost instinctive assumption that his systems and ideas about the world are the most desirable, and further, that people who do not aspire to them, or at least think them admirable, are savages or enemies" (Jones: 7).

Thus, even though the slaves's encounter with Christianity was an important factor in the creation of the postcolonial response of the spirituals, it was not the only one. Although the nature of the language of the spirituals cannot be separated from the reality of slavery in which it participates, there is a reality—an historical, pre-colonial African consciousness—that lies behind the presence of the biblical language with which the spirituals are imbued. As John Lovell explains, the spirituals "dealt with all manifestations of life from the all-encompassing religious position of the African ancestral group" (17). Cheryl Kirk-Duggan's postcolonial analysis of the spirituals links the strategies of the creators with an Afrocentric concept of theodicy. Identifying Afrocentrism as as "a holistic ideology central to all analysis involving African erudition," Kirk-Duggan's exploration of how the spirituals document the reality of the oppressed and the oppressor in the context of slaveholding America leads her to identify the spirituals as a "catalog" of "political and religious Afrocentric experience." And the kind of Afrocentric perspective displayed in the spirituals is a postcolonial one, because it "radically critiques an environment that involves a ruling Eurocentric ideology" while fusing it "with an Afrocentric social and intellectual milieu" (150).

Christianity may have offered a new text for the creators of the spirituals, but the musical form and its transformative power was already present in the consciousness of enslaved Africans. Because "Afrocentricity compels an inquiry of slavery" (Kirk-Duggan: 150), retaining these African elements constituted an important gesture of postcolonial resistance on the part of enslaved people. As soon as they made the transition from Africa to America and from their native language to their adopted language, enslaved people "naturally continued" what they had been doing all along—"making songs about [their] life and [their] religion" (Lovell: 9). That is why the distinguishing musical aesthetic of the spirituals derives from West African percussive forms, multiple meters, syncopation, a call and response structure, extensive melodic ornamentation, and an integration of song and movement, each involving improvisation. Call and response is most important because it embodies the foundational principle behind the performance of the spirituals, denoting the ritual requirement of what is necessary for completion. The soloist was viewed as a mystic whose call inspired the participating group to respond.

This full sense of process and communication reinforces the communal identity and its belief that art is an appropriate response to oppression. Very much a ritual act, when enslaved people sang spirituals they amplified their desire for liberation and created conditions of sacred space and time wherein the biblical stories were transformed and the history of the ancient past became the history of the present. As one contemporary reviewer described them, the spirituals were "God's image in Ebony." In creation as well as performance they exhibited the essential characteristics of spontaneity, variety, and communal interchange. The form of the spirituals was flexible and improvisational, thereby able to fit an individual slave's experience into the consciousness of the group, creating at once an intensely personal and vividly communal experience.

Joining Albert Raboteau, Lawrence Levine, and many others who have written about slave religion, Anthony Pinn underscores the importance of slave holders' inability to erase the African's creative resistance.

> [They] were unable to fully monitor the coded musical articulation of an African-American world view. That is, the slaves brought to religious services music heavily influenced by their African cultural patterns—which lyrically wove together enslavement realities, pieces of scripture, and folk wisdom... [their] worship services echoed with the dissonant tones which arose out of the life conditions faced by enslaved Africans. (22)

Pinn's observation leads to a consideration of other creative elements in the spirituals that demonstrate a form of resistance. In *Conjuring Culture: Biblical Formations of Black America*, Theophus H. Smith describes the sacred text of western culture, the Bible, as "a magical formulary for African Americans: a book of ritual prescriptions for reenvisioning and, therein, transforming history and culture" (3). Smith sets forth an analysis of African-American culture that reveals it to have combined biblical interpretation with postcolonial discourse in such a way that the result is a "magical transformation." As he explains: "What is innovative is a remarkable efficacious use of biblical figures, with a historically transformative and therapeutic intent, in the social imagination and political performances of black North Americans." (3) For Smith conjure is the dominant metaphor "that circumscribes black people's ritual, figural, and therapeutic transformations of [the dominant] culture" (4).

More than a cultural performance, conjuring actually transforms reality and functions as a "curative" mode of resistance for people oppressed by a colonial legacy. This conjuring or othering practiced by enslaved people on the Bible became a characteristic feature of black cultural production and was first identified by Zora Neale Hurston as "the will to adorn" (1983, 49), a process by which African-Americans take what the dominant culture has offered and ornament it for their own use. In following the will to adorn, "Even the Bible was made over to suit our vivid imagination" (Hurston, 1978, 5). Hurston's insights are echoed by Smith when he elaborates on how the spirituals' use of biblical figures operates covertly, representing a "collective strategy to cloak, mask, or disguise conjurational operations by employing approved religious content—namely biblical and Christian content" (115).

The Bible, therefore, was not seen by slaves as an inviolable hegemonic text but, like everything else, subject for the conjuring "will to adorn." It is not surprising, therefore, that in his analysis of the biblical influence on black sacred music, Charles Copher observes that "in the Spirituals one may find characters and events from different periods in biblical history mixed together. Moreover, in a single Spiritual one may find characters and events that span the whole course of Biblical history, from creation to the last judgment portrayed in the book of Revelation" (76). As an expression of the free exercise of the will to adorn, these kinds of adaptations of biblical material constitute a significant form of resistance to internal colonization. John Lovell explains, "A close comparison with the real people and happenings of the Bible will reveal the slave poet's broad or delicate emphases and variations, his outright departures, and something very important, the biblical items, events, and people he does not emphasize" (258–62).

How the slaves determined what not to emphasize of the Bible occurred in secret "hush arbor" meetings where slave families formed their own "invisible church." There the creators of the spirituals established the theological freedom to create meaning by which to make sense of and endure daily sufferings. There they critically reflected on the dichotomy presupposed by slaveholding religion and the Bible on which it was based. "From the seeds of paradox . . . slaves recognized the inherent conflict between 'baptism and bondage'" (Byrd: 204). There in the hush arbors enslaved people chose which biblical texts were most relevant to them. They spurned the sermons they received elsewhere on obedience to authority as a central tenant of Christianity in favor of a religion of the oppressed that promised them deliverance and gave them direct forms of empowerment.

In her narrative *Incidents in the Life of a Slave Girl*, Harriet Jacobs describes an incident in which slaves rejected a white minister. When an Episcopal clergyman began holding separate services for blacks in Edenton, North Carolina, "his colored members were few;"and soon after they heard his injunction that "if you disobey your earthly master, you offend you heavenly master," all the slaves left to attend a more rousing Methodist shout (68–69). Jacobs's observations are corroborated by the remarks of a former slave, Cornelius Garner: "Dat ole white preacher jest was telling us slaves to be good to our marsters. We ain't keer'd a bit 'bout dat stuff he was telling us 'cause we wanted to sing, pray, and serve God in our own way" (Perdue: 100). As Anthony Pinn explains: "The process by which slaves made this juxtaposition of their condition and biblical accounts involves the use of a hermeneutic of suspicion and identification . . . Slaves looked at the existential condition and were not satisfied with the so-called 'Christian' explanations provided by slaveholders and their ministers. Many slaves could not believe that God condoned their condition and rejected their efforts at liberation. Obedience to unjust practices and laws could not be consistent with the divine design of a loving and just God. This suspicion resulted in the slaves 'looking into' scripture themselves in order to find the answers to the questions posed by the hardships of life, and treating with scorn practices which did not line up with biblical precedence" (33).

The differences between black and white Southern uses of the Bible are significant because they reveal enslaved people as subjects whose behavior helped shape their own lives rather than merely respond as passive victims of white action. Especially in the creation of the spirituals did enslaved people demonstrate this "order of animacy" (Mackey: 96) denied them by the dominant culture. They took their oppressive conditions and shaped them to their advantage, exploiting the marginal position they occupied to create liminal spaces in which to receive and interpret scripture for themselves. But as the spirituals document, they did more than receive and interpret, they created a form by which to testify. Since "the vast majority of slaves could not read," the spirituals "were their channel to the word of God" (Raboteau: 264). Because their social status and lack of literary skills prevented them from engaging in the public and intellectual discourse about the morality of slavery, the creators of the spirituals did not debate the issue abstractly. Rather they existentially confronted it daily and eventually fashioned their own creative response out of "the imagery and symbolism of scripture and Christianity" (Pinn: 29).

Despite "all the biblical characters, incidents, parables, sermons, and historical features to choose from, the slave, in thousands of songs, selected relatively a few and turned these to only a few ends" (Lovell: 257), leading to three themes that dominate spirituals and which all are sourced in the Bible: the desire for freedom, the desire for justice, and strategies for survival.[1] God is liberator who is involved in history, and as "Wade in the Water" suggests, God will "trouble the waters" of oppression. Although God's liberating work was not always concretely evident, enslaved people were confident that "You Got a Right" to "the tree of life." Jesus represents both an historical savior and whoever helps the oppressed. Jesus functions in a more personal way than God, as deliverer and comforter, because "you may have all the world," but "Give Me Jesus." He is affirmed both in his divinity and humanity, especially his identification with the oppressed who believe that "A Little Talk With Jesus Makes It Right." Hence his birth is an occasion to "Rise Up Shepherd and Follow," and "Go Tell it on the Mountain," and his life on earth a reminder to "Rise, Mourner, Rise."

Of the many spirituals like "Joshua Fit the Battle of Jericho" and "Didn't My Lord Deliver Daniel?" that are drawn from biblical narratives, most stress God's involvement in the liberation of the oppressed but also show the oppressed as active agents in their own redemption. Other songs also stress a need for enslaved people's own participation in God's liberation, to be "Singing With a Sword in My Hand." Enslaved people did not just choose which biblical events to rehearse, they were also selective about which historical events they would allegorize. They viewed their cry of "Let My People Go" as answered with the Emancipation Proclamation, when "Slavery Chain Done Broke at Last," and believed that God makes justice for the righteous and the unrighteous because "All God's Children Got Wings,"

---

[1] Space does not permit me to indulge in detailed analysis of the many instances of biblical appropriation employed by the creators of the spirituals. Readers who wish to trace specific biblical allusions are directed towards Dixon, Cone, and especially Lovell.

but "everybody whose talking about heaven ain't going," and anyone who stands against liberation is called to account: "Were You There When They Crucified my Lord?"

Songs like "Steal Away" and "Let Us Praise God Together On Our Knees" may have served as a means to convene secret resistance meetings, while "Deep River, My Home is Over Jordan" may imply a wish to cross over to Africa or the North. But getting to freedom is what occupies many of the lyrics that take as a theme a tired sojourner struggling through a hostile landscape while leaning and depending on God. Portraying a struggle against oppression in a variety of metaphors, many spirituals focus on the difficult movement through space and time, but with the confidence to cheer the "Weary Traveler." In his analysis of African-American forms of artistic othering, Nathaniel Mackey observes a characteristic "privileging of the verb, the movement from noun to verb," which "linguistically accentuates action among a people whose ability to act is curtailed by racist constraints" (79). Thus the spirituals are imbued with spatial and temporal metaphors of movement employing a variety of methods—sailing, walking, riding, rowing, climbing—all appear for a people "Bound to Go," urging them to "Travel On." The spirituals actually and symbolically moved a people towards liberation when they sang, "We Are Climbing Jacob's Ladder," even if they could only "Keep Inching Along."

Noting the threat of adverse physical conditions, the creators appropriated symbols from their own situation and describe searching for God in the wilderness, rocks, darkness, storms, and valleys. Lyrics from songs such as "O Stand the Storm," "Sinner, Please Don't Let This Harvest Pass," or "Hold On!" gave inspiration to endure. Although an enslaved person often felt "Like a Motherless Child," lost where "I Couldn't Hear Nobody Pray," and for whom "Nobody Knows the Trouble I've Seen," faith is always affirmed because "All My Troubles Will Soon Be Over." Sometimes a lonely sojourner is aided by heavenly transportation, as in "Swing Low, Sweet Chariot," or the activity of the underground railroad that invites "Get on Board, Little Children." But the destination is always freedom, sometimes construed as Africa, the North, or heaven, as in "Roll, Jordan, Roll." The role of the community—often expressed in concepts of home as in "I Got a Home in That Rock," or as a heavenly reunion with family as in "Band of Gideon," or as a place of safety in "There is a Balm in Gilead"—is also reinforced.

III.

Constituting a form of resistance, the spirituals provide the basis for both a theology and an aesthetic. African-American liberation theologians like James Cone and womanist theologians like Cheryl Kirk-Duggan both have embraced the spirituals as foundational for their systems. Their analyses are based, in part, on the rhetorical form of the spirituals that was engendered by a postcolonial and a biblical situation. As a visionary and rebellious response to oppression, the spirituals constitute a "genre" of sacred writing that like its model, the Bible, "was salvific in character" (Mabry: 82). James Byrd, Jr. draws correlations between the spirituals and first-century apocalyptic literature. Viewing the spirituals as a kind of apocalyptic discourse, Byrd notes how they share with biblical apocalyptic literature a similar situation, an analogical mode of expression, and a corresponding rationale (199). What the creators of the spirituals were able to accomplish through this rhetoric, whether we see it as analytical or biblical, apocalyptic or constituting its own genre, was nothing less than the redemption of postcolonial Christianity. In rewriting history, including biblical history, enslaved people transformed an oppressor's tool into a vehicle for redeeming their own abused humanity.

That the spirituals are an appropriate site in which to locate a postcolonial biblical challenge is reinforced by Susan VanZanten Gallagher; she draws attention to the "many powerful and provocative interconnections" (3) between postcolonial literature and the biblical call for justice. Despite the fact that the scriptures of the Christian tradition have often been associated with evils of colonialism, Gallagher and the scholars she includes in this volume find interconnections especially in postcolonial literature's "relationship to the prophetic biblical text, which calls societies and individuals to new ways of life. Like the Bible, [postcolonial literature] is prophetic art" that is "simultaneously its echo and mirror but also possesses an awakening prophetic power which can have far-reaching and profound effect" (20). Similarly, the spirituals echo and mirror the realities of postcolonial slaveholding America while they attempt—both in their thematic concerns as well as in their very existence—to awaken their audience to the need for justice. The spirituals combine "several hermeneutical voices" (Wimbush: 45) that are present in the liberating dimensions of the Bible. These voices include the voice of suspicion that opposes African-Americans' exclusion from the Bible's communal salvation; the voice of remembrance that connects the prophetic God with contemporary suffering; and the voice of creative actualization that involves and empowers the listeners. All these voices combine as an act of resistance. Although the message of the spirituals was biblical, its applicability was contemporary. And it was prophetic, applying to God's covenant with his people in any historical situation.

The call for justice that Gallagher identifies as the link between biblical and postcolonial writing is articulated in many forms in the Bible. Nearly every instance of biblical narration of justice was used as a liberating example by the creators of the spirituals. From the Old Testament Exodus story which begins with the divine command to "let my people go," to the New Testament affirmation of Jesus as the prince of peace, to the apocalyptic texts of Daniel and Revelation where God's kingdom is envisioned as one in which justice reigns, the creators of the spirituals exploited many instances of biblical precedent to challenge the scriptural justification for their enslaved condition. Biblical rhetoric was appropriated by creators of the spirituals as proper and empowering for their situation. Furthermore, such an appropriation in a postcolonial setting was not a "mindless absorption of the dominant culture but rather a careful discernment of cultural limits" (Gallagher: 24) that allows one to see and understand the postcolonial world of the textmaker. Especially when they relied on the apocalyptic strains in biblical writing, the creators of the spirituals were establishing their work as concrete gestures of hope and acts of intervention. What Lois Zamora says of Latin American literature applies to the spirituals as well: ". . . their writings are apocalyptic literature in the biblical tradition of apocalypticism, for they share the belief that old worlds can be supplanted by new ones, that current injustices can be remedied" (Gallagher: 109–10).

These connections between postcolonial writing and the biblical call for justice demonstrate for many Christians how God enables people to reach salvation through their own cultural and racial customs. They also demonstrate how creation itself is a mode of resistance. Echoing Martin Luther King, Jr., it is not just the absence of oppression that creates the conditions of justice, but the presence of peace. In embracing the biblical call for justice we need to go beyond a perspective that focuses on salvation to include the pursuit of increased appreciation of the world so as to enrich human life. Justice, therefore, involves for the oppressed the freedom to create works of art and to explore them creatively; likewise, encountering these works of art and the voices they amplify can be for the oppressor an act of justice. It is not enough to endure and survive: one must also create and appreciate to fully exercise one's humanity in the face of oppression. This the creators of the spirituals achieved, as Howard Thurman testifies: "The existence of these songs is in itself a monument to one of the most striking instances on record in which a people forged a weapon of offense and defense out of a psychological shackle. By some amazing but vastly creative spiritual insight the slave undertook the redemption of a religion that the master had profaned in his midst" (36).

In 1925, Alain Locke edited the anthology *The New Negro* to announce the arrival of a distinctive African-American aesthetic. He affirms the transformative power of the spirituals. Although Locke draws attention to the originality and distinctive richness of the spirituals, he emphasizes how their function is not limited by race consciousness but affirms a universal ideal for the whole American nation. For in the African-American mode of call and response, the call extended is meant to be heard and spoken not just by the oppressed but by the oppressor as well. As Eric J. Sundquist points out, the call extended by African Americans in the spirituals and other cultural forms has always been responded to, if not acknowledged, by the dominant culture. Using the spiritual "My Lord, What a Mourning"—chosen by Du Bois as an epigraph in *The Souls of Black Folk*—Sundquist reveals how the spiritual announces the "(re)awakening of present generations of black Americans to their own hidden history in slavery and beyond," and how it serves as a call to "wake the nation" not only of black Americans but the nation of the United States as a whole (2). The ultimate postcolonial response of the spirituals is perhaps best summed up in the lyrics to "Oh, Freedom," which evoke the spirit of a people struggling to be free and willing to pay the ultimate price for resistance, a people who asserted that "Before I'll be a slave/ I'll be buried in my grave/ And go home to my Lord and be free." James Cone has observed that "Black history is a spiritual" (33), but it is history as rewritten to correct our ideological assumption of error as truth.

Works Consulted

Bergesen, Albert
    1979   "Spirituals, Jazz, Blues, and Soul Music: The Role of Elaborated and Restricted Codes in the Maintenance of Social Solidarity." Pp. 333–49 in *The Religious Dimension: New Directions in Quantitative Research.* Ed. Robert Wuthnow. New York: Academic.

Byrd, James Preston, Jr.
    1992   "The Slave Spiritual as Apocalyptic Discourse." *Perspectives in Religious Studies* 19:199–216.

Cone, James
    1972   *The Spirituals and the Blues.* New York: Seabury.

Copher, Charles B.
    1986   "Biblical Characters, Events, Places and Images Remembered and Celebrated in Black Worship." *The Journal of the Interdenominational Theological Center* 14:75–86.

Courlander, Harold
    1963   *Negro Folk Music, U.S.A.* New York: Columbia University Press.

Dixon, Christa K.
    1976   *Negro Spirituals: From Bible to Folksong.* Philadelphia: Fortress.

Douglass, Frederick
    1981   *Narrative of the Life of Frederick Douglass, An American Slave.* 1845. New York: Penguin.

Du Bois, W. E. B.
    1961   *The Souls of Black Folk.* 1903. New York: Fawcett.

Epstein, Dena J.
    1977   *Sinful Tunes and Spirituals: Black Folk Music to the Civil War*. Urbana: University of Illinois Press.

Fanon, Frantz
    1963   *The Wretched of the Earth*. New York: Grove.

Faust, Drew Gilpin, ed.
    1981   *The Ideology of Slavery: Proslavery Thought in the Antebellum South, 1830–1860*. Baton Rouge: Louisiana State University Press.

Fox-Genovese, Elizabeth and Eugene D. Genovese
    1987   "The Divine Sanction of Social Order: Religious Foundations of the Southern Slaveholder's World View." *JAAR* 55:211–33.

Gallagher, Susan VanZanten
    1994   *Postcolonial Literature and the Biblical Call for Justice*. Jackson: University Press of Mississippi.

Gates, Henry Louis, Jr.
    1988   *The Signifying Monkey*. New York: Oxford University Press.

Gunn, Giles, ed.
    1983   *The Bible in American Arts and Letters*. Philadelphia: Fortress.

Hurston, Zora Neale
    1978   *Mules and Men*. 1935. Bloomington: Indiana University Press.
    1983   *The Sanctified Church*. 1934. Berkeley: Turtle Island.

Jacobs, Harriet A.
    1987   *Incidents in the Life of a Slave Girl*. 1861. Ed. Jean Fagan Yellin. Cambridge: Harvard University Press.

Johnson, James Weldon and J. Rosamond Johnson
    1969   *The Books of American Negro Spirituals*. 1925, 1926. New York: De Capo.

Jones, Arthur C.
    1993   *Wade in the Water: The Wisdom of the Spirituals*. New York: Orbis.

Jones, LeRoi (Amiri Baraka)
    1963   *Blues People*. New York: William Morrow.

Kirk-Duggan, Cheryl A.
    1993   "African-American Spirituals: Confronting and Exorcising Evil Through Song." Pp. 150–71 in *A Troubling in My Soul: Womanist Perspectives on Evil and Suffering*. Ed. Emilie M. Townes. New York: Orbis.

Kolchin, Peter
    1993   *American Slavery: 1619–1877*. New York: Hill and Wang.

Levine, Lawrence W.
    1978   *Black Culture and Black Consciousness: Afro-American Folk Thought from Slavery to Freedom*. New York: Oxford University Press.

Locke, Alain
    1968   *The New Negro*. 1925. New York: Atheneum.

Lovell, John
    1972   *Black Song: The Forge and the Flame*. New York: Macmillan.

Mackey, Nathaniel
    1995   "Other: From Noun to Verb." Pp. 76–99 in *Jazz Among the Discourses*. Ed. Krin Gabbard. Durham: Duke University Press.

Marbury, Carl
    1983   "Hebrews and Spirituals: Soulful Expressions of Freedom." Pp. 75–96 in *God and Human Freedom: A Festschrift in Honor of Howard Thurman*. Ed. Henry Young Richmond: Friends United.

Perdue, Charles L. et al., eds.
    1976   *Weevils in the Wheat: Interviews with Virginia Ex-Slaves*. Charlottesville: University Press of Virginia.

Pinn, Anthony B.
    1995   *Why, Lord? Suffering and Evil in Black Theology*. New York: Continuum.

Proctor, Henry Hugh
    1988   "The Theology of the Songs of the Southern Slave." *The Journal of Black Sacred Music* 2:51–63. Reprint. *Southern Workman* 36 (1907):584–92, 652–56.

Raboteau, Albert J.
    1970   *Slave Religion: The "Invisible Institution" in the Antebellum South*. New York: Oxford University Press.

Sernett, Milton C.
    1985   *Afro-American Religious History: A Documentary Witness*. Durham: Duke University Press.

Spencer, Jon Michael
    1990   *Protest and Praise: Sacred Music of Black Religion*. Philadelphia: Fortress.

Smith, Theophus H.
    1994   *Conjuring Culture: Biblical Formations of Black America*. New York: Oxford University Press.

Spivak, Gayatri Chakravorty
    1987   *In Other Worlds: Essays in Cultural Politics*. New York: Methuen.

Sundquist, Eric J.
    1993   *To Wake the Nations: Race in the Making of American Literature*. Cambridge: Harvard University Press.

Thurman, Howard
    1983   *Deep River and the Negro Spiritual Speaks of Life and Death*. Richmond: Friends United.

Wilmore, Gayraud
    1983   *Black Religion and Black Radicalism: An Interpretation of the Religious History of Afro-American People.* New York: Orbis.

Wimbush, Vincent
    1989   "Historical/Cultural Criticism as Liberation: A Proposal for an African-American Biblical Hermeneutic." *Semeia* 47:43–55.

GREEN ANTS AND GIBEONITES: B. WONGAR, JOSHUA 9, AND SOME PROBLEMS OF POSTCOLONIALISM

Roland Boer
United Theological College

ABSTRACT

The issue on which I focus is the dialectic of postcolonial voices, or the question of who can speak in a postcolonial situation. To examine these questions, I juxtapose some contemporary Australian writing and a biblical text, two texts linked by their foregrounding of the problem of essentialism and nominalism, and by their problematizing of the identity of the writer. The Australian writing is that of Sreten Bozic, a marginalized Serbian immigrant to Australia and writer of novels and short stories in the name of Banumbir Wongar, sometimes a woman. These novels problematize the very distinctions they seem to set up: European and Aboriginal narratives, Serbia and Australia, white European and black Aboriginal, white male and aboriginal female, conquest and reconciliation. In many repects Bozic's work embodies the contradictions of postcolonial cultural production and the ambiguities of postcolonial identity.

Over against these works is Joshua 9, a story about the deception of the invading Israelites by the Gibeonites. I read this text in terms of both the motifs of deception and reception. These in turn give rise to at least two ways to understand the text: a postcolonial text that celebrates the duping of the invading forces by the indigenous inhabitants, and a complex reflection on Israelite identity, especially from an exilic perspective. Here the constantly shifting subject positions of Bozic's text and the biblical text intersect. The paper closes with some reflections regarding the nature of the essentialism/nominalism opposition.

The basic problem of this essay is the relation between biblical studies and the discourses of postcolonialism, or, more specifically, the way some of the problems of postcolonialism may affect biblical interpretation. Without being exhaustive, a list of such problems might include the contrast between interpretation from metropolitan centers and (post)colonial places; the absence or presence of metropolitan modes of reading in those places; the status and (ab)use of the Bible as a source for texts of colonialism and of liberation; the relationship between postcolonialism, postmodernism, and globalization; the uniqueness of postcolonialism; the (il)legitimacy of subject positions and identities; and the question of essentialism. The two problems that interest me here are the final two—subject positions, which I will frame in terms of speaking voices and identity, and essentialism. Since I have found that dialectical methods are often the most fruitful ones, it seems useful to set together in some sort of tension both a biblical text and a postcolonial text, distant from each other in time of composition and reading habits but also curiously similar in that the questions of speaking voices and essentialism are important for both texts.

The biblical text is Joshua 9, a story about the deception of Joshua and the invading Israelites by the Gibeonites. The postcolonial text (or rather, texts) is the written corpus of Sreten Bozic, a Serbian immigrant to Australia, writer of poetry, short stories, and a number of novels in the name of B. Wongar, an Aboriginal person, sometimes female. But before I consider these texts more closely I need to indicate what is meant by vocal dialectics (as a frame for the question of subject positions and identity). This refers to the continual movement or slippage in the nature of the "voice" (although I need to be suspicious about that word too) of postcolonial speakers or subjects. That is, those who speak within/to/from—that is, with some sort of prepositional relation to—postcolonial situations find that their ability to speak or write is always (over)determined by a range of conflicting factors, derivative mostly from the former colonial contexts themselves. For example, the very ability to be heard outside one's own context is paradoxically enabled (and then limited) by the language and connections bequeathed by the former colonial masters—an ambiguity embodied in the famous "what have the Romans done for us?" sequence in the *The Life of Brian*.[1]

One of the reasons for my attraction to Wongar/Bozic is that he provides me with a means to write my own troubled situation in a postcolonial country into this text: a desire for reflection on postcolonialism takes place within the context of my European origins, although they are Teutonic rather than Anglo-Celtic (the predominant racial construct of Australian colonization). I am both colonizer and colonized, a supporter of Aboriginal redress and power in politics, society and economics, yet also a pale male who feels the increasing pressure against speaking for and with Aboriginal people. And so Bozic/Wongar, the marginal European who writes as an Aboriginal and who raises questions about identity and essence is the site for my own investment in this paper. For this reason I begin with Wongar/Bozic after my reflection on essentialism and nominalism, for in a sense the troubled and ambiguous presence of Bozic/Wongar is the persona (the allusion to theatre is not accidental) who will read Joshua 9.

---

[1] In this scene, the leader of the revolutionary group, played by John Cleese, asks at a cell meeting, "What have the Romans done for us?" One by one various members of the group list the things the Romans have done—aqueducts, hospitals, education, peaceful streets—so that Cleese is forced to include an increasing number of concessions: "Apart from . . . . . , what have the Romans done for us?" It seems to me that colonialism is similarly ambiguous.

Essentialism and Nominalism

Part of the attraction of a dialectical method is that it requires one to "step back" and seek out the possible reasons for a particular problem. In this case the question to be asked is why the issues of subject positions, identities, and speaking voices are issues in the first place, to which an initial response might be to move more explicitly into the realms of philosophy and history. The whole area of the slippage of speaking voices, and its related question concerning subject positions, have peering over their shoulders the philosophical problem of essentialism, a problem visited with increasing frequency in certain areas of the discourses of postmodernism and postcolonialism. That this is paired with a resurgence of nominalism is something I want to suggest a little later on, but it is essentialism and the closely related questions of the subject and identity that I will place in detention for a while and subject to some systematic interrogation.

It is with the political emergence, or at least naming, of particular groups characterized by social, racial, sexual, and gender difference (from the pale male hegemony) that the problem of essentialism has become most acute. What does it mean to be identified as poor, black, indigenous, gay, lesbian, or feminist? An initial avenue is then provided by an essentialist explanation: the key is to locate that which makes a person or a group of people distinct, that which marks off individual and group identity from other identities. And it turns out that what we are looking for is some essential quality, some deeper "thing" (to evoke Žižek and Lacan) or "essence" that serves as an explanation for the nature of the person or group in question. The search for essence is often intimately bound up with origin: the location of the origins of a particular group of people or of a person then becomes a major component in specifying the identity of the group or person in question. This may happen in all sorts of complex ways: for instance, at a popular level it is common to explain a particular character trait or psychological state in terms of ethnic affiliation—the Dutch are arrogant, Australians are laid back, and so on. But essentialism has also been important in the older waves of feminism over the last century, or in the self-perception of lesbians and gays, or in the postcolonial political consciousness of indigenous peoples. Thus gender, aboriginality, ethnic identity, or sexual orinentation become the determining features of identity and psychological makeup.

The political gains of essentialist group identities have been significant, yet the basic strategy of such an approach as a whole is that it wants to claim existing terms and then reinvest them with a range of different meanings; but this merely leaves the structure of such terminology intact. It has accepted the terrain of its enemy, as it were, in order to engage in the struggle, for there is little that is *formally* distinct between the claim, for example, that indigenous people are essentially lazy alcoholics and the claim that they are deeply spiritual people with long and profound cultural and religious histories. The substance is distinct and has often seemed to be worth battling over, but both statements operate on the essentialist assumption of a deep aboriginal essence—it is what constitutes the essence that is contested, not the question of essentialism itself. If there have been political gains with such a position, then there have also been some drawbacks, the most urgent of which is the restriction of people to specifiable groups and behavior patterns. If some attributes are identified as essentially male, female, indigenous, or ethnic, then these attributes and behaviors are not open to any other group. This has dire consequences for any political action that wishes to effect social change, since the aim to which the change is directed—for example, non-hierarchical social structures—may simply not be possible for a vast majority.

So it would seem that the traps of essentialism may be too great in the long run, which then opens up the possibility that the "notion of an essential self—a self presumed to have its origins in a specific culture, ethnicity, or nation—is debunked by the performative and discursive configurations that participate in the production of these selves" (Sawhney: 216). The problem then becomes one of recognizing difference without recourse to essentialism, something more obvious in the postmodern debates surrounding the subject and what has been termed anti-essentialism. The by now commonplace observations about the subject, that it is decentered, disintegrated, dispersed and so on (and always has been so), bear with them the assumption that without an illusory essence, any pretense at integration and unity has now quietly slipped out the back door. It is of course Donna Haraway's "A Manifesto for Cyborgs" that powerfully claimed this discourse for Marxism and feminism, but in speaking of the subject and anti-essentialism in the context of postcolonialism, I am edging closer to the remarkable essay of Gayatri Chakravorty Spivak, "Can the Subaltern Speak," as well as its partner "Subaltern Studies: Deconstructing Historiography," in which the question of what it means to speak of a postcolonial subject rises to the surface. An accomplished interpreter of both Marx and Derrida, Spivak affirms a resolutely anti-essentialist position, arguing strongly for the sheer constructedness of what once counted as "real," for the inescapable artificiality of institutions, experiences, ways of thinking and feeling, and especially the constitution of the subject. In a characteristic Derridean move,[2] in which an opposition is reversed in order to problematize the opposition, Spivak speaks of a "subaltern subject-effect":

> A subject-effect can be briefly plotted as follows: that which seems to operate as a subject may be part of an immense discontinuous network ("text" in the general sense) of strands that may be termed politics, ideology, econom-

---

[2] But she also notes its presence in Deleuze and Guattari's *Anti-Oedipus*, which is "[t]he most, perhaps too, spectacular deployment of the argument" (1988a:200 n.16).

ics, history, sexuality, language, and so on. (Each of these strands, if they are isolated, can also be seen as woven of many strands.) Different knottings and configurations of these strands, determined by heterogeneous determinations which are themselves dependent upon myriad circumstances, produce the effect of an operating subject. Yet the continuist and homogenist deliberative consciousness symptomatically requires a continuous and homogeneous cause for this effect and thus posits a sovereign and determining subject. This latter is, then, the effect of an effect, and its positing a matalepsis, or the substitution of an effect for a cause. (1988a:204)[3]

In the light of such an anti-essentialist construction of the subject, Spivak concludes, after a long consideration of the ambiguous abolition of *sati*, or widow sacrifice, in India, that the subaltern, the postcolonial subject, for Spivak the colonized Indian woman, cannot indeed speak, since this requires an essentialist approach to the subject in question; or rather, she cannot speak since that which serves to construct her subject denies her speech. The subject is thus both dispersed and overdetermined. And yet, in order to attain positive political results, Spivak speaks, in her discussion of the Subaltern Studies Group, of a *"strategic* use of positive essentialism in a scrupulously visible political interest" (1988a:205; see also 206–7), a sort of limited identification of an essential will or consciousness which recognizes at the same time that that subject, the "subaltern," is itself an unstable category (see Sharpe: 17). This may be read in at least two ways: a sort of anti-essentialist essentialism on the one hand, a voice that takes on an identity for a few moments only to move on soon afterwards; or a condescension to people in colonial spaces, in which they are permitted to be essentialist if it suits their purposes. For those in sophisticated metropolitan zones it is no longer appropriate (see Larsen: 22).

Yet, anti-essentialism may also be understood as a postmodern retooling of the older philosophical option of nominalism, worked out in great detail in the fourteenth century by William of Ockham and his followers but now, in what has become a standard postmodern pattern, mutated in certain critical ways. Ockham's nominalism undermined Thomism's natural theology and metaphysical psychology through a rejection of the assumption that universals were things (and thus existed independently of their names) and a focus on individual particulars which are intuited directly by the mind (universals having formerly been inferred from particulars). Universals thus "exist" only as names, or conceptual terms.[4] Ockham and his followers emphasized the

---

[3] I have quoted this at length since it has significant repercussions not only for the discussion of Bozic's work, but especially for my consideration of the "subject" Israel when I turn to Joshua 9.

[4] Logically, only individual things can exist; it is a contradiction to assert that universals exist (see further, Copleston: 49–61; 122–52 on the Ockhamist movement).

probability of that which in the thirteenth century had the status of clear demonstrations, in particular the logical inference from one thing to the existence of other things (other people, God, etc.). This led both to a split between the synthesis of philosophy and theology, but also to a greater emphasis on the role of faith, as well as the liberty and omnipotence of God (Luther saw himself as a disciple of Ockham). In order to ensure such divine freedom and power, Ockham sought to banish the theory of essences derived from classical Greek thought, and it is here that contact is made between fourteenth century nominalism and my own discussion of essentialism.

Whereas the older nominalism attacked in the name of logic the metaphysics of Aquinas and Scotus, its revived postmodern form comes into its own with the complexities of deconstruction. In a somewhat lengthy consideration of the work, not of Derrida (although that is coming too), but of Paul DeMan, Fredric Jameson (217–59) has argued for the return to nominalism in DeMan's deconstruction, mediated through the latter's work on Rousseau. While Jameson traces in detail DeMan's interest in metaphor in Rousseau's work, it is the tension with the other category in the *Second Discourse* (on language) that suggests nominalism—naming, understood as a designation of the particular and the distinct, and then as a generalizing activity enabled by the very act of naming distinct particulars with the same name. Thus, in the standard example, "tree" names a distinct particular while providing simultaneously a general category. Such a connection between particulars is then none other than the use of metaphor, and here the relation between metaphor and language opens up the link with nominalism. In postmodernism the reappropriation of nominalism is tied with the drive towards immanence (the philosophical equivalent of the now well documented depthlessness of postmodernism) and the refusal of transcendence (modernism's depth).

If the connection is made between postmodern immanence and deconstruction's interest in the constructedness of all that was once held as essential, then nominalism seems to be the most appropriate positive philosophical term for what has generally gone by the negative designation of anti-essentialism. Spivak's emphases will then take on a different hue if they are understood as an elaborate working out of the implications of nominalism in postmodern and postcolonial theory. The political dimensions of nominalism are, not unexpectedly, ambiguous, although Ernesto Laclau and Chantal Mouffe (Laclau and Mouffe; Mouffe 1988; 1993) have been working hard at what an anti-essentialist socialist politics might look like. If what counts is the named, or "staged," identity, then it is possible for a political operator to shift and mix various possible identifiers. This has the positive import of enabling allegiances across various micro-groups who would otherwise not look beyond their own, inevitably limited, constituencies, but the negative one of losing an older political stability (given certain data, you used to know where everyone stood).

I have dealt with the opposition between essentialism and nominalism, between authentic identity and between staged identity, in a more formal way, since it seems to me to be a crucial dimension of the material I will discuss in a moment. Yet I don't want to come down on either side of the divide, although much cultural criticism at the moment seeks out and destroys the last vestiges of essentialism wherever possible. The end result here is to slip into some sort of moral approbation or condemnation, rather than ask the question that seems far more interesting to me: why is this an opposition in the first place, and what it is about this historical situation that has highlighted the issue once again?

Green Ants...

The consequences of the essentialism/nominalism opposition, and its manifestation in the question of speaking voices, are not insignificant for postcolonial theory. Indeed, most discussions of colonialism and postcolonialism have assumed that it is possible to postulate essential colonized and colonizing subjects. This has been crucial not only for the perceptions of the colonizing nation-states, but also for the movements of decolonization, where the needs and desires of the colonized peoples became the focus of attention. This often expressed itself in terms of a rediscovery or return to preconquest origins and a rewriting of the post-conquest histories. Yet it seems that nominalism may provide a rather different way of understanding the dialectic of voices that I have hinted already exists in postcolonial discourse.

These issues are still at the heart of the critical and popular reception of the work of B. (variously Banumbir, Birimbir, Boro, but also Bozic) Wongar. In Australia the initial reaction to Wongar's work was guarded, particularly since the identity of the writer was not clear (although it seems to have been so in some of the European circles with which Bozic had an acquaintance). The suspicions came to written expression in the *Bulletin* article by Robert Drewe. The charges of deception, literary fraud, and misrepresentation voiced in this article make the expected essentialist assumptions about integrity and authenticity, something that seemed to be less of a problem in the reception of Bozic's earlier work overseas.[5] Yet the debate raises the issue that

---

[5] As I write the "authenticity" of Mudrooroo Narogin Nyoongah (Colin Johnson until 1988) has been called into question in print, although rumor has been circulating for some time. The issue has not unexpectedly been clouded by the importance of origins—was he taken as a child from the Nyoongah people and sent to the U.S.A., or is he African American?—and the implications for an authentic identity. Yet what is interesting is not so much the appearance yet again of tired old terms, but the response to the accusations by some aboriginal writers, who claim him by and large for themselves. As Ruby Langford 'Ginibi' writes, "[s]o if his own family disowns him, I'll claim him as one of mine! . . . Besides, look at B. Wongar—he's not an Aboriginal but his

is my own focus here, although I will treat it in a very different way: the construction of identity in the work of B. Wongar, or the construction of the "subject-effect," to borrow Spivak's terms.

A few biographical details might be in order here (a first step in ascertaining the total subject-effect). Sreten Bozic seems to have been born circa 1936, most likely in Serbia, although some stories place his birth in Australia with a return as a child to Serbia. His father had been in Australia, but his mother is unknown. Given the turmoil of the Second World War and the remote location of the home where he was raised, his formal education was minimal. Some time after the war he wandered through a still devastated Europe until he ended up in Paris, working in an auto factory and involved in the circle associated with *Les Tempes Modernes,* especially Simone de Beauvoir. Sometime in the late fifties (some put it in 1958), he arrived in Australia, doing the same sort of thing he did in Europe, wandering around. He seems to have spent time in Arnhem land (northern Australia), the central deserts, including Maralinga (the zone in South Australia where the British undertook nuclear testing in the 1950s), and then on into Victoria. He taught himself English, but also learnt significant slabs of Aboriginal languages, particularly from Arnhem land. While there (approximately ten years according to Bozic), he also married an aboriginal woman, Djumala, who later died along with the children before they could follow him to Victoria. The earliest stories began appearing in *Les Tempes Modernes,* especially those now collected in the *The Track to Bralgu,* but eventually the writing moved over to English. After a banned photo exhibition in Parliament House in Canberra on the nuclear testing at Maralinga in South Australia, Bozic found it difficult to get his aboriginal stories accepted for publication in Australia, and so B. Wongar, "messenger of the spirit world," arrived on the scene. The profound ambivalence over the publication of aboriginal stories by a Serbian immigrant meant that initial publication took place overseas: the University of Illinois Press, University of Ohio Press, and Dodd, Mead are some of the early publishers. Only recently has the Angus and Robertson imprint of Harper Collins in Australia taken him on as a writer, reissuing earlier works and publishing the newer material.

There are any number of ways of dealing with Wongar's work, such as the recurring motifs of the transformation from human to animal or plant, the compound or jail (claustrophobia and confinement), uranium mining

---

stories about us Aboriginals are sold all over the world! So don't be too quick to judge Mudrooroo" (12). The diametrical comparison between Mudrooroo and Wongar takes another twist in all of this, since Mudrooroo has been one of the more aggressive transformers of European and American literary forms in the light of aboriginal literature. Both Wongar, in adopting aboriginal literature, and Mudrooroo, as one who takes on European forms, now find the focus on their slippery identities.

and natural devastation, the spirit world and the relief of death, sexual exploitation, the complicity of police, clergy, and mining interests; but also of the healer (or Marngit), survival and knowledge of the land, and the frog with life-giving water in its belly. In fact, I would like to pick up this final motif, particularly since it appears to be a marginal feature of these narratives, as a sort of organizing device for the others. For what is interesting about the frog episodes is their repetition in story after story—a sort of nervous tic or compulsive act, even finding its way into autobiographical comments (see the interview with Willbanks: 203–4), that signals other things going on within and beyond the text. The situation of the incident is one of extreme thirst in a desert environment; a non-Aboriginal traveler faces a severe shortage of water; an Aboriginal person arrives and digs up from some sand a frog (in semi-hibernation awaiting the next downpour of rain) and from its belly a mouthful of water is extracted by cutting it open. With thirst only partially quenched but death averted, the traveler is then able to proceed on the journey, now accompanied by the Aborigine but at the expense, presumably, of the frog's own wellbeing.

Although I am slightly guilty of Althusser's expressive causality, this repeated episode highlights a number of elements that are important for my own concerns here. There is, to begin with, the promise of death from dehydration, which is formally connected with the theme of claustrophobia and the inevitable death that the prison cell brings. And then there is a glimmer of healing, chthonic knowledge, and survival against all the odds. In other words, the repeated frog episode provides a focus for all the negative and positive features of Wongar's narrative and poetic structures:[6] onto the ones I have just listed may be added those other elements I noted a little earlier—natural and sexual devastation, the various levels of exploitation, as well as the relief of the spirit world and the release of being able to go there. Yet ultimately what is interesting about Wongar's work is not so much these individual items themselves but the transitions between them, and in the life-giving frog water there is the basic transition from death to life, linked then with the shift from devastation to restoration, claustrophia to release—however tenuous that may be and whatever form it might take. Even this is highly unstable: the life is granted only until the next supply of water and food. Yet it is in this way that I want to focus on the profound ambiguity of Wongar's speaking position, mediated through the formal device of a tenuous transformation.[7]

The formal device of transformation manifests itself as content in the stories of the shift back and forth between animal and human form. The most

---

[6] Ross (36) emphasizes the destructive and regenerative forces as well.

[7] I am indebted to Livio Dobrez for the idea of metamorphosis or transformation in Wongar's work.

common of these is the transition between dingo and human, one (at least the shift from human to dingo) that often signifies death, although the dingo as human relative stays with the camp (as, for example, "Poor fellow Dingo" in 1992b:29–37, or "Five-dog Night" in 1982:80–85). Otherwise, the interchange takes place with a cockatoo (1982:18–26), or a crocodile (1982:27–38), or an emu (1982:94–99), and so on. In these and other stories, death seems to be merely a transition from one state into another, so that the nature of death is always ambiguous. At other times the interchangeability of animal and human weaves them all into a vast and somewhat amorphous mass. Such interchangeability is part of the structure of many of the short stories in the various collections (*The Track to Bralgu, Babaru, Marngit,* and *The Last Pack of Dingoes*), although some of the motifs appear in the longer works as well.

However, while the question of speaking positions is signalled in the sorts of transitions I have been discussing, the question itself is also directly broached in what may perhaps best be characterized as a comprehensive reworking of an older point-of-view approach. Although such an approach appears in the short stories—often written in the first person—it becomes more sustained in the novels themselves. The best example comes from the fifth novel, *Raki* (an earlier version is reported to have been confiscated by the Victorian police [see Pullan]). The novel shifts back and forth between a war-torn Serbia and Aboriginal Australia. In Serbia the story is told from the perspective of a boy during World War Two (the autobiographical echoes should not be neglected here), although patterns of suffering from the long oppression by the Ottoman empire and the war in the Balkans of the 1990s also make their presence felt. In Australia it seems to be the same person, but now in prison with other Aborigines, who produces art works for the prison director. A mother figure appears, apparently his Serbian mother but mistaken for an Aboriginal mother by the director, who forces her to plant konopla, or hemp plants, traditionally used in Serbia for clothing over the winter. Indeed much of the focus in the Serbian location is ensuring an adequate konopla crop. In the end it is taken by the Germans in the form of rope to bind up prisoners, in the same way that a rope is the way prison inmates in Australia escape from their cells, after the tribal healer, or Marngit, has called.

What comes through in *Raki,* as also in the other works to a lesser extent, is the sheer inability to nail down what sort of position this novel speaks from. This is not merely the case with the inability to specify particular characters whose identities keep shifting, but also in the nature of the writing itself. It is not pure, or essential, Aboriginal writing, something that the earlier short stories attempt more directly, nor is it conventionally metropolitan or European writing. The oppressors in Serbia, Turks, Germans, neighbors, line up alongside those in Australia, especially prison officers, police and benevolent anthropologists, and Aboriginal workers. If there is an essentialist dimension to this, then that comes from the story being told from the perspective of poor Serbian peasants and Aboriginal people, continually seeking out survival tactics yet at the same time, with a sort of wise naïveté, showing goodwill to even the most callous of people. Yet, just when this seems to be a good way to read this material, we realize that its language is English, the language of colonialism and not that of either Bozic himself, Serbian peasants, or Aboriginal people. It is, in fact, a learnt language, one that comes with colonial associations for the very stories Wongar writes, and yet one that is required in order to be heard.

The speaking voice is less scrambled and more monolithic in the earlier novels (*The Trackers, Walg, Karan, Gabo Djara*), yet even here the ambiguities continue to appear: in *Walg* (womb), the first novel of the nuclear trilogy, Wongar takes on the persona of a woman, Djumala, who escapes the breeding compound and flees to her tribal ground in order to have her child, all the while pursued by various police and authorities.[8] Some of the short stories are written in a similar way—as a mother about to give birth, a mother transformed into an animal and trying to care for her young, and so on (see "Yudu, the Children" in 1982:69–79; "The Ant-woman" in 1992a:29–37; "Walpadja, the Storm-Maker" in 1992a:39–49; "Miralaidj" in 1993:11–12; "The Tortoise" in 1993:81–82; "Baru, the Crocodile" in 1993:89–103). *Karan* reverts to the more conventional male, this time an Aboriginal male, Anawari Mallee, who is in all respects "white." After some tribal initiation markings mysteriously are incised on his chest overnight, he sets out to find their meaning, first on the computers at the Tribal Research and Assimilation Center where he worked, and then on a journey to his tribal land. Relentlessly pursued he finally turns into a tree as the ruined land floods. A similar theme is found in *The Trackers*, although this time an Asian immigrant, Dao Ba Khang, begins to regain his lost color and then ends up, while persistently pursued, identifying with some Aboriginal people who are themselves being destroyed. Finally, in *Gabo Djara*, the animal dimension of many of the stories returns: here it is the mythological "Dreaming" figure of the green ant that finds itself in numerous points of contact with power (parliament, queen of England, mining tycoons, a general, the Pope, etc.) in a white world only to destroy it in what appears to be a nuclear explosion. In these cases, as well as in *Raki* and in the varying perspectives of the short stories, the ambiguities of the vocal dialectics are pushed to the extreme: European and Aboriginal narratives, Serbia (or the Netherlands) and Australia, colonizer and colonized, white European and black Aboriginal, white male and Aboriginal female, human and animal. These normally—at least, according to essentialist perceptions—mutually exclusive categories find themselves operating together

---

[8] For Connor and Matthews (715) the complex interaction of frame and text in *Walg* troubles any notion of a fixed identity. Gunew (8–9) develops this issue further.

in Wongar's work. All of this is then epitomized in the duplicity of self-designation—B. Wongar and Sreten Bozic. In Spivak's terms, B. Wongar is as much a "subject-effect" as Sreten Bozic.[9]

In order to set up a wider theoretical context in which Wongar's work might be placed, I want to draw some comparisons (with their own post-colonial logic in the [re]turn to England) between Wongar's work and a similar case in England that has been dubbed the "Vicar and Virago Affair." In this case some stories written under the name of Rahila Khan, a feminist from the Indian subcontinent, about young South Asian girls and adolescent white boys in Thatcher's Britain, were accepted by the British Broadcasting Corporation (BBC) and Virago, the Woman's Press. When pressured to make some public appearances, the author turned out to be a middle-class Anglican white male vicar, Toby Forward. An autobiographical article in *The London Review of Books* basically ended the story, with Forward discredited and the press embarrassed. The similarities and differences between Forward and Wongar probably balance out, although it is worth indicating the vast difference of the established vicar and the marginalized Wongar. However, my interest is the way the Vicar and Virago affair has generated what may well be the two possible critical responses to the situation of both writers. These are articulated in papers by Dympna Callaghan and Sabina Sawhney in the collection *Who Can Speak? Authority and Critical Identity.*

For Callaghan, Forward's effort replicates in new forms an old pattern whereby white heterosexual males colonize and dominate the cultural expressions and identities of women, non-European and especially colonized peoples, gays, and lesbians. Perhaps the strongest argument in this position is that the white heterosexual male assumes that all others are marked in some fashion by gender, sexual orientation, socio-economic status, ethnic affiliation, education, religion, and so on, except for the white male himself, who is *tabula rasa,* as it were, or at least not affected by any of these factors. He thus assumes that he is able to take on the identities of others in a situation of commodified ethnic identity—particularly since whiteness has lost its racial specificity and is equated with blankness—in what can only be regarded as more sophisticated forms of control. The catch in all of this is that "endeavors to compensate for the exclusion of racial 'minorities' from the means of literary production can become the very means for continuing this exclusion" (197). Ultimately, for Callaghan identities are produced in terms of race,

---

[9] In an allusion to Spivak's "Can the Subaltern Speak?" Sneja Gunew concludes her paper with "'Wongar' may neither speak nor write" (12; Spivak begins her last paragraph with "The subaltern cannot speak" [1988b:308]). This happens when the "god author" becomes the dominant issue: "One is refusing textuality in terms either of interpretation or of the processes whereby meanings become constructed. In this case it both refuses the overt political meanings of this text and refuses to acknowledge the ways in which these meanings are consistently denied" (Gunew: 12).

gender, and sexuality, but she wants to keep the political resonance of the category of identity. For Sawhney, on the other hand, this smacks a little too much of the sort of essentialism I have discussed earlier, despite the weight of Callaghan's arguments for oppositional politics. Her examples include not only the case of Toby Forward but also a joke by Spivak that makes a play on her Indian origins as a basis for the spurious cultural practice of interruption in excited discussion. The very difficulty Spivak's listeners have in discerning a "spurious" cultural practice or Forward's readers have in distinguishing the work of an English vicar from that of a somewhat naive Indian girl signals the deeply constructed nature of the various factors that go to make up any identity, "the extent to which any cultural identity is part of a performance, a staging of the self" (Sawhney: 216). This of course spills over into Callaghan's position, although perhaps not with the consequences that she anticipates: the nominalism (to revert to my earlier terminology) implicit in Sawhney's argument applies as much to the pale breeder male as to the others whom he emulates. Yet Wongar/Bozic has an advantage over Forward in that the chronic uncertainty of his identity makes its way into the form and substance of his writing. His biological existence as a white heterosexual male is by no means an unexamined and comfortable one, being as uncertain and transitional (for me as for Bozic/Wongar) as the other identities found in the various stories and novels. He produces in the end a very unstable subject-effect.

I have so far been favoring an anti-essentialist or nominalist position in my discussion of Wongar/Bozic, and that position seems to make it easier to understand the various contradictions and mutually exclusive dimensions of Wongar/Bozic's life and work. Each of these mutually exclusive positions may then be reread as constructed identities, comparable to those identities continually assembled by Wongar in narrative and poetic form. Once we understand the constructed nature of terms such as "European," "Aboriginal," "white," "black," "woman," "man," "English," "Serbo-Croatian," as well as "first generation Australian," "heterosexual," and "homosexual," then it seems as though we have gone a long way towards releasing the antagonisms that these terms generate. Yet I want to reiterate one question from the previous section and add another to it: why is it that nominalism and essentialism seem to be the only two options available for us at this postcolonial moment? And what is it about our socio-economic situation that makes an anti-essentialist or nominalist position more attractive? I will return to these questions in my conclusion.

... And Gibeonites

The strange thing is that the issues I have raised are not restricted to postmodern or postcolonial texts like those of Wongar/Bozic, since it seems now that we can read ancient texts, such as those in the Hebrew Bible, in the same way. It is as though the Hebrew Bible (and many other ancient texts for that matter) contains postcolonial texts *avant la lettre*, that its authors have had access to the same theoretical material we have, that they have read Derrida, Foucault, Spivak, Laclau and Mouffe, and Haraway, and that they express ideas we thought were only newly discovered. This is the sort of impression I get when reading Joshua 9 in the Hebrew Bible, particularly when it is juxtaposed with the work of Wongar/Bozic; or, to put it more starkly, it is the way I, whose subject-effect is now in part determined by and whose blockage in reading has been written into this text through Bozic/Wongar, read this biblical text. I have chosen Joshua 9 because it has a postcolonial feel about it: not only has the material in Joshua been used time and again to justify invasion and colonial expansion, but the idea of a ruse by the indigenous peoples makes it attractive for a consideration of issues in postcolonialism as well.[10]

As with my discussion of the work of Wongar/Bozic, my main focus is on the way identities are constructed in the text, or, to use Spivak's terminology, the way various strands or lines come together to generate the subject-effect. In some respects Joshua 9 explicitly foregrounds the issue of identity (like the work of Wongar/Bozic), and I will consider this a little later, but my concern for the moment is that which builds up the identity of Israel and that of the Gibeonites. I have selected two motifs, deception and repetition (one concerned with content and one with form), and a way of organizing those motifs, namely, ideology.

Yet, before I reflect on these different areas, I need to give some consideration to more conventional historical criticism, which normally distinguishes between three layers of activity, although there have been various suggestions as to multiple layers of the text. Identification of these layers normally follows the designations of leadership or negotiators with whom the Gibeonites deal: the oldest layer is determined by the dominance of "men of Israel" (אִישׁ יִשְׂרָאֵל, vv. 4–6, 7, 11–14, 16), followed by Joshua (vv. 3, 8–10, 15a, 22–27), and completed with the "princes of the congregation" (נְשִׂיאֵי הָעֵדָה, vv. 15b, 17–21). The first forms the basis and the others serve as supplements to this foundation. More details may be found in the work of Noth, Gray, and Sutherland, although what interests me more in their work is not so much the historical critical suggestions themselves as the signals such suggestions

---

[10] The texts of Joshua have been forbidding territory for many critics, preferring as they do the storytelling excellence of Judges and Samuel within this smaller horizon of biblical narrative. Apart from those with an interest in military exploits and the techniques of destruction and occupation, it is in many respects the very content that causes problems for those who find stories of divinely ordained destruction problematic. This ethical problem has been explored by Stone.

give out about their modernist presuppositions and realist relics.[11] There is, however, another dimension to historical critical study that owes a significant debt to conventional reading habits and the bulk of literary critical activities both within and outside biblical studies. I am thinking here of the focus on character and plot that dominates so much literary reflection, a domination that is worth unsettling and questioning because of the very natural feel that such readings have. This is one of the main reasons why I have opted for the alternative categories or strands noted above.

There are two elements in the construction of the deception, the spatial and the domestic: untruth attaches to the claim to have travelled from "a very far country" (v. 9; see v. 6) and to the claim that the provisions and clothes have worn out on the journey (vv. 12–13). The request for a treaty (vv. 6, 12) and the reiteration of Yahweh's deeds (vv. 9–10) are not deceptive as far as the story is concerned.

As far as space is concerned, my interest is specifically in the function of journeying or travel:[12] the Israelites are presented in the words of the Gibeonites as having been in Egypt (v. 9), while the Gibeonites themselves pretend to have travelled a long distance (vv. 6, 9, 22), having in fact travelled for only three days (or rather, this is how long it takes the Israelites to travel to Gibeon from Gilgal [v. 17]). Joshua's reproach in v. 22 is cast in terms of space and distance: "Why did you deceive us, saying, 'We are very far from you,' while in fact you are living among us?" Space then becomes an element in the deception of the Gibeonites themselves, the purpose of the worn out sacks and wineskins, the patched sandals, worn out clothes and moldy supplies is to give the impression of having travelled over a great distance. Indeed, these items become the proof called upon in the negotiations for a treaty in vv. 9–13. The converse of this is not so much the lack of real distance between the Israelites' present location and Gibeon, but rather the sugges-

---

[11] By this I mean the modernist assumption of a depth model: the text then becomes a deceptive surface (in its projection of a unified story about Joshua et al.) that needs to be overcome or bypassed in order to see the "real" picture "beneath" it. In this case the "real" situation is a complex and fragmentary textual history that competes with the unifying effect of the surface (this problem of the fragmentary and total is a modernist problem in itself, cranked up to another level in postmodernism). The realist assumption is that the history of the text, once uncovered, approximates fairly closely with "what really happened"—an ideological frame of mind that persists in many areas of scholarship and popular culture.

[12] Other spatial features are as follows: the kings of 9:1 come from the hill country beyond the Jordan and from the coastal plains as far as Lebanon; Gibeon is but one place in this expanse, ominously associated with the now defunct Jericho and Ai in 9:3; Joshua and company are in Gilgal in 9:6; the stretch from Egypt to Heshbon and Bashan appears in the recital of Israel's journey in 9:9–10; Gibeon is joined by Chepirah, Beeroth, and Kiriath-jearim in 9:17, and it is at Gibeon that the final dialogue takes place. These spatial items are also the concern of historical critics seeking, with a deep desire to make some tangible connection with the real, to identify places and construct maps with the assistance of archaeological data.

tion that news of the deeds of Yahweh on behalf of Israel have traversed this fabricated distance to the "very far country" of Gibeon. That this is a confession of the type found in other stories of the conquest (see, for example, Rahab's confession in Joshua 2:9–11) is not of immediate interest here, although I will return to this later. What is significant is the way such a narrative statement of Yahweh's deeds becomes part of the deceptive strategy of the Gibeonites. The ambiguity of finding a perfectly acceptable (at least in terms of the ideological structures of Joshua, if not the Deuteronomistic History as a whole) confessional statement used to enhance the deception—Yahweh's deeds are so stunning that even we have heard of them in our far-flung corner—is one of the more appealing dimensions of this story.

So the confessional statement joins space as integral to the beguiling of the Israelites. But there is also what might be termed the domestic, or the homework economy, normally regarded as a peripheral device to the main story line. Yet if Freud has left any legacy at all, then part of it would have to be the significance of the insignificant, the function of the peripheral symptom in the structure of dreams, literature, or any dimension of culture. By "domestic" I refer to the interest in the provisions for the constructed journey of the Gibeonites—the bread, wine, wineskins, sandals, and cloaks that are each qualified by adjectives describing their status in the cycle of economic production and reproduction. At first mention (9:4–5) they are worn out (בָּלוֹת/בָּלִים), torn (מְבֻקָּעִים), tied up (מְצֹרָרִים), patched (מְטֻלָּאוֹת), dry (יָבֵשׁ) and moldy or crumbly (נִקֻּדִים), only to become fresh or hot (חָם) and new (חֲדָשִׁים) in the mouths of the Gibeonites as they relate their story (9:12–13), and then once again dry, burst, worn, and old. In terms of the chapter as a whole (although that in itself is a troubled division) the newness of the provisions and clothing is only in the words of the Gibeonites and thus part of their deception, yet the cycle itself, when removed from its context, indicates the basic pattern of economic reproduction, the needed replenishment and replacement of food and clothing. Now, while it is true that there is something reasonably permanent about this cycle, it is also worth reflecting on the way different socio-economic systems, or modes of production, have formed in order to deal with the production of essential and unessential items, as well as provide the social circumstances for the dominance of certain groups or classes over others. Yet what is interesting in Joshua 9 is only partly covered by reflecting on the roles of the various negotiating persons in Israel (men of Israel, Joshua, or the princes of the congregation; see Sutherland), or on the marks and traces of the Asiatic mode of production (see Boer: 187–91). The other dimension to this is the heavily gendered nature of the supply and deterioration of the provisions: the focus is squarely on the homes where the supplies are hot, fresh, and new—that is, recently produced—and then on the distance from home which sees them become worn out, dry, and torn. That it is the men who make the journey and who are then in the presence of the worn-out material acts as a strong symptom that the women are involved in the process of domestic (re)production, in the homework economy. But this is a highly conventional pattern; the men travel and work outside the home, the women remain in the *domus* and work there or in its near environs.

Thus, there are all the marks of a domestic mode of production here, but all of this forms part of the deception by the Gibeonites. In other words, while the *domus* is apparently present, or at least implied, in the freshness of the Gibeonites's provisions at the beginning of their journey, that journey itself has been fabricated as far as the narrative is concerned. This means that the narrative itself excludes women at another level, that of the narrative action. The provisions have always been worn out, torn and dry, twice removed from their initial domestic production, yet they form the major evidence in the Gibeonite ruse, their current status attesting, in the mouths of the Gibeonites, to the distance they have travelled from when they were first produced. It is curious, then, that a more conventional historical criticism should discount the story of the provisions—its possible historical reference and therefore usefulness is almost always discounted—in inverse proportion to their importance. The story would collapse without them.

I want to ask eventually what sort of contradiction might be lurking in the need for a story of deception about taking the land (itself constructed out of spatial and domestic codes), but I also want to pursue on a more formal level any other significant (as in "that which signifies") features, and this is where repetition comes into play. The most obvious place to begin is the double ending of the story. An initial reading indicates nothing untoward: the first ending in vv. 18–21 flows reasonably well into the second one (vv. 22–27), although there is a difference between the "leaders of the congregation" in the first and "Joshua" in the second that I have noted earlier. Even so, the narrative moves quite nicely from a deliberation between the leaders and the congregation first, and then a subsequent summons of the Gibeonites by Joshua, who questions them and delivers the verdict. The feel of unity jars, however, when the reader's eyes reach the final verse of the second story: "But on that day Joshua made them hewers of wood and drawers of water for the congregation and for the altar of Yahweh, to continue to this day, in the place that he should choose" (9:27). Yet this seems to have been decided already. Compare 9:21: "The leaders said to them, 'Let them live.' So they became hewers of wood and drawers of water for all the congregation, as the leaders had decided concerning them."

Apart from the issue of who is responsible for decision making in this story, a reconsideration of the two endings shows a significant difference of emphasis. In the first, the "leaders of the congregation" are concerned to hold firm to the treaty "sworn to them by Yahweh, the God of Israel" (9:18, repeated in 9:19). Its sanctity is affirmed three times in succession (vv. 18, 19, 20), with the consequences of its breach being Yahweh's wrath (v. 20). The decision to make the Gibeonites "hewers of wood and drawers of water" is thus a resolution of the dilemma generated by the unbreakable treaty or oath and the pressure from the congregation which "murmured against the leaders" (v. 18). The content of the treaty is never disclosed, except for the crucial piece of information that it guaranteed them their lives (v. 15). This seems to be all that is needed for the narrative to move along to the next stage, any further details only confusing the issue, which then becomes the crux of the dilemma in the first ending.

In the second ending the shift is marked by those with the privilege of reported speech in the narrative: only the leaders do any speaking in the first ending of vv. 18–21, although it seems to be in response to the congregation as such (see v. 19), while in 22–27 it becomes a conversation between Joshua and the Gibeonites. Joshua immediately takes the high moral ground and accuses the Gibeonites of deception; he decisively states that they are cursed (vv. 22–23). The Gibeonites back peddle, claiming self defense, yet putting themselves at Joshua's mercy (v. 25), who now becomes their savior, keeping them from death at the hands of the Israelites. In this second ending, notable for the inclusion of the house of God and the altar of Yahweh as places for hewing and drawing, the treaty is much more distant, never mentioned and only alluded to in the initial question, "Why did you deceive us?" Thus, apart from the massed tide of vengeful but mute Israelites and the final punishment, the two endings are quite distinct in emphasis, dialogue partners, and tone. At the same time they finish on virtually the same note.

Rather than pursue the implications of such a repeated ending, both different and yet the same in terms of sources and their redaction, I want to make use of a Freudian idea, namely, the "compulsion to repeat" as a mark of something else going on, or of something that has happened in the past. For Freud the traumatic neurosis comes about through the ego's effort to protect itself from the full consequences of the trauma. It does so by repeating the traumatic situation in dreams and thereby continually drawing the person back into the situation (see Freud: 314–15, 428–29). All of this begs to make the transition to literary and cultural criticism, where the search becomes one for a textual trauma that generates the repetition in the text. I am going to suggest that such a "trauma" may be the issue of Israel's own formation, and here deception has a crucial function.

Two further repetitions in content rather than form enhance the suggestion of a trauma regarding origins. Both are indicated by a sort of narrative tic, nervous repetitions with some small variations between them. The first of these is the treaty or oath itself, concerning which the verb "to swear" appears three times in succession: נִשְׁבַּע, "they swore," in v. 18, and נִשְׁבַּעְנוּ, "we swore," in vv. 19 and 20. The nervousness of the text over such a treaty, or rather the insistence on its inviolability, may fruitfully be connected with the role of the "confession" that I noted a little earlier—to provide a means whereby entry into Israel is enabled. But then the dialectical twist here is that treaty and confession have something other to say about the formation of Israel itself. A similar point applies to the other textual tic, in this case the triple appearance of the phrase "hewers of wood and drawers of water" (חֹטְבֵי עֵצִים וְשֹׁאֲבֵי מָיִם; 9:21, 23, 27), which, while it indicates a clear colonial subjugation of an invaded people, may also reflect a displaced awareness of the origins of those who called themselves "Israel."

I did, however, promise a third category, which is that of ideology. My call upon the ideological as a final phase of analysis for Joshua 9 is intended to indicate the import of deception and repetition in the text. In doing so I am going to make use of two ideas from Marxist literary interpretation. The first is that ideology is inevitably conflictual. This has its material conditions in class conflict for which ideology then functions as class discourse, articulating the hopes and fears of particular social groups. The second is that texts, narratives, and ideological formations may be described as imaginary resolutions of social and economic contradictions. At the same time the traces of such contradictions leave their marks in the texts in question, and this takes place in the very act of attempting a resolution. The paradox here is that the text would not exist if it were not for the attempted resolution, yet by undertaking such a task it necessarily shows the signs of the very thing it attempts to overcome.

I want to argue, then, that the text of Joshua 9, in particular the two items of deception and repetition, signals both ideological conflict and functions as an imaginary resolution of a social contradiction. This ideological conflict and social contradiction are tied, it seems to me, to the question of Israelite origins. The imaginary resolution operating in Joshua 9 is then the story as it is: the Gibeonites are indigenous people, or at least the "first nations" of Canaan, ensuring their own survival through a ruse. Joshua and company are therefore deceived by the natives into preserving their lives, despite the colonial command of God. At this level the text may become a postcolonial celebration of the duping of dull colonial forces. Yet I have already suggested that deception and repetition are symptoms of other things happening with this text. Deception may here be understood in a curiously self-referential fashion: the story of the invasion of the land and the deception by the Gibeonites is itself a deception over Israel's own origins. Similarly the trauma both denied and continually repeated is, I would suggest, the same issue of origins and a troubled identity. It is then possible to offer a second reading of Joshua 9, in which a possible social contradiction rises to the surface. In this case the Gibeonites may be understood as Israelites, or rather their story indicates a secondary narrative concerning the process by which "Israel" itself is gradually constituted in the text. The way the Gibeonites become part of "Israel" is one example of the way various groups constitute "Israel" in the first place, as do Rahab and her family in Joshua 2. This suggestion has echoes in the model which sees Israelite origins as an amorphous mix of different peoples who retreated into the highlands of Judea, perhaps with the occasional revolutionary conflict. But the resonance may also be heard with arguments such as those of Philip Davies in which "biblical Israel" (over against the "Israel of history" and "ancient Israel"), is a construct of Persian period scribes. If I follow this line, then what appears in Joshua 9 with my reading are some of the contradictions inherent in such a construct, marked by both deception and repetition. These contradictions would themselves be the traces of class conflicts, although whether such class conflicts (constructed inevitably in line with certain theories) are more characteristic of the alternative origins of my first echo or of Davies's proposal requires further work.

The very effort to construct a dominant story of origins brings the discussion back to anti-essentialism or nominalism, since the various items I have traced enact a dialectic of voices, pointing to a profound uncertainty about Israelite identity, to the possibility that "Israel" is a discursively constructed entity. Deception therefore has, not unexpectedly, a double role to play: it indicates the duplicity of Israel's own perception of the taking of the land, and it acts as a trace of the social contradiction that the story attempts to resolve. The repetition of the endings is then a second symptom of this double story, now from the perspective of a hidden trauma. Thus, deception and repetition indicate that Israel's overt textual presentation of its origins is part of the construction of its own identity: "Israel" exists only when it is named. In this light the other items also fall into place: it is not so much the Gibeonites who are "hewers of wood and drawers of water," but the Israelites, or rather the Gibeonites as Israelites; the treaty is important not so much for the Gibeonites but for the various elements that make up Israel.

It would seem that this text is also about the question of speaking positions. Whom do the Gibeonites represent? Conquered native people who avoid death by a trick? Or Israelites uncertain about their own identity? As with the material of Bozic/Wongar, this ceases to be a problem if "Israel" itself is understood as a construct, as a name given to very diverse and constantly shifting entity. We are, of course, back with the problem of essentialism and nominalism, and it seems to me that Joshua 9 reads better as a nominalist text than an essentialist one. Sawhney's comments apply as much to Israel and the Gibeonites as to contemporary subjects such as Wongar/Bozic: "[i]mpersonation in any manifestation of cultural articulation demonstrates the manner in which such articulation is constructed, thus subverting the notion of a homogeneous or transparent identity.... Constituted as we are, through a multiplicity of subject positions—some of which may be contradictory—any attempt to fix identity relies on a denial of these contradictions and self-differences" (216).

Conclusion

I have set up this reflection on postcolonialism, Wongar/Bozic and Joshua 9 in terms of speaking voices, subject positions, and identity, all of which is generated out of the opposition between essentialism and nominalism. I have argued that Wongar/Bozic's work insistently foregrounds the question of identity and, with the particular subject-effect that I have named Bozic/Wongar peering over my shoulder or even using my eyes, that Joshua 9 indicates the presence of a similar question through deception and repetition. What comes through in my readings is the profound ambivalence of the question of identity in both postcolonial and biblical texts, as well as in the postcolonial interpreter. It is of course the ways of thinking associated with postcolonialism that have raised these sorts of issues for both contemporary interpretation and that of the Hebrew Bible.

In conclusion I want to pick up another dialectical step and return to a problem I have mentioned on a couple of occasions in my text, namely, why the problem of essentialism and nominalism should have arisen in its old-yet-new postmodern/postcolonial form. I have by and large been favoring an anti-essentialist or nominalist line, since it seems at this historical conjuncture to provide better interpretive options, particularly from a left materialist perspective. Yet I need to ask why it seems to be so now (and I am by no means the only one to prefer such an approach). An answer might begin with the acknowledgement that the problem itself is an intellectual one, thereby finding its place in what is termed in Marxist thought the superstructure. The search is then on for something in the base or infrastructure to which such a tension or problem is a response. In many respects the favoring of nominalism signals what appears to be a final break between signifier and signified, the link between them being that upon which essentialism relies. In a world of free-floating signifiers, only nominalism is possible. But this itself is part of the complex interweaving of economic, social, and intellectual elements that are dominated by the commodity form. Is not nominalism then a necessary transferal or translation of commodification into the realm of thought, in particular in literary and cultural analysis? It is perhaps for this reason that we find nominalism so much more obvious and desirable, saturated as we are with the rampant commodification of late capitalism. Yet, assuming a desire finally to overcome such a situation (capitalism and its associated cultural forms), the question becomes one of the means to take a step beyond both anti-essentialism or nominalism, to move past or sublate the opposition itself, without reverting to essentialism or resorting to a futile conservative reaction. In doing so postcolonialism itself may become the basis of something better.

Works Consulted

Boer, Roland
    1996   *Jameson and Jeroboam.* Semeia Studies. Atlanta: Scholars.

Callaghan, Dympna
    1995   "The Vicar and Virago: Feminism and the Problem of Identity." Pp. 195–207 in *Who Can Speak? Authority and Critical Identity.* Ed. Judith Roof and Robyn Wiegman. Urbana and Chicago: University of Illinois Press.

Connor, Michael and David Matthews
    1989   "In the Tracks of the Reader, in the Tracks of B. Wongar." *Meanjin* 48/4:713–21.

Copleston, Frederick
    1963   *A History of Philosophy.* Volume III. *Ockham to Suárez.* London: Burns and Oates.

Davies, Philip
    1992   *In Search of 'Ancient Israel.'* JSOT Supplements 148. Sheffield: JSOT Press.

Dobrez, Livio
    1990   "Wongar's Metamorphoses: *The Track to Bralgu.*" Pp. 161–72 in *Aspects of Australian Fiction: Essays Presented to John Colmer.* Ed. Alan Brissenden. Nedlands: University of Western Australia Press.

Drewe, Robert
    1981   "Solved: the Great B. Wongar Mystery." *The Bulletin Literary Supplement* 21 April:2–7.

Freud, Sigmund
    1973   *Introductory Lectures on Psychoanalysis.* The Pelican Freud Library 1. Harmondsworth: Penguin.

Ginibi, Ruby Langford
    1996   "The Right to Be a Koori Writer." (letter to the editor) *The Australian* (August 7):12.

Gray, John
    1967   *Joshua, Judges, and Ruth.* London: Nelson.

Gunew, Sneja
    1993   "Culture, Gender and Author-Function: 'Wongar's' *Walg.*" Pp. 3–14 in *Australian Cultural Studies: A Reader.* Ed. John Frow and Meaghan Morris. Sydney: Allen & Unwin.

Haraway, Donna
    1991   "A Manifesto for Cyborgs: Science, Technology and Socialist Feminism in the 1980s." Pp. 257–76 in *Unfinished Business: Twenty Years of Socialist Review.* Ed. Socialist Review Collectives. London and New York: Verso.

Jameson, Fredric
1991   *Postmodernism, or, The Cultural Logic of Late Capitalism.* Durham and London: Duke University Press.

Larsen, Neil
1990   "Postmodernism and Imperialism: Theory and Politics in Latin America." *Postmodern Culture* (e-journal: http://jefferson. village.virginia. edu/pmc /contents.all.html) 1/1 (September).

Laclau, Ernesto and Chantal Mouffe
1985   *Hegemony and Socialist Strategy: Towards a Radical Democratic Politics.* London and New York: Verso.

Mouffe, Chantal
1988   "Hegemony and New Political Subjects: Toward a New Concept of Democracy." Pp. 89–101 in *Marxism and the Interpretation of Culture.* Ed. Cary Nelson and Lawrence Grossberg. London: Macmillan.

1993   *The Return of the Political.* London and New York: Verso.

Noth, Martin
1953   *Josua.* Tübingen: Mohr.

Pullan, Robert
1989–90 "In Police Custody: 200 Pages of B. Wongar's Manhunt Novel." *The Australian Author* 21:11–12.

Ross, Robert L.
1990   "The Track to Armageddon in B. Wongar's Nuclear Trilogy." *World Literature Today* 64:34–38.

Sawhney, Sabina
1995   "The Joke and the Hoax: (Not) Speaking as the Other." Pp. 208–20 in *Who Can Speak? Authority and Critical Identity.* Ed. Judith Roof and Robyn Wiegman. Urbana and Chicago: University of Illinois Press.

Sharpe, Jenny
1993   *Allegories of Empire: The Figure of Woman in the Colonial Text.* Minneapolis: University of Minnesota Press.

Spivak, Gayatri Chakravorty
1988a   "Subaltern Studies: Deconstructing Historiography." Pp. 197–221 in *In Other Worlds: Essays in Cultural Politics.* New York and London: Routledge.

1988b   "Can the Subaltern Speak?" Pp. 271–313 in *Marxism and the Interpretation of Culture.* Ed. Cary Nelson and Lawrence Grossberg. London: Macmillan.

Stone, Lawson G.
1991   "Ethics and Apologetic Tendencies in the Redaction of the Book of Joshua." *CBQ* 53:25–36.

Sutherland, Ray K.
    1992   "Israelite Political Theories in Joshua 9." *JSOT* 53:65–74.

Willbanks, Ray
    1992   *Speaking Volumes: Australian Writers and Their Work*. Ringwood, Vic: Penguin.

Wongar, B.
    1975   *The Trackers*. Collingwood: Outback.

    1982   *Babaru*. Urbana: University of Illinois Press.

    1983   *Walg*. New York: Dodd, Mead and Melbourne: Macmillan, 1986.

    1984   *Bilma*. Columbus: Ohio State University Press.

    1985   *Karan*. New York: Dodd, Mead and Melbourne: Macmillan, 1986.

    1987   *Gabo Djara*. New York: Dodd, Mead and Melbourne: Macmillan, 1988.

    1992a   *Marngit*. North Ryde: Harper Collins.

    1992b   *The Track to Bralgu*. Pymble: Harper Collins.

    1993   *The Last Pack of Dingoes*. Pymble: Harper Collins.

    1994   *Raki*. Pymble: Harper Collins.

From I-Hermeneutics to We-Hermeneutics: Native Americans and the Post-Colonial[1]

Jace Weaver

Ironic Histories: Natives and Christianity

Vignette No. 1: In 1782, Christian Delawares left their homes and their already planted fields in Gnadenhutten and moved into a new "praying town" organized by Moravian missionary David Zeisberger at Sandusky. The move had been voluntary to avoid conflict with Amer-European farmers. When the Natives returned to harvest their crops, however, they were confronted by a patrol of 100 militia from Fort Pitt. The peaceful band surrendered and explained their presence. The colonel in command ordered them bound and—in order to save ammunition—clubbed, scalped, and burned. According to eyewitness reports, the unresisting Natives sang hymns and prayed as the soldiers went about their grisly work. Twenty-nine men, 27 women, and 34 children were killed (Rausch and Schlepp: 130–31).

Vignette No. 2: In 1838, in one of the best remembered incidents of the Removal of Natives from the American Southeast, 16,000 Cherokees were forcibly marched 900 miles from Georgia to present-day Oklahoma. One-fourth of the Cherokee Nation died *en route* along what came to be called the Trail of Tears. As they walked, Christian Indians among them sang Christian hymns in their own language. The best known of these was an atonement hymn, "One Drop of Blood," which asks, "Jesus, what must I do for you to save me?" The reply is, "It only takes one drop of blood to wash away our sins. You are King of Kings, the Creator of all things." The Cherokee translation of "Guide Me, O Thou Great Jehovah," also sung on the trail, is equally poignant:

> Take me and guide me, Jehovah, as I am walking through this barren land.
> I am weak, but thou art mighty.
> Ever help us.

---

[1] I am indebted for this title to a paper delivered in 1988 at the Roundtable of Ethnic Minority Theologians by Stephen S. Kim of the Claremont Graduate School, entitled, "From I-Hermeneutics to We-Hermeneutics: A Prolegomenon to Theology of Community from an Asian-American Perspective." That I find it applicable as a title for the present article attests to the many commonalties people of color have shared in the colonial experience. This article is taken from *Unforgotten Gods: Native American Religious Identity in a Post-Christian Age*, edited by Jace Weaver (forthcoming, Orbis Books, 1998).

Open unto us thy healing waters.
Let the fiery cloud go before us
and continue thy help.

Help us when we come to the Jordan River
and we shall sing thy praise eternally. (Hofstra: 14–15)

Christian Choctaws, enduring a similar trek, sang, too. Theirs, a song of Christian hope, promised that Jesus would save them and stated, "For each of you the heavenly place where you shall dwell is there for you. Follow Jesus to the heavenly place. You will see joy such as you have never seen" (Hofstra: 39). Oklahoma proved a heavenly place for neither nation.

Vignette No. 3: In 1862, 303 Sioux were sentenced to die for their roles in an uprising against their brutal treatment led by Little Crow, an Episcopalian. President Abraham Lincoln demanded that he personally review the records of the entire proceedings. In the end, he authorized the hanging of 39 men. On the day after Christmas, in Mankato, Minnesota, 38 men (one having received a reprieve) quietly followed the provost marshal to the scaffold. They showed no fear and stood calmly as the nooses were placed around their necks. Then they broke into song. Contemporary newspaper accounts reported that they had sung their Sioux death chant. In reality, a good many were Christian. They were singing the hymn "Many and Great, O God." As the trap dropped, they grabbed for each others' hands and sang, saying "I'm here! I'm here!" It was the greatest mass execution in United States history (Noley, 1991:165–66).

Vignette No. 4: In his book *Custer Died for Your Sins*, Vine Deloria, Jr. (Standing Rock Sioux) describes an encounter in 1967 with the Presbyterian minister in charge of that denomination's Indian missions. Deloria listened to the clergyperson describe missionary work among the Shinnecocks of New York's Long Island and then asked how long his church intended to continue such work among a tribe that had lived as Christians for more than 350 years. The impassive reply was, "Until the job is done" (112).

Vignette No. 5: From 1845 to 1848, it was a criminal offense in the Creek Nation to profess Christianity. The penalty for infraction was 39 lashes from a cowhide whip.[2] When less than 20 years old, Samuel Checote was so punished. According to one account, "While blood flowed to his ankles, he was asked 'Will you give up Christ?' He replied 'You may kill me but you cannot separate me from my Lord Christ.'" He later served as chief of the Nation and a clergyman. He was instrumental in having the ban on Christianity lifted. Out of respect for his people, he never admitted having suffered at the whipping post for his Christian confession (Noley, 1991:198–200).

---

[2] The number itself is ironical, perhaps deliberately. Jewish law allowed the imposition of 40 lashes as punishment. More was considered cruel and possible to cause death. Thirty-nine were regularly administered to allow for counting errors (Deut 25:3; 2 Cor 11:24).

These five brief vignettes, spanning 200 years, which could be replicated many times over, attest to what Marie Therese Archambault (Hunkpapa Lakota), herself a Catholic nun, describes as the "terrible irony" of being both Native and Christian (Weaver, 1993a:40). During the eighteenth and early nineteenth centuries, by necessity, Natives in the eastern United States made great efforts to adapt to and accommodate the Amer-European culture that had engulfed them. Many converted to Christianity, the borrowed religion of the foreign invader. They thought that these things would protect them from further depredations. They were wrong. The attempts at acculturation did not matter. The profession of Christianity did not matter. In the end, it only matter that they were Indian. Their continued occupation of their homelands served as both a rankling reminder of a brutal conquest not yet complete and an impediment to its final completion. In the process by which Natives were dispossessed, Christian missionaries were often no less culpable than those wielding rifle or plow. As historian Homer Noley (Choctaw) states, "On the one hand, church denominations geared themselves up to take the souls of Native American peoples into a brotherhood of love and peace; on the other, they were part of a white nationalist movement that geared itself up to take away the land and livelihood of Native American people by treachery and force" (Noley, 1991:85).

Though numerous non-Native historians have produced well-documented treatments of the Native\Christian encounter (most notably Henry Bowden's *American Indians and Christian Missions: Studies in Cultural Conflict* and John Webster Grant's *Moon of Wintertime: Missionaries and Canadian Indians in Encounter Since 1534*), scholarly discussion of these events by Natives has been lacking. In the early 1990s, two volumes attempted to begin to fill this lacuna: *Missionary Conquest: The Gospel and Native American Cultural Genocide* by George Tinker and *First White Frost: Native Americans and United Methodism* by Noley.[3] Although there are many areas of basic agreement between the two authors, a comparison of the two works yields important differences and provides an illustration of the complexity involved in rehearsing Native religious history.

While Tinker is willing, at least in the case of historic missions, to give missionaries the benefit of the doubt for their good intentions, Noley is less generous in his overall interpretation. Tinker declares, "To state the case baldly and dramatically, my thesis is that the Christian missionaries—of all denominations working among American Indian nations—were partners in genocide. Unwittingly no doubt, and always with the best of intentions, nevertheless the missionaries were guilty of complicity in the destruction of Indian cultures and tribal social structures—complicity in the devastating impoverishment and death of the people to whom they preached" (4; Tinker,

---

[3] Although the history of Natives and Methodism is Noley's primary focus, the volume is much fuller, providing a broad history of Native\Christian interaction.

1994:174). This was so because "the kerygmatic content of the missionary's Christian faith became confused with the accoutrements of the missionary's cultural experience and behavior" (Tinker, 1993:4). Putting aside the difficulty of attributing intentionality, it must still be noted that the systemic nature of racism, of which Tinker himself makes quite a lot, organizes and structures personal intent (however good) so as to mask the racist ends it may serve. By contrast, Noley asks how the missionaries, whose work, as Tinker notes, was clearly so destructive, could *not* have known what they were doing (Noley:191). He declares, "Given the political intrigues that spanned most of the eighteenth century . . . the integrity of missionaries and their mission was in doubt. The biblical dictum 'You cannot serve God and Mammon' (Matt 6:24) was set aside as missionaries, on the one hand, offered a religion of love and eternal life, and colonists, on the other hand, were forming militia to kill tribal people or drive them from their homes in order to take their lands and crops" (43). Intellectual and historiographic rigor force the question of how different the missiological experience would have to be before Tinker would surrender his assertion as to the "best intentions" of the missionaries, since such a belief cannot be reconcilable with *any* amount of Native suffering and *any* amount of culpability on the part of the evangelists. In the end, I suspect, Tinker's claim is empty because, given the grimness of the historical record and the role of missionaries in it, absent the improbable "smoking gun" stating baldly a divergence between stated and actual goals, it seems apparent there could be no circumstance, real or imaginary, that would dislodge Tinker from his much-repeated faith in the European and Amer-European bearers of the gospel (see Flew: 96ff.).

The second major difference between Tinker and Noley, dealing as it does with the way they approach their material, is more fundamental. Tinker limns the history of evangelical activities among Natives by focusing on the stories of four prominent missionaries from different regions and eras (John Eliot in Puritan New England; Pierre-Jean De Smet in the Northwest; Junípero Serra in old California; and Henry Benjamin Whipple, Episcopalian bishop of Minnesota during the second half of the nineteenth century). Other exemplars could have been chosen, but, for Tinker, the unrelenting sameness of the stories makes further renditions unnecessary (125–26). Tinker hopes that his study "becomes a contribution to our understanding of why Native American peoples have generally failed to enter the American mainstream and continue to live in poverty and oppression, marginalized on the periphery of society. By and large, Indian people have not found liberation in the gospel of Jesus Christ, but, rather, continued bondage to a culture that is both alien and alienating, and even genocidal against American Indian peoples" (5).

Tinker's method has an unintended and unfortunate consequence. By concentrating exclusively on the four non-Natives of his case study, he erases Natives from the picture. In the process, Native agency is destroyed and Native subjectivity is damaged. The missionaries are portrayed as the only actors in the story. Indians are passive recipients, merely acted upon (see Grant: 239). Noley agrees—it would be impossible for him to do otherwise—that Natives

> were not involved in the preliminary discussions and planning sessions that took place prior to the deployment of missionaries to mission assignments. Their lot was to respond to the implementation of strategies that they had nothing to do with in the planning stages. They were not party to the assessments of their needs and the consequent decision making about how to go about meeting those needs. They were not involved in interdenominational agreements about who could work among which people. It is no wonder that they often became incredulous spectators of events that drastically affected their lives and reflected on their status as intelligent human beings.
>
> From the very beginning of the major missionary movements, when the American Board of Commissioners for Foreign Missions debated heatedly on the subject of whether to "civilize" the Indian first and then "Christianize him," or vice versa, to Reconstruction Era top-to-bottom mission deployment . . . Native people have generally been unwilling spectators of the frustrating results. (Noley:205–6)

In contrast to Tinker, Noley depicts the broad sweep of missiological history. He discusses the many prominent Native missionaries and clergy (e.g. Peter Jones, George Copway, John Sunday, Harry Long) who labored, and continue to labor, effectively among their own people. Natives were, of course, actors in the drama as well. A response *was* required of them. Remarkably, despite brutality, a great many Natives did willingly embrace the alien faith, and some of them went on to carry the message to others. This difference between Noley's and Tinker's accounts is crucial. In it lies the question of whether Natives were (and are) self-determined or selves-determined (see Folk).

In their colonialist drive to assimilate Natives, missionaries told those whom they converted that to become Christian meant to stop being Indian. Exemplary is the experience of Natives after the purchase of Alaska by the United States. In 1897, Dr. Sheldon Jackson, a Presbyterian missionary, was appointed the first Territorial Commissioner of Education. With the support of his colleague Dr. S. Hall Young, Jackson set eradication of Native culture and language as a priority and established boarding schools along the Carlisle model. They encountered a basic problem: these Natives did not fit their stereotypes of Indians. Instead of "rude savages," they found Alaska Natives who already literate and multilingual, already educated in a Western sense, and already Christian and theologically astute. In fact, the Aleuts had been sending missionaries to other tribes for generations (Oleska: 21–24).[4]

---

[4] The Russian Revolution of 1917 threw Russian Orthodox missions in America into a turmoil that would not end fully until 53 years later when the Russian Patriarch recognized the American church as autocephalous.

The first response of these "uncivilized" Natives was to send letters of protest to the Russian ambassador in Washington and to President McKinley. It did not work. In the place of the bilingual education system created by the Russians, Amer-Europeans taught the same self-hatred and internalized loathing that characterized American boarding schools.

Today, only between 10 and 25 per cent (depending on what set of statistics one chooses to believe) of Natives consider themselves Christian. Missions still often are conducted in a manner unchanged in over a hundred years. Natives are still taught that "Christian Indian" is an oxymoron. For all too many, to become Christian still means to cease being Indian. Because of the intimate connection between culture and religious traditions for indigenous peoples, an additional irony is that converts are often told the same thing by their traditional relatives. For those who choose to practice Christianity, the result can be ostracism and isolation from community as illustrated by the story of Samuel Checote above. Referring to the brutal assimilationist methods of Christian evangelism, traditionalist and peyotist Leonard Crow Dog (Sicangu Lakota) states, "Indians became Christian by force. Often they were killed if they did not convert. Indian Christians have a very hard time these days as they are caught between two ways of seeing the world. I feel sorry for those of you who don't know who you are" (Treat: 18).

Ironic Readings: Natives and Biblical Hermeneutics

William Baldridge (Cherokee) confirms these ironic histories as well as their continued contemporaneity: "[M]any missionaries served as federal agents and in that role negotiated treaties which left us no land. Most missionaries taught us to hate anything Native American and that of necessity meant hating our friends, our families, and ourselves. Most refused to speak to us in any language but their own. The missionaries functioned as 'Christ-bearing colonizers.' If it were otherwise the missionaries would have come, shared the gospel, and left. We know, of course, that they stayed, and they continue to stay, and they continue to insist that we submit to them and their definitions. The vast majority of Native people have experienced the missionary system as racist and colonial . . ." (25).[5] Much of that racism can be traced to the biblical hermeneutics of those who came to colonize the Americas and the theological anthropology that flowed from those interpretive systems. From the outset of the invasion of the continent, the Bible was read in a manner oppressive of indigenous peoples and employed to justify conquest.

In his paper, "Native Americans and the Hermeneutical Task," Homer Noley stresses the role of "theological presuppositions and constructions

---

5 Baldridge's original title for the article in which this statement appeared was "Christianity After Colonialism."

which were put in place by Colonial America to describe Native Americans in the nation's theological themes" (Noley, 1988). Jonathan Edwards was one of many who spoke of the western hemisphere as a "promised land" whose inhabitants were "wholly possessed of Satan until the coming of Europeans." John Rolfe proclaimed in 1616 that the British were "a peculiar people, marked and chosen by the finger of God" for the colonial enterprise "to possess [the Americas], for undoubtedly he is with us" (Miller: 119).

Both Alfred A. Cave, in his article "Canaanites in a Promised Land: The American Indian and the Providential Theory of Empire," and Djelal Kadir, in his book *Columbus and the Ends of the Earth: Europe's Prophetic Rhetoric as Conquering Ideology*, have demonstrated that biblical language was used to spawn and spur the colonial enterprise. Cave quotes Sir George Peckham, a prominent Catholic nobleman who envisioned America as a refuge for Catholics. Peckham regarded the Native population as the Canaanites inhibiting conquest of the Promised Land; these heathens would either be exterminated or, like the Gibeonites, submit "as drudges to hewe wood and carie water" (287). Kadir shows conclusively that colonizers crossed the Atlantic convicted of the fact that they were exercising their God-given right to lands held in escrow for them from the foundation of the world. Reverend Alexander Whitaker of Henrico, Virginia, exemplified this opinion when he wrote in 1613 that "this plantation, which the divill hath so often troden down, is by the miraculous blessing of God, revived . . . God first shewed us the place, God first called us hither, and here God by his special providence hath maintained us" (Cave: 288). Anders Stephanson shows in *Manifest Destiny: American Expansion and the Empire of Right* that such beliefs did not cease with the end of the colonial experience but persisted in the American Republic well into the 19th century (15–65). When Natives were not conceptualized as Canaanites, they were viewed simply as part of a hostile landscape that needed to be ordered and tamed by European civilizers, little more than one more type of fauna to be either domesticated or driven toward extinction. Typical, and illustrative of such a mindset, was the declaration of Eliphalet Stark in a letter to a relative in 1797: "The Yankees have taken care of the wolves, bears, and Indians . . . and we'll build the Lord's temple yet, build it out of these great trees" (Grinde and Johansen: 7; Weaver, 1996:14–15). The roots of such racism were sunk deep in biblical exegesis.

In March 1493, the Church was suddenly presented with a problem. Columbus returned home from the "New World" with captives who appeared to be human. The question immediately arose as to how to account for this when the biblical account of creation in Genesis clearly mentioned only three continents (Europe, Asia, and Africa), each populated by the progeny of a different son of Noah after the Deluge. In response, Pope Alexander VI issued his encyclical *Inter Caetera*. The bull sanctioned the conquest, reading, "Among the works well pleasing to the Divine Majesty and cherished in our heart, this assuredly ranks highest, that in our times especially the Catholic faith and the Christian religion be exalted and everywhere increased and spread, that the health of souls be cared for and that the barbarous nations be overthrown and brought to the faith itself" (Tafoya and De Boer: 17).

The papal instruction did little, however, to answer the basic question concerning the humanity and origins of the indigenes of the Americas. Some considered Natives merely human in form but devoid of a soul. Some contended that the newly discovered Natives must be "sons of Ham," the same stock therefore as the racially inferior peoples of Africa (Weaver, 1995: 234–35). Still others, observing the degree of civilization among their cultures, declared the Indians to be the Lost Tribes of Israel. Though all three ideas co-existed, the last gradually became dominant and persisted relatively unchallenged until well into the 19th century. John Wesley, for instance, merely echoed the prevailing opinions of the day when, addressing the urgency of Christian missions to Natives, he fretted:

> One thing has often given me concern.... the progeny of Shem (the Indians) seem to be quite forgotten. How few of these have seen the light of the glory of God since the English first settled among them! And now scarce one in fifty among whom we settled, perhaps scarce one in an hundred of them are left alive! Does it not seem as if God had designed all the Indian natives not for reformation but for destruction? Undoubtedly with man it is impossible to help them. But is it too hard for God? Pray ye likewise the Lord of the Harvest and he will send out more laborers into his Harvest. (Noley, 1991:43–44)

The argument over Native humanity itself was not finally resolved until 1512 when Pope Julius II, faced with "mounting evidence of man-like creatures inhabiting the Americas," declared that Native peoples were indeed human beings, descended from Adam and Eve through the Babylonians (Noley, 1991:18). Thus by the grace of God and declaration of the Holy Pontiff, Indians were found to possess divine souls and were thus eligible for salvation.

Europeans' first reaction to inhabitants of the Americas was thus not alterity but sameness. Behind the debate over origins was a belief not only in the literal truth of the biblical witness but also that no people could attain any degree of civilization—even language—unless they could be shown as springing from the same roots as those of the known, "Old World." They were not Other but Same. Yet, while the debate over the humanity of indigenes was settled, at least nominally, in the Natives' favor, questions as to the value of their cultures were not so resolved.

Edwards was hardly alone in proclaiming American Natives "wholly possessed of Satan" until the arrival of Europeans. Regardless of the country from which they came, colonists and missionaries universally regarded Native cultures and religious traditions as pagan and diabolic, to be eradicated and replaced with Western values and lifeways. Even Russian missionaries, who, on the whole, were more sympathetic to the Native cultures they encountered could not transcend and escape this Eurocentric bias.

An 1894 letter from an Orthodox bishop discussing the traditional beliefs of the Aleuts and Kodiaks states that the morality and religious views of these people "are in essence similar to the Bible stories." The cleric considers this proof of the common origins of all humanity from a single pair of progenitors as depicted in the Hebrew scriptures. He concludes, "The incomplete and fragmentary nature of the religious views of the Aleuts and Kadiaks [sic] can simply be explained by the fact that they have been too long . . . removed from the direct influence of God's Revelations, which alone can communicate to people in all its fullness the knowledge they need to have about God and the World, whereas originally God's Revelation was limited in all its purity to the European peoples alone. It must be noted that in accordance with God's Holy Revelations the Aleuts and the Kadiaks were not completely bereft of God's Grace, as a result of which there remained with them a sense of morality which prevented them from falling into ultimate sin" (Oleska: 71).

In daring to admit that there was something of the divine in Native religious traditions, albeit fractured and diminished, Bishop Petr was affirming the classical doctrine of the *logos*, which had been interpreted so that the ancient Church could cast itself as the "heir of the pagans" and claim for itself the wisdom of the Greek philosophers—a doctrine that Edwards and others implicitly denied when they saw only deviltry in indigenous traditions. The Gospel of John begins, "In the beginning was the Word [*logos*], and the Word was with God, and the Word was God." It then continues that this *logos* is "the true light, which enlightens everyone" and that it became flesh and lived among humanity (John 1: 1, 9, 14). According to historian Justo González, "Since this Logos enlightens everyone, it follows, so the ancients said, that wherever people have any light, they have it because of this eternal Word of God, who became incarnate in Jesus Christ" (43). If the Church had been consistent in its treatment of the *logos*, the doctrine should have provided a means to affirm indigenous cultures. Of course, it was not so consistent.

> If the Word incarnate in Christ is the true light which enlightens everyone, it follows that the Word of God can be found wherever humans have any light whatsoever. . . . Once it attained a position of power within the Roman Empire and Greco-Roman culture—partially through its use of the doctrine of the Logos—it did not even consider the possibility that the same Word may have illumined those whom the "best" of culture considered "barbarians." *They* had no Logos. The Word had to be taken from them. Ever since, Christians seem to have remembered the doctrine of the Logos only when approaching cultures and civilizations they had no possibility of overpowering. When, on the contrary, they faced cultures or civilizations they were

determined to overrun, or which had not advanced the art of killing as Western civilization had, they saw in those cultures and civilizations nothing but idolatry and ignorance. (Gonzáles: 43)

Not until the Second Vatican Council did significant theologians take seriously the notion that indigenous peoples might have something to contribute to understanding of ultimate reality. In the wake of Vatican II, Italo-German theologian Romano Guardini queried whether truths might not "require their own soil in order to develop?" Articulating a doctrine of division of labor among religions, he wrote:

> Here too we might discern a kind of division of labor, by which, for example, certain truths became clear in India whereas Europeans had not yet grasped them. Hence we might find in the spiritual realm of the Vedas some insights which could be useful for a deepening of the doctrine of the Trinity, or it might be that in Buddhism—the strict Buddhism of the south—experiences emerged clearly which might be valuable for the problem of the "negative" knowledge of God?
>
> And what of the matter of mythology; indeed the whole question of myth? Shall we simply reject it, and shall those concerned about the purity of the message confine themselves to freeing this message from its mythical elements? Or is it not possible that a way of experiencing and thinking, in which all peoples lived for a time, should contain images which could contribute to a deepening of the Christian faith? (Guardini: 8–9)

Such expressions, while falling unfortunately short of setting Native traditions on an equal footing with Jewish/Christian traditions, are nonetheless far more accepting than earlier attitudes.

Nonetheless the older ideas persist. Views of Native religious traditions as worthless and demonic and of seeing Natives as the progeny of Ham remain staples of fundamentalist Christianity. The myth of the Ten Lost Tribes remains alive in the Mormon description of American Indians as the Lamanites and continues to recur in popular discourse. Successionist, fulfillment, and anonymous Christ theologies continue to claim a superior position for Christianity over Native cultures. Even conceptualizations of Natives as Canaanites impeding the *eisode* have yet to die out completely. Noley notes that in *The Light and the Glory*, Peter Marshall and David Manuel claim that the divine scheme that America should be the "new Jerusalem" was "to be worked out in terms of the settlers' covenant with God and with each other." In such a plan Natives are listed along with droughts, smallpox, and wild animals as "enemies from which God delivered his people" (Noley, 1988). Worse yet, Amer-European missionaries, continuing the ironic history, still teach such theologies and the biblical interpretations that support them to their Native American charges. As George Tinker observes, it is not unusual for entire Indian congregations to remain faithful "to the very missionary theology that was first brought to them, even when the denomination has long ago abandoned that language for a more contemporary articulation of the gospel. One must at least suspect that the process of Christianization has involved some internalization of the larger illusion of Indian inferiority and the idealization of white culture and religion" (1993:3). When such self-hatred has been internalized to its fullest extent, the conquest will finally be complete.

Ironic Philosophies: Natives and Post-Colonialism

For Native Americans, perhaps the most pervasive result of colonialism is that we cannot even begin a conversation without referencing our words to definitions imposed or rooted in 1492. The arrival of Columbus marks the beginning of colonial hubris in America, a pride so severe that it must answer the charge of blasphemy. (Baldridge: 24)

The idea of the "post-colonial," referring to "a general process of de-colonisation which, like colonisation itself, has marked the colonising societies as powerfully as it has the colonised (of course, in different ways)," has gained a great deal of currency in academic circles and exerted an important influence on the developing discipline of cultural studies (Hall: 246). It has been most fully articulated by literary critics. To a certain extent this is natural because "[l]iterature offers one of the most important ways in which these new perceptions are expressed and it is in their writing, and through other arts such as painting, sculpture, music, and dance that the day-to-day realities experienced by colonized peoples have been most powerfully encoded and so profoundly influential" (Ashcroft, Griffiths, and Tiffin: 1). Yet this also has posed a limitation for post-colonial analysis because these same literary scholars "have been reluctant to make the break across disciplinary (even post-disciplinary) boundaries required to advance the argument" (Hall: 258) or, indeed, to truly test its utility as a way of apprehending the lived reality of persons and peoples.

On its face, the concept has much to recommend it to Native scholars engaged in American Indian Studies or religious studies, including biblical hermeneutics. As William Baldridge's statement above demonstrates, Native cultures were decisively different after the ruptures of invasion and colonization. It is self-evident that they were different from how they would have developed in isolation. New and extreme pressures, erratic and oppressive government policies, and the reduction of indigenes to less than one percent of the population have led to new constellations of identity.

Stuart Hall, a leading force in cultural studies, observes,

The argument is not that, thereafter, everything has remained the same—colonisation repeating itself in perpetuity to the end of time. It is, rather, that colonisation so refigured the terrain that, ever since, the very idea of a world of separate identities, of isolated or separable and self-sufficient cultures and economies, has been obliged to yield to a variety of paradigms designed to capture these different but related forms of relationship, interconnection and discontinuity. (252–53)

While I do not want to be accused of the charge of "banal reductionism" which Hall hurls at critic Arif Dirlik, I do believe that there are potentially troubling aspects of post-colonial discourse that must be seriously debated before American Natives can determine whether it is useful to hop aboard the post-colonial bandwagon.

If Ella Shohat is correct about the ahistorical, universalizing, depoliticizing effects of the post-colonial, there is nothing in that analysis for Natives. If Ruth Frankenberg and Lata Mani are right in their assertion that too often the sole function post-colonial analysis seems to serve is a critique of dominant, Western philosophical discourse—"merely a detour to return to the position of the Other as a resource for rethinking the Western self"—then Natives will want little part of it (101; Hall: 248–49). Unquestionably, as Dirlik states, "post-coloniality represents a response to a genuine need, the need to overcome a crisis of understanding produced by the inability of old categories to account for the world" (353). The "old categories" of Western discourse, though, never accounted for Native worldviews, and since the time of the first contact with Europeans American Indians' reality has been all too much monotonously the same, controlled by those who conquered them.

A basic question concerning postcoloniality is that raised by Hall in the title of his essay "When Was 'the Post-Colonial'? Thinking at the Limit." Shohat has pointed out the "problematic temporality" of the term. Bill Ashcroft, Gareth Griffiths, and Helen Tiffin, in their volume *The Empire Writes Back: Theory and Practice in Post-Colonial Literatures*, contend that the post-colonial is that period that commences at the moment of colonization and continues to the present day (2, 6). Hall, for his part, maintains that one thing the post-colonial is not is a periodization based on epochal stages "when everything is reversed at the same moment, all the old relations disappear for ever [sic] and entirely new ones come to replace them" (247). For him the term is not merely descriptive of "there" versus "here" or "then" versus "now." Nevertheless, in Hall's thinking, as for many post-colonial critics, the term has a temporal scope much more limited than that given to it by Ashcroft, Griffiths, and Tiffin. "Post-colonial" truly represents a time *after* colonialism and temporally means that time post-independence of the former colonial world, even if the struggle for decolonization is not yet complete.

The problem is that for much of that Two-Thirds World colonialism is not dead. It is not living merely as "after-effects" as Hall implies. Native Americans remain a colonized people, victims of internal colonialism. "Internal colonialism" differs from classic colonialism (sometimes called "blue water" colonialism) in that in colonialism's classic form a small group of colonists occupy a land far from the colonial metropolis (*métropole*) and remain a minority, exercising control over a large indigenous population, whereas in internal colonialism, the native population is swamped by a large mass of colonial settlers who, after generations, no longer have a *métropole* to which to return. Today Native American life is characterized by the same paternalistic colonialism that has marked it for over a century. The heavy hand of federal plenary power still rests heavily upon their affairs.

An ironic aspect of post-colonial critique for Natives is its relationship to post-modernism. Post-structuralist discourse provides its "philosophical and theoretical grounding," and like post-structuralism, it is "anti-foundational" (Hall: 255–56). To understand the irony of this predicament, one must turn back to the previous century. In the late 19th century two great rationalizing sciences rose to prominence, sociology and anthropology. The former purported to study that which was normative in the dominant culture. The latter, which Claude Lévi-Strauss labels "the handmaiden of colonialism," studied the Other and advised colonial masters in the manners and mores of native peoples that they might be more effectively controlled (Said, 1993:152). In like manner, in the late 20th century, two systems of critical thought have arisen to explain the world. It is no coincidence that just as the peoples of the Two-Thirds World begin to find their voices and assert their own agency and subjectivity, post-modernism proclaims the end of subjectivity. By finding its theoretical roots in European intellectual discourse, post-colonialism continues, by inadvertence, the philosophical hegemony of the West.

Like post-modernism, post-colonialism is obsessed with the issues of identity and subjectivity.

> Questions of hybridity, syncretism, of cultural undecidability and the complexities of diasporic identification . . . interrupt any 'return' to ethnically closed and 'centred' original histories. Understood in its global and transcultural context, colonisation has made ethnic absolutism an increasingly untenable cultural strategy. It made the 'colonies' themselves, and even more, large tracts of the 'post-colonial' world, always-already 'diasporic' in relation to what might be thought of as their cultures of origin. (250)

Putting aside for the moment the diasporic nature of much of modern Native existence, one must nevertheless admit that there is something real, concrete, and centered in Native existence and identity. Joseph Conrad can become a major figure of English letters and Léopold Sédar Senghor a member of the French Academy, but one is either Indian or one is not (King: x). And certain genuine consequences flow from those accidents of birth and culture. It is part of the distinction drawn by Said between filiation and affiliation (1983:19–20).

The problem is that at base post-colonial discourse *is* depoliticized. As Shohat notes, in its legitimate and sincere effort to escape essentialism, "Post-colonial discourse sometimes seems to define *any* attempt to recover or inscribe a communal past as a form of idealisation, despite its significance as a site of resistance and collective identity" (Hall: 151). Its error, like that of post-modernism, is that it mistakes having deconstructed something theoretically for having displaced it politically (Hall: 249). Jacqueline Rose observes that the postmodern in its "vision of free-wheeling identity . . . seems bereft of history and passion." Said responds, "Just so, particularly at a moment when, all over the globe, identities, civilizations, religions, cultures seem more bloodily at odds than ever before. Postmodernism can do nothing to try to understand this" (1996:7). The same case could be made against post-colonialism.

After more than 500 years of ongoing colonialism, Native Americans wrestle with two different pulls of identity, one settled and the other diasporic (Said, 1996:7). The settled is that of traditional lands and a continent that was once wholly theirs. The diasporic is that of new homes to which they were exiled by their conquerors, of urban existence far removed from even those territories, and a grim realization that their colonizers are here to stay. Only the most winsome dreamer and the most prophetic visionary believe that Amer-Europeans are going anywhere—short of the success of the Ghost Dance or cataclysmic destruction brought upon themselves. Post-colonial critique provides a useful tool for analyzing Native literatures, which reflect these divergent pulls on identity, and for deconstructing the ironic and destructive biblical readings that have been imposed upon us. But as long as those readings and the theologies that spring from them are still taught, as long as denominational factionalism and Amer-European missionization continue to divide families and force Natives to choose between their communities and their religion, the post-colonial moment for Native Americans will not yet have arrived.

Dissolving Irony: Searching for a Community Hermeneutic

In *The Irony of American History*, Reinhold Niebuhr delineates three distinct types of history: the pathetic, the tragic, and the ironic. Pathos is that element of history that inspires pity but deserves neither admiration nor contrition. Suffering resulting from purely natural consequences is the clearest example of pathos. Tragedy is the conscious choice of evil for the sake of good. For Niebuhr, writing at the height of the Cold War, that the United States supposedly had to have and threaten to use nuclear weapons in order to preserve itself and its allies was tragic. Irony "consists of apparently fortuitous incongruities of life which are discovered, upon closer examination, to be not merely fortuitous" (Niebuhr: vii–viii). It is distinguished from the pathetic in that humans bear responsibility for it. It is distinguished from the tragic in that the responsibility rests on unconscious weakness rather than conscious choice. Irony, unlike pathos or tragedy, must dissolve when it is brought to light. It elicits laughter. American history for Niebuhr is ironic: there is a gap between the ideal of America's self-image and the reality of its history and existence (Weaver, 1995:233–34). Natives have been representing themselves in print for more than 200 years and have striven to bring to light, in the hope of dissolving them, the ironic histories, readings, and philosophies that have been imposed upon them by the dominant culture. Without falling into the post-colonial/post-modernist naïveté of believing that theoretical deconstruction necessarily means ultimate efficacy, they have asserted their own subjectivity and have attempted to develop and spell out their own histories, readings, and intellectual discourse in a way that affirms their personhood.

Noley (1988) states, "If the Native American clergy are satisfied with their training, there may not be an interest in a new basis for Native American ministries. If they are not satisfied, there is a place for Native American Biblical scholarship." He remains skeptical because most Native clergy "reflect the fundamentalism of rural white non-Indian Christianity." The remarks are consonant with Tinker's contention that Natives often adhere to the missionary theology first brought to them generations ago. In point of fact at least a few Native clergy and laity always have expressed their dissatisfaction with the transmitted biblical interpretation of the dominant culture.

The work of William Apess (Pequot), written in the 1820s and 1830s, must be viewed as resistance literature, repeatedly employing indirection and signification to affirm Indian cultural and political identity over against that dominant culture.[6] For example, in his autobiography, *Son of the Forest*, he rejects any use of the term "Indian" as a disgrace. Looking to the Bible, he finds no reference to "indians" "and therefore deduces that it is a word imported for the special purpose of degrading us." He concludes, "But the proper term which ought to be applied to our nation, to distinguish it from the rest of the human family, is that of :'*Natives*'—and I humbly conceive that the natives of this country are the only people under heaven who have a just title to the name, inasmuch as we are the only people who retain the original complexion of our father Adam" (10). Here Apess' subversion through rhetoric can be seen clearly. He invokes the language of evangelical Christianity with its appeal to the Bible. In all his writings, he constantly throws

---

[6] For further discussion of Apess's work as resistance literature, see Laura Donaldson, "Son of the Forest, Child of God: William Apess and the Scene of Postcolonial Nativity," in *Postcolonialism and American Culture*, ed. Richard King (Urbana: University of Illinois Press, forthcoming).

up the norms, language, and tools of Christianity into the face of Amer-Europeans in order to expose their racism and to subvert their use of the same material for racist ends.

A key example of Apess' use of signification can be found in his use of the contention that America's indigenes are the Ten Lost Tribes of Israel. As quoted above, Apess states that Indians are the only people with Adam's original complexion, an assertion he repeats, a reference to his belief that Indians were the Lost Tribes. As such, they, like the Jews whom he considers people of color, would be Semites and thus closer to Adam's coloring than the pale Anglo-Saxons. He includes a lengthy appendix to *Son of the Forest*, outlining all the various arguments in favor of this thesis. He returns to the theme in a sermon, "The Indians: The Ten Lost Tribes." Far from using this myth of dominance to slur his own people, however, Apess uses it to claim their common humanity. If Natives are the 10 Lost Tribes, they are every bit as human as their Amer-European invaders. If they are human, they are entitled to equal treatment. Beyond this, if they share a common ancestry with Amer-Europeans, how is there any basis for racism against them? In a scathing pun, Apess looks at Amer-Europeans' complexion and their treatment of Indians and concludes that their Christianity must be only "skin-deep" (34ff.).

Likewise, Peter Jones (Anishinaabe), writing in the decades immediately after Apess, examines the biblical text and employs it against the established order. Jones concludes that Whites have more to atone for in their treatment of Natives than they will ever be able. In language reminiscent of Apess, he looks to the ultimate judgment, writing, "Oh, what an awful account at the day of judgment, must the unprincipled white man give, who has been the agent of Satan in the extermination of the original proprietors of the American soil! Will not the blood of the red man be required at *his* hands, who, for paltry gain, has impaired the minds, corrupted the morals, and ruined the constitution of a once hardy and numerous race." Such judgment, however, extends to crimes far more numerous than the introduction of liquor. Jones declares sarcastically, "When I think of the long catalogue of evils entailed on my poor unhappy countrymen, my heart bleeds, not only on their account, but also for their destroyers, who, coming from a land of light and knowledge, are without excuse. Poor deluded beings! Whatever their pretensions to Christianity may have been, it is evident the love of God was not in their hearts; for that love extends to all mankind, and constrains to acts of mercy, but never impels to deeds of death" (29–30).

One hundred and fifty years later, Marie Therese Archambault declared, "When we read the Gospel, we must read it as *Native people*, for this is who we are. We can no longer try to be what we think the dominant society wants us to be.... We must learn to subtract the chauvinism and cultural superiority with which this Gospel was often presented to our people. We must, as one author says, 'de-colonize' the Gospel, which said we must become European in order to be Christian. We have to go beyond the *white gospel* in order to perceive its truth" (135). For Robert Warrior, in his important and widely reprinted article "Canaanites, Cowboys and Indians," the Native experience *is* that of the biblical Canaanites, dispossessed of their homeland and annihilated by a foreign invader. His argument takes on added force in the case of the tribal groups who were subjected to a genocidal reverse Exodus from country that was for them, literally, the "Promised Land." Thus, for Warrior, to read the biblical witness as a Native, as Archambault suggests, is to read it with "Canaanite eyes" (Weaver, 1993b:40).

Tinker, trained as a biblical scholar, contends that a Native biblical reading "presents an interesting challenge to the predominant, Eurocentric tradition of biblical scholarship." It will differ, he avers, from "Euro-American" hermeneutics in three ways: "First, the theological function of the Old Testament in a Native American context will differ. Second, the sociopolitical context of Native American peoples will characteristically generate interpretations that are particularly Native American. Moreover, the discrete cultural particularities of cognitive structures among Native Americans will necessarily generate 'normatively divergent' readings of scripture" (Tinker, 1994: 174). Each of these points requires some elaboration.

According to Justo González:

> The "modern" world view is so prevalent, and so successful in its manipulation and the exploitation of the natural world, that in many circles it currently passes for the only rational or reasonable understanding of the world. The net result in theology, and in particular in biblical interpretation, has been the need to demythologize, as Bultmann correctly pointed out—or perhaps better, to re-mythologize into the myth patterns of the twentieth-century Western technocratic myth system. Passages in the Bible dealing with miracles, demons, and divine intervention in human and natural affairs, many of which have been sources of strength for believers throughout the centuries, have become problematic for many in the dominant culture—and, precisely because of the dominant power of that culture, for many in other cultures. (48)

Needless to say, however, the "modern" worldview is not the only possible way of seeing reality, nor is its logic as inescapable as its proponents would have one believe. "Traditional societies, as have existed since *homo sapiens* first appeared, have almost universally shared certain common attitudes toward fundamental experience. They perceive time, space, and nature in ways remarkably different from those of the post-Renaissance West . . ." (Oleska: 7–8). Native worldviews are, in fact, much closer to the worldview of the ancient Israelites than that of the modern West. After all, Yahweh was first and foremost the tutelary, local tribal deity of the Hebrew people, whose acts they recognized in their lives. Stan McKay (Cree), former moderator of the United Church of Canada, writes, "For those who come out of the Judeo-Christian background it might be helpful to view us as an 'Old Testament People.' We, like them, come out of an oral tradition which is rooted in the Creator and the creation. We, like Moses, know about the sacredness of the earth and the promise of land. Our creation stories also emphasize the power of the Creator and the goodness of creation. We can relate to the vision of Abraham and the laughter of Sarah. We have dreams like Ezekiel and have known people like the Pharaoh. We call ourselves 'the people' to reflect our sense of being chosen" (52).

These divergent worldviews will generate culturally relevant and specific interpretations of the biblical text. Native Christians give authority to scripture specifically because it resonates with their experience. Even while reading with Canaanite eyes, they locate themselves and their perceptual experience in the story. They report relating to Moses trudging up Sinai to meet the divine as one about to embark on a vision quest. They recognize Mary, the mother of Jesus, because she is *la Virgen de Guadalupe*, or White Buffalo Calf Woman, or Corn Mother, or *La llorona* refusing to be consoled at the death of her child. They can chuckle knowingly at the exploits of Jacob because he is the trickster familiar to them as Coyote, or Raven, or Iktomi. This is not the hermeneutics of professional exegetes. Rather, it is the "folk theology" upon which Christianity at the ground level has always thrived as a living faith. This process of appropriation of the text is no different than that which goes on in the lives of ordinary Christians anywhere in the world. Native Christians give authority to the biblical witness because, to paraphrase Coleridge, there is something that "finds them" where they live their lives.

Any post-colonial biblical hermeneutic for Natives must affirm traditional religious expressions, which previously have been denied and denigrated. As Steve Charleston (Choctaw), former Episcopal bishop of Alaska, reminds, Natives had a covenant with the Creator lived long before missionaries came to them. According to Charleston, that original covenantal relationship forms the "Old Testament of Native America" (54–55). Yowa of the Cherokee, Wakan Tanka of the Lakota, the Great Energy of the Gwich'in, and countless other manifestations are as much *logoi* as any of the faces of deity in the Jewish-Christian tradition. Noley (1991:187) explicitly rejects the assimilationist, missionary hermeneutic that speaks of Native missions in terms of the parable of the tares (Matt 13:24–30, 36–43). In such an interpretation, the tares sown by the enemy are Natives who continue to adhere to their indigenous religious traditions or those who practice religious dimorphism (a very common occurrence among Native peoples), whereby a person participates in Christianity but also still participates in his or her traditional culture and ways without mixing the two. A post-colonial hermeneutic rejects any interpretation that divides Native community.

A post-colonial hermeneutic also will take seriously the importance of land for Native peoples. This imperative has several layers. First, Natives tend to be spatially oriented rather than temporally oriented. Their cultures, spirituality, and identity are connected to the land—and not simply land in a generalized sense but *their* land. The act of creation is not so much what happened *then* as it is what happened *here*; it is the story of the formation of a specific land and a particular people. Thus, when Indian tribes were forcibly removed from their homes, they were robbed of more than territory. Taken from them was a numinous world where every mountain and lake holding meaning for their faith and identity. For example, the Cherokee word *eloh'*, sometimes translated as "religion," also means, at precisely the same time, "history," "culture," "law"—and "land" (Weaver, 1996:12).

George Tinker has written repeatedly about this spatiality. He claims that a Native reading of the Greek scriptures "begins with a primarily spatial understanding of the *basileia*." In the predominant Western biblical scholarship, since the late nineteenth century when eschatology emerged as a central aspect of interpretation of the Greek scriptures, the *basileia tou theou* (the realm of God) has been seen almost exclusively in temporal terms. According to Tinker, "That is, the only appropriate question to ask about the *basileia* has been When?" For Natives, however, thinking spatially, "It is natural to read *basileia tou theou* as a creation metaphor." It is an image of the ideal of harmony and balance. Tinker concludes, "To this extent, the ideal world is the real world of creation in an ideal relationship of harmony and balance with the Creator. It is relational, first of all, because it implies a relationship between the created order of things and its Creator, and, second, because it implies a relationship between [sic] all of the things created." It is the real world within which we hope to realize the ideal world of harmony and balance (1994:176–80).

Naturally flowing from this is the question of humanity's relationship to the earth as a creation of the Creator. Natives traditionally do not relate to the land as landscape. Landscape is related to the German *landschaft*, "a territory shaped by people, a working country carved by axe and plough" (Daniels: 8). It is a word rooted in a belief that the earth must be subdued by human effort before it has worth (Though many Natives have "tooled" the land, by irrigating it or clearing it for crops or pasture, for instance, there is not the concomitant view that it is inferior or worthless without such ministrations). In that sense, it shares a common origin with the injunction of Genesis 1:28 to have dominion over the creation. By contrast, in traditional Native cultures, the relationship to the creation is quite different. There is no superiority assumed or claimed for humanity, and humanity is, in some sense, undifferentiated from the rest of the created order. The world around the Native is a point of communion with the divine because it is a visible expression of the one who created it and still undergirds it.

Finally, when one speaks of land, the issue arises as to ownership. Before the advent of Europeans and the imposition of foreign notions of land tenure which divided up the land that it might be rendered tame, land was not "owned" in a modern sense. It was held in common by all. It was not property but community. Once again, the affinity with the worldview of the ancient Hebrews is evident. Such a belief compares readily to that expressed in Lev 25:23: "And the land shall not be sold in perpetuity; for the land is mine: for ye are strangers and sojourners with me." When he attempted to rally the Native nations into a grand alliance to halt White expansionism, Tecumseh (Shawnee) declared, "The only way to stop this evil is for all the red men to unite in claiming a common and equal right in the land, as it was at first, and should be now—for it never was divided, but belongs to all. No tribe has a right to sell, even to each other, much less to strangers, who demand all and will take no less" (Noley, 1991:71–72). This raises the ultimate question of ownership of land, namely that of how it was wrested from its original occupants. Noley states the matter bluntly, "The fundamental question has never been addressed, even after two hundred years of white presence on this continent: namely, the validity of white presence on a continent already possessed and cultivated" (1991:71–72). A post-colonial hermeneutic must take account of Native land claims.

The final fundamental, and most basic, element of a post-colonial hermeneutic is its communal character. As is often said, community is the highest value for Native peoples, and fidelity to it is a primary responsibility. Native religious traditions are not practiced for personal empowerment or fulfillment, but, rather, they are practiced to ensure the corporate good. There is generally no concept of salvation other than the continuance of the people, and the closest approximation of the Jewish-Christian doctrine of sin is a failure to live up to one's obligations to the people. A post-colonial hermeneutic for Natives rejects the individualistic interpretations brought by assimilationist missions in favor of more communal and communitarian methods and understandings.

No professional exegete or theologian can say what a text means, let alone *should* mean, for Native communities. Only the communities themselves, gathered in dialogue (though modern mass communications may permit them to be geographically distant) can perform that task. The community as the proper locus of the hermeneutical task means that what emerges resembles what Justo González, for Hispanics, labeled *Fuenteovejuna* (sheep trough) theology, "meaning ... a theology undertaken with such a sense of community that it belongs to the community itself, and at the end no one knows who first proposed a particular idea" (53). In traditional cultures, the thought that an idea or a story could belong to an individual—belong to such an extent that he or she would have enforceable proprietary rights in it—would seem as irrational and bizarre as a single person owning the land.

A post-colonial Native hermeneutic, a "we-hermeneutic," however, "goes far beyond the proposal that Scripture is best understood within the circumstances of a community, and when interpreted by a community" (González: 54; Kim). Community is not only a tool or a framework for the hermeneutical task but also its ultimate goal.

> Thus, the community is not just a hermeneutical tool and a necessary context in which to understand a text, but also the goal of every interpretation and every text to be interpreted. Without such a perspective, we fall into I-hermeneutics, which fails, not merely because it misinterprets its text, but also because it misinterprets its task. The task of hermeneutics is not merely for an individual—or even for a community—to understand a text, but is even more for building the community. . . . (González: 54; Kim)

I have called such an approach "communitist" (a combination of "community" and "activist"). A truly post-colonial we-hermeneutic is communitist because it possesses a pro-active commitment to Native community. The community itself "stands at the very center" of such an interpretive system (González: 54).

Though such a hermeneutic will, of necessity be culturally specific (Natives have too long been subjected to the universalizing impulses of Western discourse), as Hall claims for the post-colonial critique in general, it moves beyond the "clear-cut politics of binary oppositions" of "us" versus "them" (Hall: 244). Though it seeks to be inclusive, as much as possible, of the entire Native American community, it does not stop there. Nor does it stop at the entire human community but, rather, seeks to embrace the entire created order, plants, animals, Mother Earth herself.

In his book *Tribal Secrets: Recovering American Indian Intellectual Traditions*, Robert Warrior speaks of the need and ability of American Natives to assert their own "intellectual sovereignty" (1995:97–98). What exactly a post-colonial we-hermeneutic will mean for Natives must emerge out of the community itself as we critically reflect upon our own communitist commitments. If we are ever to dismantle the colonial paradigm and move to a place "after" and "beyond" colonialism (Hall: 253–54) and the imperialist readings it engenders, we must have hermeneutical sovereignty as well.

Works Consulted

Apess, William
    1992   *On Our Own Ground: The Complete Writings of William Apess, a Pequot.* Ed. Barry O'Connell. Amherst: University of Massachusetts Press.

Archambault, Marie Therese
    1996   "Native Americans and Evangelization." In *Native and Christian: Indigenous Voices on Religious Identity in the United States and Canada*. Ed. James Treat New York: Routledge.

Ashcroft, Bill, Gareth Griffiths and Helen Tiffin
    1989   *The Empire Writes Back: Theory and Practice in Post-Colonial Literatures*. London: Routledge.

Baldridge, William
    1993   "Reclaiming Our Histories." In *New Visions for the Americas: Religious Engagement and Social Transformation*. Ed. David Batstone. Minneapolis: Fortress.

Bowden, Henry Warner
    1981   *American Indians and Christian Missions: Studies in Cultural Conflict*. Chicago: University of Chicago Press.

Cave, Alfred A.
    1988   "Canaanites in a Promised Land: The American Indian and the Providential Theory of Empire." *American Indian Quarterly* (Fall 1988).

Charleston, Steve
    1990   "The Old Testament of Native America." In *Lift Every Voice: Constructing Christian Theologies from the Underside*. Ed. Susan Brooks Thistlethwaite and Mary Potter Engel. San Francisco: Harper & Row.

Daniels, Stephen
    1996   "This Land Was Made for Us." *Times Literary Supplement*, August 9.

Dirlik, Arif
    1992   "The Postcolonial Aura: Third World Criticism in the Age of Global Capitalism." *Critical Inquiry*: (Winter 1992).

Flew, Anthony
    1955   "Theology and Falsification." Pp. 96–130 in *New Essays in Philosophical Theology*. Ed. A. G. N. Flew and A. C. MacIntyre. London: S.C.M.

Folk, Holly
    1996   "Indian Missionaries Among the Anishinaabe Tribes of the Great Lakes Region: Selves-Determined or Self-Determining." Unpublished paper (Columbia University, Spring 1996).

Frankenberg, Ruth and Lata Mani
    1992   "Crosscurrents, Crosstalk: Race, 'Postcoloniality' and the Politics of Location." *Cultural Studies* 7:2.

González, Justo
    1992   *Out of Every Tribe and Nation: Christian Theology at the Ethnic Roundtable*. Nashville: Abingdon.

Grant, John Webster
    1984   *Moon of Wintertime: Missionaries and the Indians of Canada in Encounter Since 1534*. Toronto: University of Toronto Press.

Grinde, Donald A., Jr. and Bruce E. Johansen
    1995   *Ecocide of Native America*. Santa Fe: Clear Light.

Guardini, Romano
    1966   *The Church of the Lord: On the Nature and Mission of the Church*. Chicago: Henry Regnery Company.

Hall, Stuart
    1996   "When Was 'the Post-Colonial'? Thinking at the Limit." In *The Post-Colonial Question: Common Skies, Divided Horizons*. Ed. Iain Chambers and Lidia Curti. London: Routledge.

Hepburn, Ronald W.
    1958   *Christianity and Paradox*. London: Watts.

Hofstra, Marilyn
    1992   *Voices: Native American Hymns and Worship Resources*. Nashville: Discipleship Resources.

Jones, Peter
    1861   *History of the Ojebway Indians: With Especial Reference to Their Conversion to Christianity*. London: A.W. Bennett.

Kadir, Djelal
    1992   *Columbus and the Ends of the Earth: Europe's Rhetoric as Conquering Ideology*. Berkeley: University of California Press.

Kim, Stephen
    1988   "From I-Hermeneutics to We-Hermeneutics: Prolegomenon to Theology of Community from an Asian-American Perspective." Paper delivered at Roundtable of Ethnic Minority Theologians.

King, Thomas
    1990   *All My Relations*. Toronto: McClelland & Stewart.

McKay, Stan
    1996   "An Aboriginal Christian Perspective on the Integrity of Creation." In *Native and Christian: Indigenous Voices on Religious Identity in the United States and Canada*. Ed. James Treat. New York: Routledge.

Miller, Perry
    1957   *Errand Into the Wilderness*. Cambridge: Harvard University Press.

Niebuhr, Reinhold
    1952   *The Irony of American History*. New York: Charles Scribner's Sons.

Noley, Homer
    1988   "Native Americans and the Hermeneutical Task." Paper delivered at the Roundtable of Ethnic Minority Theologians.

    1991   *First White Frost: Native Americans and United Methodism*. Nashville: Abingdon.

Oleska, Michael
    1987   *Alaskan Missionary Spirituality*. New York: Paulist.

Rausch, David A. and Blair Schlepp
    1994   *Native American Voices*. Grand Rapids: Baker.

Rose, Jacqueline
    1996   *States of Fantasy*. Oxford: Clarendon.

Said, Edward
    1983   *The World, the Text, and the Critic*. Cambridge: Harvard University Press.

    1993   *Culture and Imperialism*. New York: Alfred A. Knopf.

    1996   "Fantasy's Role in the Making of Nations." *Times Literary Supplement*, August 9.

Shohat, Ella
    1992   "Notes on the Postcolonial." *Social Text* (31/32)

Stephanson, Anders
    1995   *Manifest Destiny: American Expansion and the Empire of Right*. New York: Hill and Wang.

Tafoya, Terry and Roy De Boer
    1981   "Comments on the Involvement of Christian Churches in Native American Affairs." in *Christians and Native Americans in the Late 20th Century*. Ed. Marilyn Bode. Seattle: Church Council of Greater Seattle.

Tinker, George
    1993   *Missionary Conquest*. Minneapolis: Fortress.

    1994   "Reading the Bible as Native Americans." *New Interpreters Bible*. Vol. I. Nashville: Abingdon Press.

Treat, James
    1996   *Native and Christian: Indigenous Voices on Religious Identity in the United States and Canada*. New York: Routledge.

Warrior, Robert
    1989   "Canaanites, Cowboys and Indians." *Christianity and Crisis*, Sept. 11.

    1995   *Tribal Secrets: Recovering American Indian Intellectual Traditions*. Minneapolis: University of Minnesota Press.

Weaver, Jace
    1993a   "Native Reformation in Indian Country?" *Christianity and Crisis*, Feb. 15.

    1993b   "A Biblical Paradigm for Native Liberation." *Christianity and Crisis*, Feb. 15.

    1995   "Original Simplicities and Present Complexities: Reinhold Niebuhr, Ethnocentrism, and the Myth of American Exceptionalism." *JAAR* 63:2.

    1996   *Defending Mother Earth: Native American Perspectives on Environmental Justice*. Maryknoll, NY: Orbis.

TROPES OF TRAVEL

Miriam Peskowitz
University of Florida

ABSTRACT

Various efforts in scholarship, popular culture and tourism industries produce a certain region of Western Asia ("Palestine," "Israel") into a biblical Holy Land of interest to Christians and Jews. Professors of Biblical Studies lead summertime study and excavation tours to Greece, Turkey, and Israel, while Holy Land theme parks in the United States use the latest philological and archaeological research to publicize their accuracy.

This paper is part of what Nicholas Thomas calls "the continuing re-interpretation of colonial histories and representations." It attends to the crossings between biblical studies scholarship and public culture, and queries the enmeshment of both in colonial and neo-colonial privilege. Part of this privilege is the nostalgic premise that "you can be there" and the assumption that "you belong there," two claims that implicitly guide scholarly exercises in "reconstructing" biblical antiquity and in different ways, popular attempts to replicate biblical geography in United States settings. The paper considers what various refusals of these remnants of colonial culture might be.

As her essay "The Maps in My Bible" begins, Minnie Bruce Pratt is at a Franciscan Monastery. She has come to see the "Holy Land of America," a miniature replica of Jerusalem that fills the monastery garden. As she strolls, she sees tombs from first-century Palestine, and then, the Stations of the Cross. But not really. The limestone is fake. Concrete and cement trick the eye. Marble pillars are made from plaster and brick.

Walking in the garden of real replicas, Pratt writes about other reproductions of biblical lands and about how we conceive of certain lands as "biblical." "When I was growing up, Protestant, Presbyterian, 'The Holy Land' was the only foreign land I received any detailed education about. When I was seven-and-a-half, my parents gave me my own Bible, with my name in gold on the leather cover. I found in this book wonderful maps of that Land in pastel yellow, pink, blue." One of these softly colored maps showed "The Probable Settlements of the Descendants of Noah." Yellow designated Africa and Ham. Saudi Arabia was in green, but the rest of the Middle East was yellow, in order to separate Shem into Arabs and Jews. The northern areas that stretched from Europe toward China were colored pink, for Jafeth. As Pratt sees them now, the maps convey several messages.

> Their details proved what I was learning in my religion, that there was a place whose terrain, cities, buildings corresponded to the words of a Bible that was to be believed literally and absolutely. The place existed and it was *mine:* mine to imagine being in, traveling to, mine to experience the blood, wars and drama of; mine, because Christ had given it to me through the sacrifice of his life. [The colors that distinguished Noah's sons, and assigned land to specific groups were] proof to me, as a child, of what I had been taught, the God-ordained separation of people into separate races, by blood.... Poring over the maps in the late 1950s, I wished I could travel to this Land I felt so connected to, unaware that my maps were a hundred years out-of-date, unaware of my enmeshment in a history that had drawn and re-drawn them. (193)

The colored maps use land and place-names to demonstrate the Bible's authenticity and literal truth. They establish familiarity with faraway places and offer a sense of having a home there, of belonging, of abstract ownership. With the softness of pastels the maps claim a biblical genealogy for the separation of people into peoples.

Positing Palestine as somehow belonging to the Christian/West (in a related and different mode from Jewish/Zionist discourse and practice) is not something that belongs solely to the traditions to which Pratt responds. It is a cultural commonplace, one expressed in various terms through a range of media. Nor are Pratt, or myself, alone in responding critically. Ted Swedenburg includes this personal account in his anthropology of the anticolonial revolt of Palestinians against British occupation in 1936–1939:

> My early relationship to Palestine/Israel was largely determined by religion. I was raised in a Christian home by a Methodist minister and his devout spouse, and read and studied the Old and New Testaments at church services, in Sunday School, and—after Arthur Godfrey was shut off—virtually every morning over oatmeal or Cheerios. One of the favored texts of my bookwormish childhood was a Bible atlas, which I pored over, locating place-names on the maps that corresponded to stories in scripture. Palestine (the Holy Land, Israel) was hardly "foreign" to me—I was almost as familiar with its geography as with that of any of our fifty states. But I imagined it primarily as a biblical space whose sites held meaning because of events recorded in the Old and New Testaments. I did have a vague notion about its contemporary history, mainly that, after protracted suffering in exile, Jews had finally "returned" to the Holy Land. I knew this primarily from *The Diary of Anne Frank* and the graphic depictions of her life and the Holocaust in *Life* magazine—a weekly that in the fifties had the cultural impact of all three television networks rolled into one. (1995:xv–xvi)

Similarly, Neil Postman places the imperial imagination of certain geographies into a broader setting that includes Western fascination with positing its origins in Bible and in Greek classical texts: "The smallest details of the geography of two tiny chopped-up countries, Greece and Israel, have imposed themselves on our consciousness until they have become part of the map of our imaginative world, whether we have ever seen these countries or not" (Postman: 17, citing Frye).

When Pratt explores her consciousness of maps and Bibles, she turns the tables on the easy relationship a reader can have with the places it names and the people it divides. She makes strange the knowledge that scripture has provided, doing so because the consequences of these biblical mappings have been so damaging. The repetitions of these stories of being there have led people of the West to occupy, visit, celebrate, and claim as home a part of the world they would otherwise (and sometimes simultaneously) denigrate as "the Orient" and "the East." Palestine/Israel is crafted into a spiritual home—as the "Holy Land" or "Eretz Yisrael" or "the Homeland" or the "Land of the Bible." Familiarization is effected through various media, from liturgical repetition, to the popular culture of Holy Land replicas, travel advertising, souvenir kitsch, study slide-sets and travel writing, to the scholarly writings of Biblical Studies. From this angle, the distinctions between popular and scholarly merge into an overlapping biblical culture, in which Professors of Biblical Studies lead summertime travel tours to Israel, and Holy Land theme parks use the latest philological and archaeological research to assure their accuracy.

I wish to engage in the traffic and tropes of this travel, to see the efforts that make these lands home for Americans, and the efforts that bring these lands home to America. Much of this is part of what Nicholas Thomas calls "the continuing reinterpretation of colonial histories and representations"(2), and part of my own attempts to think through the silent colonial and neo-colonial commitments of Biblical Studies and biblical culture in the United States. As such I am not particularly interested in transhistoric religious claims that, by antique birthright, certain people belong in certain places. Nor am I interested in comparing claims grounded in biblical passages repeated throughout the liturgical year by people within various traditions. I am interested in how geopolitical shifts of the nineteenth century made it newly possible to claim a place called "the Holy Land" as home for the Christian/West and in the legacy of these shifts. The disciplines of biblical studies and of biblical archaeology developed during the heyday of European colonization of Asia and Africa. Assyriology, Egyptology, archaeology, philology—these and other cognate disciplines to Biblical Studies trace their genealogies directly to the inroads made by France and Britain in the eastern Mediterranean in the nineteenth century, and later, to the travels of American biblical scholars such as Edward Robinson. Napoleon's expedition to Egypt in 1798 included teams of research scientists to collect inscriptions, artifacts, and art. These and other treasures were to be shipped back to France to fill the Louvre. When the British captured Egypt from the French, these things were confiscated. Instead of being returned to Egypt they were taken to the British Museum in London (Larsen: 21–22). As it developed, Biblical Studies rested on the growing stature of science in Europe and the United States, a science that was intimately related with the culture and practice of colonization. From the nineteenth century onward, American Bible scholars imported new scientific knowledge about the Bible from Europe and produced their own. All these scholars worked amid their nations' ongoing colonial ventures and formal and informal imperialism. The conjunction of scientific interest and growing European influence and control of Western Asia made biblical archaeology and philological language study possible. These privileges largely remain hidden in the discipline's self-presentation as neutral science. In the years since formal decolonization and national independence movements, without conscious and committed attention to the entangling of Biblical Studies and colonial culture, Biblical Studies continues within these foundations and its colonial legacy.

Holy Land Replicas

Pratt was visiting the Franciscan Monastery in Washington, D.C. The garden tombs and the pathway through the Stations of the Cross are not the only elements of the Holy Land there. Inside the monastery visitors are guided underground. We begin in Nazareth, wind our way through the Roman catacombs, and just after stopping at the Shrine of the Nativity in Bethlehem (where the tour guide offers to take our pictures), we climb the stairs back to the main sanctuary. This is not the only Holy Land replica in the United States. The next one of which I learned was the Ave Maria Grotto in Cullman, Alabama. My guidebook, *America's Religious Treasures*, has the following to say:

> On the campus of St. Bernard College on U.S. 278 is an amazing "little Jerusalem" in miniature created by Benedictine monk Brother Joseph. A native of Bavaria, he came to study at St. Bernard College in 1892 and then entered the Benedictine order. When assigned to the abbey power plant in 1910, he began his hobby of creating miniature shrines in his spare time. Soon they attracted so many people, it was decided to move them to a more adequate site. The present location was officially dedicated May 17, 1934, and since then thousands have come each year to view more than 100 authentic shrines in the 4-acre park. In addition to the cement replicas of the Holy City, Brother Joseph added internationally famous shrines like Our Lady of Fatima, Our Lady of Guadalupe, and the American missions. The accurate proportions of St. Peter's in Rome never cease to amaze visitors. (Vuilleumier: 107)

The replicas are built with materials that range from semiprecious stones to castoff soup cans. Brother Joseph, they say, never visited the Holy Land. His replicas—said by many to be extremely accurate—are based on books and pictures, as well as what another travel book calls "Divine Inspiration" (*Foder's* 97:25–26).

Another Holy Land replica was established in Lucedale, Mississippi, in 1960. According to its brochure, Palestine Gardens is "a scale model of the Promised Land where Jesus walked. After crossing the river Jordan, see the lowest point on the earth: the Dead Sea. Stroll past Bethlehem and Jerusalem as you journey to Caesarea Philippi. You will enjoy seeing many other biblical sites as you follow in Jesus' footsteps." This replica claims to keep intact the scale relation of buildings and mountains and valleys. The perceived perfection of the scale in part causes a sense of wonderment and appreciation for their "realness." What changes is the relation of humans to the buildings and landscape. The buildings are no longer larger than people. Instead, women and men can walk among, around and over the twenty acres of biblical attractions. Even if the scale of the model remains constant, people become giants in relation. The view is panoramic and controlling (Sayre; Foucault; Gregory).

Several kinds of biblical landscape have been built in Eureka Springs, Arkansas. *America's Religious Treasures* describes the set for the Great Passion Play, which is located across from the Christ Only Art Gallery and near the Christ of the Ozarks, a seven-story high statue of Jesus. Dedicated in 1966, the statue was built "to withstand 500-mile-an-hour winds" and is said to be strong enough "that an automobile could be suspended from either wrist without affecting the statue" (Vuilleumier: 118–19). The Passion becomes a landscape, nestled into the Ozark's hills and staged in an amphitheater with seats for 4000 viewers each night. The guidebook: "Across from the art gallery, the traveler will see a duplicate of the streets of Jerusalem, for here each summer the events of Christ's last week on earth are repeated. In a beautiful outdoor amphitheatre the Palm Sunday procession, the scenes leading to the crucifixion, burial, resurrection, and ascension are reenacted, with a cast of thousands. On a nearby slope, a replica of the Holy Land is under construction which will have a location for baptisms on the banks of the new River Jordan" (Vuilleumier: 118–19).

Eureka Springs is a small resort town in the Ozarks. It has been the subject of a fair number of travel articles. These articles are aimed at a general audience, imagined to be predominantly secular and not religious Christians. Accordingly, most travel articles do not mention Eureka Springs' Christian pageantry nor refer to the Christocentric monuments there. Writing in *Ms. Magazine* in 1986, Crescent Dragonwagon almost nearly repeats this pattern. Her article emphasizes Eureka Springs as a place of communal harmony. She offers its steady population of two thousand as a model for how people with different politics, religious identities, experiences, educations, and sexualities can live together kindly and democratically. Almost parenthetically she mentions that "American fascist, Gerald L. K. Smith . . . selected Eureka Springs as the site for his 'Sacred Projects' which include a 70-foot-tall Christ of the Ozarks and a Passion Play depicting Christ's last week on earth—but that's another story." What strikes me is the deferral within her article. Gerald L. K. Smith, fascism, Christ statues and the Passion Play—and we can add, questions about how knowledge of the Holy Land's Arkansan geography, topography, and landscape have been reproduced—are "another story." That which made the replica possible is simultaneously mentionable (broadly and parenthetically) and unmentionable (in any detail).[1]

Eureka Springs contains two kinds of Holy Land replicas: the set and seasonal performance of the Great Passion Play, and a landscape replica called the New Holy Land. The 1976 guidebook to religious treasures is a bit out-of-date. "The New Holy Land" has since been completed. Now, the multimedia Great Passion Play is the site's main draw. In a 1993 article in *The Saturday Evening Post*, travel writer Holly Miller writes explicitly about the play. She loves the show and celebrates the mechanics that make it possible: the synchronized voice track, hundreds of costumes and props, herds of live animals, and hoisting devices that lift actors high into the air. Yet even as she explains the mechanisms that make the fiction of reproduction possible, the pervasive mood is one of seamlessness and ease:

> Actors slip effortlessly into their roles as Jerusalem townspeople, usually taking the audience with them. The backdrop is as comfortable as the players' backyards, and the characters on stage are just as familiar as family friends. A feeling of déjà vu permeates the amphitheater within minutes of the opening processional. The hillside in Arkansas becomes the Holy Land, and 4000 spectators make the transition to participants in the world's greatest drama. "This play is no typical production," says Sharon DeLano [a woman from St. Louis who has seen the play three times]. "It reminded me of everything I have read in the Bible. It was so real that I felt I was right there. For two hours I was living in those times." (82–84)

The monastery in Cullman offers replicas rebuilt from bottle caps, cement, and semiprecious stones. Palestine Gardens promises a forty-five minute walk that crosses over the Jordan River and lands one in Bethlehem. Bound maps in a cherished childhood Bible tender colorful and memorable cartographic designs for traveling the world. The Great Passion Play trades on backyard comfort, familiarity, and a sense of seeing what one already viscerally knows. A small plot of Arkansas becomes the Holy Land and offers

---

[1] On Gerald L. K. Smith and his links to racist and antisemitic politics and to American Nazism, see Glen Jeansonne, *Gerald L. K. Smith: Minister of Hate* (New Haven: Yale University Press, 1988); David Bennet, *Demagogues in the Depression* (New Brunswick: Rutgers University Press, 1969), and Arthur Frommer, *Arthur Frommer's Branson* (New York: Macmillan, 1995), 292–95.

up the fiction that reproduction becomes reality: it was "so real I felt I was right there . . . living in those times." Place and time are conflated. In this chronology, the progression of time does not cause change. In fact, the reverse: this place is imagined to be preserved "as it was." Sitting in one's seat on the lawn, one travels in time to first-century Palestine, to a pristine moment in a Christian and an American past.

These are elements of a widespread nostalgic desire expressed in biblical terms. By one definition, nostalgia is "a wistful desire to return in thought or in fact to a former time in one's life, to one's home or homeland, or to one's family and friends." In another, it is "a sentimental yearning for the happiness of a former place or time." To fulfill the desire to return home, one must first posit a certain place as home. Yet the return visits are not reality but reality-effects, to be exposed for the damage that positing selective pasts and attempting to live them out inflicts on those not included in the dream, and those actively maligned by it. Nostalgia has been actively enmeshed with colonial projects and their imaginaries. Reacting in part to the notion that Europe was both exhausted (and paradoxically, still powerful), for white Europeans engaged in colonial culture, the colonies were part of a future that was imagined in a direct continuum with a Christian biblical past. The Americas were to be the New Jerusalem. The New World would provide virgin homes, places to settle, and a new start in a different time. Colonies there were imagined as long lost homes to which Europeans "rightfully" return, homes that are pristine, uncorrupted, and fresh, homes that have withstood a process of time that has affected and caused decay to other places. Nostalgia within a colonial and neocolonial vein contains the assumption that one belongs wherever one imagines one's home to be, no matter who else is displaced in the process.

My great-grandparents' immigration from the poverty of their lives in eastern Europe has meant that whereas in another trajectory I might have been Hungarian or Russian or socialist or not born at all, instead I was born and raised in the United States and benefit from its power and privilege. Thus, for me, reading biblical texts critically in a postcolonial ethos means refusing their claims to universal privilege and recognizing their Eurocentric value (Felder). It means noticing how colonial legacies still function. Things that now seem normal and natural and "the way things are" have had their origins in colonial relations. Even texts and images that existed prior were refracted and revalued so that their meanings are inseparable (at least in dominant usage) from colonial relations and their neocolonial legacies. For those of us who wish not to be engaged in these and other inequities (at minimum), and for those who wish more actively that our intellectual life refuse these terms and be part of a decolonization of imagination (Pieterse and Parekh), this means looking again at how disciplines of knowledge contribute to these inequities, even unknowingly and against all intentions. And because the texts, stories, and metaphors of the Bible are simultaneously problematic and pleasurable, asking what keeps some of us attached to them is imperative. What dissociations from other people's sufferings (or our own) are going on when we take a stance that is critical of biblical texts and their uses, but remain committed to Euro-American and white privilege so that we are unable to give up the biblical canon. In a so-called postcolonial period that is rife with neocolonial culture (although Palestine cannot yet be spoken of as postcolonial), what forms will a refusal of attachment to these travels and travails take?

TRAVEL ADS

The promise that you can be there, and that "there" is also "home," is elemental in Holy Land replicas tucked away off the highways of various states. The promise also appears in major national magazines and the travel ads that fill them. Commissioned by the Israel Ministry of Tourism, one advertisement appeared in several magazines in the United States. The image is a shot of the Masada fortress against a dusk-lit background. The accompanying text reads: "High above the western shore of the Dead Sea lives a testament to just how high the human soul can soar. Come experience Masada and hear its ancient heart beat." The words give life to the ruins, as if ancient fortress-palaces have human hearts. The ad links ancient stone ruins and living people. It makes each a point on the same continuum. "From the age-old vibrance of its people," the caption continues, "Israel will become part of you. And the closer you get, the deeper it will move you." Here, archaeologically excavated ruins associate living humans with a nation-state (Israel), which itself becomes a normal and a natural part of the landscape, in part by linking the living with the ancient and dead (Abu el-Haj, 1995 and forthcoming). The language is intimate: closer, deeper, part of you. The image and text offer land as a gesture of friendship and belonging; the final slogan reads "No one belongs here more than you." The slogan announces this place as accessible to Western travelers who seek refuge from modernity and alienation in a home drawn from past time. The slogan that promises home to travelers from the United States and elsewhere promotes a nation-state that denies that its lands are home to many whose families have lived there for generations and centuries.

Another advertisement in the same series features dusty stone walls and a maroon-toned sunset. This ad pitches Israel explicitly to Christian tourists.[2]

---

[2] This ad campaign was designed by the New York firm AC&R. The campaign included sixty-second radio spots and print ads in upscale magazines. It was aimed at both "general travelers" and at Christians, and replaced the earlier "Hope to see you soon, Love, Israel" campaign. According to *Advertising Age*, the new campaign meant "to convey Israel's place in world history [as well as] the profundity of the travel experience." AC&R President Steve Bennett explains

It invites a visitor to "Follow in Jesus' exact footsteps, and feel the events of two thousand years as if they had just occurred." A tourist is promised that the changes of time will be made negligible, if not entirely effaced. Travel leads to another space and to another time. Other advertisements deliver past time to those who will join the traffic of travel imaginatively, from their usual and lived-in homes. The CD-ROM "Dead Sea Scrolls Revealed" allows users to "travel through an interactive three-dimensional reconstruction of Khirbet Qumran as it stood in the Second Temple period and learn about the people who were associated with this site and the neighboring caves." A Biblical Archaeology Society bestseller, the "New Testament Archaeology Slide Set" contains "180 stunning slides vividly depicting the world of Jesus, Paul and early Christianity." These slides "Bring the world of the New Testament—the sites, the scenes and the artifacts—into your home, classroom, church or study group."

If the virtual world of antiquity is neither wanted nor sufficient, more tactile remnants can be purchased. In this case, affordable artifacts display antiquity's accessibility. One firm sells Greek and Roman coins that can be worn as necklaces, earrings, or as buttons. Another peddles pendants with your first and last name in hieroglyphics on a "real Egyptian papyrus." The Gallery Byzantium sells candle holders and jewelry that replicate a fourth-century St. Peter's fish, a fifth-century Magi's Camel, a sixth-century Egyptian Royal Peacock and a seventh-century Georgian Angel's Cross. Corinthian columns of white plaster are available in a variety of sizes for home decorating.

In these products antiquity is not just a time, or a place, but a series of things—antiquities. Time is tangible. It can be worn as jewelry, displayed on the hutch, or moved to the dinner table in the form of candlesticks with 24 karat antique gold finish. Objects and replicas from "their" homes enter ours. In slides, past time can be seen through projected pictures. The slides show images of roofless and disconnected ruins. Ragged half-story walls and floors in centuries-old disrepair are projected and then refashioned as they were "originally" through artists drawings, plaster reconstruction, and a viewer's imagination of what they should be.

In these mementos of material culture, what beckons is the highly crafted call of identification, one-to-one correspondence, and the lure of exact and unmediated knowledge of reality. Geographic and chronological distances and cultural differences are erased. You are there. A tourist can experience "ancient Jerusalem" or "follow the exact footsteps of Jesus." Anyone with the proper computer equipment may see Khirbet Qumran "as it stood." The past

---

that he "needed a message that rang true to Catholics, Protestants and Jews, and to those who travel out of intellectual curiosity." After the February 25, 1994, massacre of Arab residents at Hebron by a Jewish man, the campaign development was speeded up, and its budget was raised in order to counteract expected negative reactions to this terrorist act (Fisher).

that from one angle no longer exists is instead, from another, constructed as animate and alive: "Its heart still beats." The language of unmediated connection and access—"the world of the New Testament enters your home"—makes antiquity seem real. This language camouflages the production of stories about antiquity, the way this past is put together, the question of who is present and who is made absent, of who will be powerful and who will be marginal, belittled, violated, or oppressed. The quaintness of antiquity—its very antiquarianness—masks the political uses made of the past, as it is "discovered" again and again, for different reasons and with different meanings and effects (Whitelam; O'Toole). The travel ads and their captions demand a closeness that effaces differences between "us" and "them," collapsing their lives into ours.

Some Genealogies of Replication

The replication of Holy Lands in the United States has a history. One of the first Holy Land models in the United States was landscaped into the edge of Lake Chautauqua. John Heyl Vincent etched the Holy Land into the dirt and stones of New York State in 1874, the Chautauqua Institute's first summer. The result, Palestine Park, was 75 feet wide by 120 feet long, "an extensive topographic model that bordered Lake Chautauqua and used the shoreline as its 'Mediterranean Coast'" (Vogel: 2). Vincent had attempted a prototype in a grove outside his congregation in Camptown, New Jersey. As part of his concern with "Singing Geography," Vincent used this visual and visceral model to train Sunday School teachers. For those too far away to attend, he distributed his Holy Land map through a two-week study course offered through the *Sunday School Journal*, which he edited (Case: 12). At Chautauqua he transformed the prototype onto a larger grid, with the added authenticity of the adjoining body of water.

> The Chautauqua model was designed to make the already familiar more "real," to turn the image of the Holy Land—already in the mind's eye—into a tangible through miniaturized landscape. The leaders of Chautauqua were confident of the degree to which people already held such an image, and they were so confident that their model was consistent with reality that they even claimed examination of the model in conjunction with a proper text would be "almost equivalent to an actual tour of the Holy Land." The model allowed viewers to process their assorted perceptions and form them into a distinct image that was consistent with popular understanding. (Vogel: 3)

Use and appreciation wore away its features, and Palestine Park was continually in need of reconstruction and rebuilding. Ongoing discussions were had at Chautauqua about what to do with Palestine Park, as it periodically decayed into muddy disrepair.

Palestine Park was several things simultaneously. As a text for outdoor classroom instruction, Sunday-school teachers would be led through the

Park and taught its geographic features. Palestine Park was a site for reflection, meditation and closeness, and Sabbath walks. Just as reading New Testament would lessen the distances between human and divine, the model could transport Christian believers to the home landscape of Jesus and the early Christians.

Palestine Park was also used by children. In written recollections by adults of their childhood summers at Chautauqua, the willingness to let its miniature features stand in for "the real" Palestine collides with a sense of playfulness. Rebecca Richmond remembers that "originally the models of the cities were made of plaster and were light enough to permit mischievous youngsters to take unholy liberties with Palestinian geography" (Morrison: 35; Richmond). Ida Tarbell elaborates. "The worst mischief in which I personally assisted was playing tag up and down the relief model of Palestine ... one rule of our game was that you could not be tagged if you straddled Jerusalem. The most serious vandalism was stealing Damascus or Nazareth or Tyre and carrying it away bodily" (Morrison: 35, citing Tarbell).

These adult stories of childhood games are playful and charming. Yet the images—picking up Tyre and running off—contain a central feature of colonial knowledge-gathering. Amid the claims of pleasure, piety, and respect is a landscape etched for the purposes of power, knowledge, and control. The cities are light enough to carry. American children become the masters of foreign cities, giants who can straddle Jerusalem and control Damascus.

Palestine Park was facilitated by the emerging science of American Biblical Studies and the new maps of Palestine. These new knowledges were conveyed by teachers and tour-guides. They were made explicit in the tent-housed museum nearby. The museum was "designed to illustrate biblical and oriental geography, costumes, and manners, and to furnish at least introductory materials for study. Its casts, books, clothing, dried flora, agricultural and domestic implements included items representing Assyria and Egypt as well as Palestine. A mummy was present, lent by Mount Union College" (Morrison: 35–36). The museum's contents were the result of the classifications of academic study and the collection of objects from Western Asia—and about such collections we must always raise the question of how these treasures were stolen. The museum's architecture of tent-housing resonated with the Romantic and Orientalist image of the "bedouin" tent. It recalled the elaborate tent-camping schemes experienced and written about by travelers from the United States to Ottoman Palestine, camping made possible by scores of native servants leading long trains of loaded-down donkeys, in order to produce luxurious dining and lodging for the foreign visitors (Rix).

On a grander scale, the 1904 World's Fair in St. Louis had a Jerusalem exhibit that spread over ten acres. The Jerusalem Exhibit Company produced this exhibit with an advisory board of Protestants, Catholics, and Jews. But knowledge of this as a reproduction was to fade for those who entered. The Exhibit Company's proposal imagined that the display, in short, will be Jerusalem itself. It is intended that there shall be at least three hundred natives to make the scene realistic. When the visitor enters the gates of the city he shall be made to feel as though he were in actual Jerusalem, with its streets, bazaars, buildings, and people forming a picture of supreme interest to those who have never been there and surprisingly familiar to those who have. There will be peasant women who will vend from native baskets the luscious oranges, lemons, dates, and grapes which so attracted the spies of Israel. These peasants will be seen in their tattered, yet picturesque garments.... There will be Bedouins from the desert, with their camel's hair fillets, bound round their heads, native Christians in blue dresses and embroidered veils, Copts, Moslems, Turks, and priests.... It is a remarkable fact that Palestine has changed little since the days of Christ, and in some respects but little, if any, since the days of Abraham. This will be vividly impressed upon the visitor to the Jerusalem exhibit. (Vogel: 214–15; Jerusalem Exhibit Company: 10–14)

The description establishes Jerusalem as the Orient. It is simultaneously exotic, different from home, and home (Grewal; Kabbani).

The reproduction merges with the actual. The American who enters the exhibit is transported not only spatially but temporally. She travels to Palestine, and Palestine travels to her. St. Louis and Jerusalem are the same. The point of destination becomes the point of departure. After all, the exhibit is about things that are imagined not to change, that in essence are the same. Palestine's residents were brought to the United States to perform living in the Palestine of Jesus' day, and to exemplify the land of Abraham in the second millennium BCE. The currently living residents traveled between these times that (in the exhibit's imaginary) were really one and the same. They travel and they do not travel. They are here and there, now and then. As such, the imported residents of Palestine embody for the Americans who viewed "Jerusalem and its residents" the possibility that they too can have access to the "then" and the "there" they desire.

The collapse of differences of time, place and manners is articulated perfectly by Bertha Spafford Vester in her memoir *Our Jerusalem: An American Family in the Holy City, 1891–1949*, published in 1950. Bertha was raised in Jerusalem; her parents founded and sustained the American Colony there. The Spaffords began their mission to Jerusalem despite the agreement among evangelical churches in Britain, France, and the United States to divide Ottoman-controlled regions according to the logic of Euro-American nationhood. In areas of Asia and Africa already controlled by specific European nations, the question of which national church could establish a mission was easily determined. For areas still controlled by the Ottoman empire, European and American churches generally abided by a plan that gave Palestine to British and French missions and limited American missions to Beirut and its environs. The Spaffords found the call of Jerusalem too pressing, and they withstood the venom of missionaries from other nations as a result.

Our Jerusalem belongs to an extensive genre of memoirs and travel narratives written by Americans who had spent time in Palestine during the nineteenth and early twentieth centuries. Visitors and pilgrims would prepare for their trips with books and pamphlets written by those who had already been there. These readings established sets of facts and data that they could repeat in the traveler's own writing. In *Our Jerusalem*, Bertha describes the education she and her siblings received at the American Colony. Books and textbooks were difficult to obtain. Yet, she writes, "we all knew the children's fairy tales, and better still, the Bible stories, for all we saw around us was straight from the Bible, and we saw them lived.... Living in the Holy Land we almost spoke in Biblical speech, and I still find myself saying, 'I verily believe.'" In this vignette the King James English of her Bible became "Biblical speech." The desire to replicate biblical life was (almost) possible to achieve. "We became archaeologists," she continues, "and all we experienced we tried to translate in Biblical terms"(6). In these archaeological ventures, the mission children were aided by visiting scholars who stayed at the American Colony's hostel, and by American diplomats and consuls posted in Jerusalem who engaged in archaeology on the side.

Pratt sits in the Holy Land of a Franciscan Monastery, calmed by the burble of a garden waterfall and remembers the maps in her Bible, pained by the human damage they make seem like a normal part of living. She ponders the meaning of maps for the present, and questions how other times and places have become part of her consciousness of the present. Taking up her query, I was moved to consider how maps had found their way into Bibles, so that today it seems natural to find them in certain Bibles, including those used for Protestant worship, and the "Study Bibles" students purchase to use in university and college courses in Biblical Studies. The earliest sustained and scientific mapping of Palestine was done by the British team Claude Condor and Herbert Kitchener. Their labor resulted in several publications, including the multi-volume *Survey of Western Palestine* (1881–1883) and the *Map of Western Palestine*. Today these are classic if antiquated texts of biblical archaeology. Once published, their maps were criticized by the British military for containing too many inaccuracies. Archaeologists and scientists found additional mistakes. Nonetheless, the cartography of Condor and Kitchener set the basis for colonial mapmaking in this region.

In the interests of calling attention to the colonial engagements of biblical scientists and archaeologists, it is necessary to notice their links not only to late twentieth-century scholars, but to the colonial projects that made their work possible and to which they contributed. Condor and Kitchener were trained at the Royal Military Academy. Both were members of the Royal Engineers. They are best known to archaeologists and biblical scholars for mapping Palestine and discussing its flora and fauna. For both men Palestine was only a small—if significant—part of their careers. Claude Condor followed a family tradition of mapmaking and travel. His paternal grandfather was a travel writer who had edited a thirty-volume series of travel guides—"The Modern Traveler"—all without stepping foot outside Britain. Condor's father had also written about Palestine and the Bible. After mapping Palestine, Condor served the British again in the mapping office of Bechuanaland. Herbert Kitchener, also a young man when in Palestine, went on to subdue revolts in British controlled West Africa. He was governor-general in the Sudan, and commander-in-chief in India. He served in Egypt, was engaged in the reconquest of the Sudan in 1896, and fought in southern Africa.

Charles Warren, another of the early British archaeologists in Palestine, worked in the mapping office in the colony of Gibraltar. The funds that supported the mapping of Palestine came in part from the British government. Other funds were raised by the Palestine Exploration Fund, itself supported substantially by donations from James Ferguson, whose wealth was amassed in indigo factories in the British colony of India. Later archaeologists were also embedded within the privilege of colonial occupation and the travel possibilities it afforded to individuals. Kathleen Kenyon, renowned as the British archaeologist who brought scientific stratigraphy to Palestinian excavation, excavated first in Southern Rhodesia (Hall). The American biblical scholar Edward Robinson, who spent several years in Beirut, was thanked profusely by William Francis Lynch, Commander of the United States Naval Expedition to the River Jordan and the Dead Sea, for his contacts and letters of introduction (Lynch).

In the nineteenth century, imperial/colonial power and its intellectual tools could refashion a textual past into a newly geographical place. Western imperial success meant that longstanding religious dreams of belonging in biblical land could be realized and reshaped. Even before the British Mandate and the beginning of direct Western control of Palestine that culminated in the State of Israel, the presence of missionaries, archaeologists and biblical scholars, among other travelers, naturalized this place as familiar to Americans and established claims of belonging there (Porter: 185). As Philip Khoury notes, "travelers and explorers did not have to become settlers in order to contribute to the colonial and imperial movements of the age" (169).

Here is another genealogy to the maps Minnie Bruce Pratt finds in her Bible. On March 6, 1522, Philip Melanchthion wrote to a friend in search of a map to include with a new New Testament translation by Martin Luther. His search seems to have been unsuccessful, since no map appeared in the 1522 Bible. Three years later Christopher Froschauer, working out of Zurich, included a map in his Old Testament. The decade of the 1520s ended with a number of Bible translations accompanied by maps, of which "The Exodus from Egypt" was the most popular. In their study of sixteenth-century maps, Delano-Smith and Ingram argue that maps appeared in Bibles printed in Dutch, English, and German, and in French-language Bibles printed in Switzerland or Swiss-influenced regions of France. Maps were not part of Bibles from predominately Catholic areas. They found none in Spanish and Italian Bibles, nor in Latin Bibles, nor in Bibles produced in Paris. Consequently, they link the currency of Bible maps with the Protestant Reformation. They argue that maps in Bibles resulted from "new attitudes towards scripture and its ancient geographical setting." With a new emphasis on literal readings of Bible, place and setting demonstrate the literal truth of biblical text. The science of maps adds to the text's truth. Literacy also had something to do with the newly mapped Bible editions. "The vernacular Bibles that the Reformation placed in the hands of individual readers, many barely literate, imposed a responsibility for informed, intelligent reading of the text that would lead readers not only to understand the details of scripture, but also to 'experience' its truth" (Delano-Smith and Ingram: xvi–xxiv). The popularity of maps in Bibles was also a selling point. Their presence was advertised on the title page. Maps were part of what publishers hoped would convince Bible readers to purchase their Bible, and not the edition of a rival publisher.

While helpful, this analysis by Delano-Smith and Ingram of the development of maps in Protestant Bibles in the sixteenth century ignores what made maps themselves more popular and possible. New developments in European travel—the so-called age of discovery—produced new information for these maps. Maps became more significant, made increasingly more "scientific" as their "blank spaces" were filled. Even within the explanation proposed by Delano-Smith and Ingram, the proliferation of maps assumes that access to the literal truth of biblical words is possible. Bible maps foster a sensibility in which the desire to be part of an ancient home can essentially be fulfilled. The maps placed in Bibles from the sixteenth century onward advertised the possibility of access to the truth of biblical words, as they bolstered the realness of that truth. Those who read and held and gazed at the Bible and its maps could find themselves at home in an ancient world.

Nostomania

For nostalgia to work, nothing can be imagined that essentially stands between now and then. However difficult to attain, one must sustain belief in the possibility of unmediated connection. So the apparent efficacy of a long-running travel ad campaign, the continued pleasure of Holy Land replicas, the ease with which Bertha Spafford Vester wrote without apparent irony that the biblical language she speaks is not Greek or Aramaic or Hebrew, but an English straight out of the King James Bible. She is home in the Holy Land and the people there speak her language. The vernacular contains no expression or communication to which she is not privy.

From within this pathway to the present, are there other possibilities? Mine is not a desire to recuperate nostalgia, recover "home," nor to find an alternative from "before" modernity. As Ammiel Alcalay writes, "To want to retrieve or recuperate memory . . . would be to concede defeat" (86). In varying ways, but within a generally continuous discourse, biblical culture rests on the possibility of identifying with and experiencing antiquity. Antiquity becomes a kind of long-lost home, to be reached through various modes and directions of travel. In this vision (selections from) its religions are part of our origins. Its men are our fathers and its women our mothers. Antiquity yields reunions with ancestors.

What happens when the starting point for thinking about antiquity is not the ability to reconstruct it and make it live again, but instead, its very demise. Antiquity is gone (as if it were ever present). There are no homes awaiting return, no former times to resurrect, no prior ways of being to recuperate. Standing at the intersection of Bible, colonialism and nostalgia, an anticolonial refusal means that we release our attachments to Bible, and in doing so, question more intently the claims and metaphors and stories that have become part of a collective Western consciousness. It means refusing the Bible's status as a privileged text of the West, and refusing to be privileged by it, because this privilege and these texts cannot be separated from an imperial history and its attendant occupations and displacements, its degradations and pain.

Nostalgia is the combination of the Greek *nostos*, homecoming or return, and *algos*, pain. A yearning for times or things past or absent. The English term derives from a colonial setting: "When first current in the eighteenth century, 'nostalgia' meant 'homesickness,' especially as experienced by Englishmen abroad. This was not a 'wistful longing' but quite a serious medical condition, resulting in severe depression and melancholy. The malaise seems to have arisen during the American War of Independence, when many Britons were certainly miles from home" (Room: 190–91).

Down the page from nostalgia most dictionaries list a second word: nostomania, defined as "intense homesickness" and "an irresistible compulsion to return home." One dictionary entry ends with the caution that nostomania is "a desire that can never be met." The OED adds 'nostomaniac,' a person affected with nostomania. As a relation to a past time and place, nostomania conveys a very different kind of emotion. It rejects nostalgia's hazy sentimentality and accedes to its pain. Its home*sick*ness uncovers the dis-ease within nostalgia's sentimental certainty that home exists. Nostalgia builds identity—for oneself, for one's group—on an imagined and deeply felt relation to faraway times, places, and people. Nostomania forces us to reconsider whether this compulsion to imagine times and places that no longer exist is in fact (ir)resistible. Admittedly, we inhabit a tensive situation, stuck between the romance of an accessible past and its nostomanic impossibilities.

Acknowledgements: I thank Musa Dube, David Watt, Laura Levitt, and Rob Baird.

WORKS CONSULTED

Abu el-Haj, Nadia
    1995   "Excavating the Land, Creating the Homeland: Archaeology, the State, and the Making of History in Modern Jewish Nationalism." Ph.D. diss., Duke University.

    1997   "The Boundaries of Belonging: Territorial Self-Fashioning and the Colonization of Palestine."

Alcalay, Ammiel
    1993   "Understanding Revolution." In *For Palestine*. Ed. Jay Murphy. New York: Writers & Readers.

Blunt, Alison and Gillian Rose
    1994   *Writing Women and Space: Colonial and Postcolonial Geographies*. New York: Guilford.

Bowman, Glenn
    1992   "Pilgrim Narratives of Jerusalem and the Holy Land: A Study in Ideological Distortion." Pp. 149–68 in *Sacred Journeys: The Anthropology of Pilgrimage*. Ed. Alan Morinis. Westport, CT: Greenwood.

Case, Victoria and Robert Ormond Case
    1970   "What was Chautauqua?" in *We Called it Culture: The Story of Chautaqua*. Freeport, NY: Books for Libraries [1948].

Davis, John
    1996   *The Landscape of Belief: Encountering the Holy Land in Nineteenth-Century American Art and Culture*. Princeton: Princeton University Press.

Delano-Smith, Catherine and Elizabeth Morley Ingram
    1991   *Maps in Bibles 1500–1600: An Illustrated Catalogue*. Genève: Librairie Droz.

Dragonwagon, Crescent
    1986   "The Strangest Small Town in America." *Ms.* 14.10 (April 1986): 59–60ff.

Doumani, Beshara
    1992   "Rediscovering Ottoman Palestine: Writing Palestinians Into History." *Journal of Palestine Studies* 21:5–28.

Felder, Cain Hope, ed.
    1991   *Stony the Road We Trod: African American Biblical Interpretation*. Minneapolis: Fortress.

Fisher, Christy
1994   "New Israel Ads Woo Travelers with Lure of Past." *Advertising Age*, 26 Mar 94:4.

Foucault, Michel
1979   *Discipline and Punish: The Birth of the Prison*. New York: Vintage.

Frye, Northrop
1981   *The Great Code: The Bible and Literature*. Toronto: Academic.

Gregory, Derek
1994   *Geographical Imaginations*. Cambridge, MA: Basil Blackwell.

Grewal, Inderpal
1996   *Home and Harem: Nation, Gender, Empire, and the Cultures of Travel*. Durham: Duke University Press.

Hall, Martin
1996   "Heads and Tales." *Representations* 54:104–23.

Jerusalem Exhibit Company
1903   *Prospectus*. St. Louis: The Company.

Kabbani, Rami
1986   *Europe's Myths of Orient: Devise and Rule*. London: Macmillan.

Khoury, Philip
1985   "Review of Yehoshua Ben-Arieh, *The Rediscovery of the Holy Land in the Nineteenth Century*." *Middle East Journal* 39:168–69.

Larsen, Mogens Trolle
1996   *The Conquest of Assyria: Excavations in an Antique Land*. London and New York: Routledge.

Lynch, William Francis
1850   *Narrative of the United States' Expedition to the River Jordan and the Dead Sea*. Philadelphia: Lea & Blanchard.

Miller, Holly
1993   "Eureka! It's Arkansas." *Saturday Evening Post* 265.2 (March):82–84.

Mitchell, Timothy
1989   "The World as Exhibition." *Comparative Studies in Society and History* 31:217–36.

Morrison, Theodore
1974   *Chautauqua: A Center for Education, Religion, and the Arts in America*. Chicago: University of Chicago Press.

Noll, Mark A.
1987   "Review Essay: The Bible in America." *JBL* 106:493–509.

Obenzinger, Hilton
1996   "In the Shadow of 'God's Sun-Dial': The Construction of American Christian Zionism and the Blackstone Memorial." *Stanford Humanities Review* 5.1

O'Toole, Fintan
    1996   "Imagining Scotland." *Granta* 56:59–76.

Pieterse, Jan Nederveen and Bhikhu Parekh
    1995   *The Decolonization of Imagination: Culture, Knowledge, and Power*. London: Zed.

Porter, Andrew
    1996   "Empires in the Mind." Pp. 185–223 in *The Cambridge Illustrated History of the British Empire*. Ed. P. J. Marshall. Cambridge: Cambridge University Press.

Postman, Neil
    1985   *Amusing Ourselves to Death: Public Discourse in the Age of Show Business*. New York: Penguin.

Pratt, Mary Louise
    1992   *Imperial Eyes: Travel Writing and Transculturation*. London and New York: Routledge.

Pratt, Minnie Bruce
    1991   "The Maps in My Bible." *Bridges* 2.1:93–116. Reprinted in Minnie Bruce Pratt, *Rebellion: Essays 1980–1991*. Ithaca, NY: Firebrand.

Richmond, Rebecca
    1943   *Chautauqua: An American Place*. New York: Duell, Sloane and Pearce.

Rix, Herbert
    1907   *Tent and Testament: A Camping Tour in Palestine, with Some Notes on Scripture Sites*. London: Williams and Norgate. Reprint. 1977. New York: Arno Press.

Robertson, George et al.
    1994   *Travelers' Tales: Narratives of Home and Displacement*. London: Routledge.

Room, Adrian
    1986   *Dictionary of Changes in Meaning*. London and New York: Routledge.

Said, Edward
    1979   "Zionism from the Standpoint of its Victims." *Social Text* 1:7–58.

Sayre, Henry
    1983   "Surveying the Vast Profound: The Panoramic Landscape in American Consciousness." *Massachusetts Review* 24:723–42.

Schwartz, Hillel
    1996   *The Culture of the Copy: Striking Likenesses, Unreasonable Facsimiles*. New York: Zone.

Swedenburg, Ted
    1995   *Memories of Revolt: The 1936–1939 Rebellion and the Palestinian National Past*. Minneapolis: University of Minnesota Press.

Tarbell, Ida
    1939   *All in a Day's Work*. New York: Macmillan.

Thomas, Nicholas
  1994   *Colonialism's Culture: Anthropology, Travel and Government*. Princeton: Princeton University Press.

Vester, Bertha Spafford
  1950   *Our Jerusalem: An American Family in the Holy City, 1891–1949*. Garden City: Doubleday. Reprint. 1977. New York: Arno Press.

Vogel, Lester
  1993   *To See a Promised Land: Americans and the Holy Land in the Nineteenth Century*. University Park: Pennsylvania State University Press.

Vuilleumier, Marion Rawson
  1976   *America's Religious Treasures: A Spiritual Heritage Travel Guide*. New York: Harper & Row.

Whitelam, Keith
  1996   *The Invention of Ancient Israel: The Silencing of Palestinian History*. London: Routledge.

RESPONSES

EL SALTO HERMENÉUTICO DE HOY

Elsa Tamez
Seminario Biblico Latino Americano

El número de Semeia "Postcoloniality and Scriptural Reading" plantea claramente el estado actual de la cuestión de la hermenéutica. Cada artículo refleja distintos desafíos a la academia. Son desafíos profundos que cuestionan radicalmente las lecturas colonialistas de los textos sagrados, y el canon mismo. Esta experiencia es un proceso que se observa en las distintas regiones del mundo. Por esa razón inició el diálogo con el sentido global de todos los artículos, compartiendo el proceso hermenéutico presente en América Latina.

Los aspectos sobresalientes de las contribuciones coinciden entre ellas mismas y también con la experiencia latinoamericana.

1. LA LUCHA HERMENÉUTICA

Un aspecto mencionado en la mayoría de los artículos es la ambivalencia en los textos bíblicos: cómplices del colonialismo y a la vez liberadores.

Esta experiencia hermenéutica colonial y anti-colonial observada en los artículos de Jace Weaver (entre los nativos americanos) y Kimberly Rae Connor (entre los afro americanos) ha estado presente en A.L. desde la invasión española y portuguesa. Algunos de los escritos de Cristóbal Colón, Hernan Cortés -el conquistador-, Motolinia y Juan Jinés de Sepúlveda, explicitan el espíritu triunfalista de los conquistadores. Por ejemplo, Toribio de Benavente, conocido como Motolinia, interpreta el sufrimiento que los españoles causaron a los nativos como castigo de Dios. Cada una de las plagas de Egipto narradas en el Éxodo es parafraseada y relacionada con algún mal como enfermedades, trabajo forzado de esclavos en las minas, tributos, matanzas, etc. En otras citas bíblicas se deduce que los invasores son los liberadores y que la conquista de Canaán es el paradigma bíblico de la invasión.

Si bien los colonizadores utilizan los textos sagrados para matar, el español Bartolomé de las Casas o el indígena Guaman Poma hacen una lectura radicalmente opuesta en favor de los indígenas. Ambos desde su perspectiva como cristianos. Curiosamente el profeta maya Chilam Balam, cuyo canon no es el libro cristiano, critica a los conquistadores por no ser coherentes con su propio canon que habla de amor. Chilam Balam es capaz de percibir la manipulación de los textos por parte de los conquistadores. De manera que la lectura colonialista de la biblia ha estado siempre presente desde la llegada del cristianismo hace 500 años, y la lectura contestataria, anti-colonialista, ha ido a la par.

Esta última aparece con mayor fuerza con la lectura popular de la Biblia, diseminada desde hace mas de 25 años en toda América Latina. Esta hermenéutica "desde abajo" ha asumido la tarea de reapropiarse de los textos bíblicos y releerlos desde un ángulo liberador. La obra de Leñero, *El Evangelio de Lucas Gavilán*, analizada por Héctor Ávalos en su artículo es un ejemplo de ella. Mientras que la lectura colonialista cree asumir la postura objetiva universal, la lectura popular asume, conscientemente, su parcialidad desde los discriminados, ya sea por clase, raza o género. En las luchas populares los pobres y las discriminadas encuentran en los textos la fuerza que les impulsa a resistir la opresión, a luchar y a fortalecer la esperanza.

Lo que en realidad ha ocurrido ha sido una lucha hermenéutica entre los cristianos, sea por mantener el dominio o por buscar la liberación. Hasta hace poco se inicia el cuestionamiento de los textos sagrados en sí. Fuera de esta lucha están los indígenas con su propia religión, que rechaza la biblia como canon para ellos.

2. El desafío del salto hermenéutico

Cuando "los sin voz" toman la palabra, nuevos desafíos aparecen. Las mujeres, los indígenas y los afro en Abya Yala cuestionan no sólo la línea colonialista de la lectura de los textos, sino también los mismos textos sagrados aun cuando se lean de manera anti-colonialista. Esto es porque la lucha hermenéutica se enmarca dentro de la cultura occidental dominante. Las vivencias cotidianas, las visiones de mundos distintas, y las experiencias múltiples de Dios no han encontrado cabida ni en las lecturas bíblicas ni en los textos bíblicos mismos. Pero el paso de la lectura de la biblia de los pobres hacia "el otro empobrecido", no es fácil.

La alteridad plantea cuestiones radicales que desbordan el canon y la ortodoxia tal y como se entienden estas oficialmente.

Los artículos de Musa W. Dube y Jon Berquist abren la pista para dar el salto hermenéutico. El salto exige reconocer primero los elementos colonialistas que han estado presentes en el proceso de redacción de los texto (como lo hace Berquist), y trascender el canon (como lo plantea la africana Torontle en el artículo de W. Dube). Jim Perkinson, en su excelente análisis de la mujer Sirofenicia, agranda la fisura del texto para introducir otros "logos", aparte del "logo de Jesucristo". Este ha sido el reclamo de "La hermenéutica india" y de los afros de Abya Yala. El diálogo ecuménico verdadero acontece cuando hay reconocimiento de la variedad de "logos" salvadores.

Por otro lado, las mujeres al vernos limitadas en el canon, empujamos hacia nuevos paradigmas. Creemos que las teorías de género, al postular un nuevo paradigma, diferente al sistema patriarcal jerárquico, abre infinitas y novedosas posibilidades para la lectura postcolonialista. En la aplicación de la nueva teoría de la reconstrucción de textos, se tiene necesariamente que romper con las fronteras del canon, recurrir a otros textos, y construir nuevos evangelios con categorías inclusivas.

3. Transversalidad desde la óptica de los excluidos

En América Latina, en los últimos años, hemos enfatizado el principio de orientar nuestros análisis con la visión de "una casa donde quepan todos y todas". El sentido fundante viene de la expresión del movimiento revolucionario indígena zapatista mexicano: "Por un mundo donde quepan muchos mundos". La frase en sí convoca a la transversalidad, es decir a incluir en los análisis todas las situaciones posibles, y a considerar el sujeto como un ser de relaciones infinitas. Hoy día el rechazo de afirmaciones como verdades absolutas lleva a asumir la complejidad de los contextos, sujetos y discursos. De hecho, esto es lo que ha facilitado la emergencia de la voz misma de quienes no tenían voz. Una mirada transversal al texto bíblico ofrece la posibilidad de que se desborde en su significación, rica y compleja, ofreciendo, quizá, un "un mundo donde caben muchos mundos". Sin embargo, la lectura será podrá ser post-colonial, si se "amarra" la transversalidad con la preocupación por los excluidos y las excluidas en su sentido más amplio.

THE HERMENEUTICAL LEAP OF TODAY

Elsa Tamez
Seminario Biblico Latino Seminario

The issue of Semeia "Postcoloniality and Scriptural Readings" clearly presents the current state of the hermeneutical question. Each one of the articles reveals a different challenge to the academy. These are thoughtful challenges which seriously question not only the colonial readings of the sacred texts but also the canon itself. This confrontational experience is a process that has been taking place simultaneously in different regions of the world. Therefore, I shall open the dialogue presenting the current hermeneutical process in Latin America as a way of addressing the articles in their global sense.

The main issues highlighted in the articles share similarities among themselves and also with the Latin American experience.

1. THE HERMENEUTICAL STRUGGLE

One of the issues addressed by many of the articles is the ambivalence of the biblical texts: they are at the same time in complicity with colonialism as well as liberating.

The colonial and anti-colonial hermeneutical experience that is observed in the articles by Jace Weaver (Native-American experience) and Kimberly Rae Connor (African-American experience) has been present in Latin America since the Spanish and Portuguese invasions. Writers such as Christopher Columbus, Hernán Cortés (the conqueror), Motolinia, and Juan Jinés de Sepúlveda made clear the triumphal spirit of the invaders. For instance, Toribio de Benavente (also known as Motolinia), interprets as divine punishment the sufferings inflicted on the natives by the Spaniards. Each one of the plagues of Egypt narrated in Exodus are associated with equivalent experiences such as sickness, slave labor in the mines, tributes, massacres, and so on. From other biblical texts it is inferred that the invaders are the liberators, and that the conquest of Canaan is the biblical paradigm that epitomizes the invasion.

Just as the colonizers use the sacred texts to kill, the Spaniard Bartolome de las Casas and the native Guaman Poma present a reading radically opposed in favor of the natives. Both of these men are Christians. Interestingly enough the Mayan prophet Chilam Balam, whose canon is not the Christian book, criticized the conquerors for being inconsistent with their canon that speaks of love. Chilam Balam perceives the manipulation of the texts by the conquerors. Consequently, the colonial reading of the Bible has existed since the arrival of Christianity 500 years ago. The resistance reading, the anti-colonial reading, has co-existed in the meantime as well.

The anti-colonial reading has emerged steadily with the popular reading of the Bible, which has been disseminated for more than 25 years all around Latin America. This "grassroots" hermeneutics has assumed the task of re-appropriating the biblical texts and re-reading them from a liberating perspective. The work of Leñero, *El Evangelio de Lucas Gavilán*, analyzed in Hector Avalos' article, is an example. While the colonialist reading believes in its objectivity and universality, the popular reading is consciously aware of its partiality that comes from those who are discriminated against, either by class, race, or gender. In the popular struggles, the poor and discriminated find within the texts the strength to resist and battle the oppression and to increase their hope.

What has occurred is a hermeneutical battle between Christians, either to keep dominion or to liberate. Only recently has the sacred text been questioned. At the same time the indigenous people have their own religion, which rejects the Bible as a viable canon.

2. The Challenge of the Hermeneutical Leap

When those "without voice" begin to speak, new challenges surface. Women, natives, and the Afro in Abya Yala question not only the colonial reading of the texts, but the very sacred texts in themselves even when they are read from an anti-colonial perspective. This is because the hermeneutical battle is framed in the dominant Western culture. The daily experiences, the perspectives from different worlds, and the multiple experiences of God have not found a place in the biblical readings nor in the biblical texts themselves. However, the transition from the reading of the Bible from one poor to the "other poor" is not easy. The otherness brings radical questions that go beyond the canon and the orthodoxy as they are officially understood.

The articles by Musa W. Dube and Jon Berquist open the way to take the hermeneutical leap. The leap demands acknowledging that the colonial elements were already present during the production of the text (as Berquist mentions) and transcending the canon (as the African Torontle does in Dube's article). Jim Perkinson in his excellent analysis of the Syrophoenician woman enlarges the fissure of the text to introduce other "logos" besides the "logos of Jesus Christ." This has been the claim of the "indigenous hermeneutics" and the Afros from Abya Yala. Truly ecumenical dialogue takes place when there is acknowledgement of a variety of salvific "logos."

On the other hand, when we women realize how limited we are in the canon, we push further towards new paradigms. I believe that the theories of gender with their new paradigms, different from the patriarchal hierarchy, open up endless and innovative possibilities for the postcolonial reading. When the new theories of text reconstruction are applied, it is crucial to cross the boundaries of the canon, search for different texts, and write new gospels with inclusive categories.

3. Transverseness from the Perspective of the Excluded

During the last few years, in Latin America, we have emphasized the principle of orienting our analysis with a perspective of "a house in which there is room for everybody." The basis for this analysis comes from the creed of the "Zapatistas," the indigenous Mexican revolutionary movement: "Towards a world where many worlds fit." The statement in itself invites to transverseness; in other words, to include all the possible situations in the analysis and to consider the subject as a being of endless relationships. Today the rejection of the absolute truths lead us to assume the complexity of the contexts, subjects, and discourses. In fact, this is precisely what has aided the emergence of the voice of "those who did not have a voice." A transversal look at the biblical text offers the possibility of overflowing its rich and complex significance, perhaps suggesting "a world where many worlds fit." At the same time, the reading will be post-colonial if the transverseness is connected to the concern for the excluded in a wider sense.

Translated by Leticiá Guardiola-Saenz

Response

Robert Allen Warrior
Stanford University

The articles in this special issue speak to the still growing gulf between the traditional practice of biblical studies and the needs of Christians around the world, Christians who are exhorted to read Christian scripture and find in it some guide to contemporary life. All too often, as many of the fine commentators gathered here attest, the biblical witness is one that testifies for a politics that justifies colonial projects, stands to the side in the battle for justice, and has no ear to hear the voices that become excluded in the formation of orthodoxies, canons, and schemes of salvation.

I have not done much biblical criticism in the past half-decade, and I am glad to say that the state of affairs that held when I last did much peering into the wide-ranging project of making sense of scripture has shifted towards a much more positive direction. My last word as an indigenous, and thus Canaanitic, critic of Christian scripture was a comment on the story of the Canaanite woman in Matthew. Jim Perkinson's quite learned article on the Markan and Matthean versions of the same unsettling story is, thus, a particularly apt reentry point for me into a discussion of scripture.

In reading "A Canaanitic Word," I was pleased to see the willingness that Perkinson and many others he cites evince in allowing the fullness of the gospel in all of its traces to be as complicated as the textual evidence indicates that it is. For, as Perkinson says, in this story of a Syro-Phoenician (Mark) or Canaanite (Matthew) woman beseeching Jesus for a cure for her daughter, Jesus, "astonishingly, loses an argument." If that weren't enough, the woman becomes in the telling of Matthew, a Canaanite, "summoning up a troubled image of polytheism, sacred prostitution, and ethnicity beyond the pale." As Perkinson convincingly argues, the presence of this woman and her audacious answer to Jesus' dismissive chauvinism (a maneuver of "silencing," says Perkinson), becomes both the "point furthest out" of the christological mission, but also turns into a return for Matthew's Jesus to the very ground of origin, the still unexplored connection between time and place at the root of his own genealogy. The displacement or subsuming of the Canaanite story as it gives way to the story of the religion of Israel and Judaism emerges, however briefly, in the transformative moment of Christian emergence. Though I may be going beyond Perkinson in saying so, it is as though the place-transcendant impulses of Christianity are given final confirmation in the place-bound person of the Canaanite, a person whose complaint has not been forgotten by the passage of time.

By reading these pericopes side by side, Perkinson is able to draw out the richest ground of biblical interpretation. His deft reading confronts the interpreter with a desire to know more, a need to understand both the self and the other in previously unavailable ways, and a sense that whatever universals are proposed within the gospels and within scripture include certain voices only as traces or absences. And whatever the gospel reader might want to know from Mark's Syro-Phoenician woman or Matthew's Canaanite woman will have to occur outside the biblical text; both of them leave the scene, returning home having proven the messiah wrong and in possession of what she had come for.

Perkinson's article is a wonderful beginning point for much of what follows since he demonstrates one instance, at least, in which the gospel witness is unable to contain itself and of a necessity crosses borders, violates boundaries, and goes far afield. Kimberly Rae Connor's careful and insightful explication of the tradition of the spirituals provides a vehicle for the same sort of necessary work of revision and correction of error. Along with providing an overview of the more widely read work in the history of the spirituals, she also explicates what various literary critics and intellectual historians have had to say about this most central African-American tradition.

Miriam Peskowitz's "Tropes of Travel" is a sometimes dazzling tour of replicated Christian touring sites. In discussing places like Eureka Springs, Missouri, and the holy land replica in Washington, D.C., she is able to show how various modes and ethics of Christian pilgrimage and tourism have been transplanted to places with no claim to Christian fame. Hector Avalos's discussion of *The Gospel of Lucas Gavilán* is remarkable for the way it demonstrates the exegetical and hermeneutical skills of non-clerics.

In "Reading for Decolonization," Musa Dube ends by showing something of a similar hermeneutical practice in southern Africa. Dube's well-argued scholarly case for an anti-imperialistic, decolonizing critical practice is an impressive effort. The scope is ambitious, but Dube makes a convincing argument that discussion of scriptural complicity in empire-building, the importance of geography to understanding the relation of religion and empire, and the necessity for understanding the ideological impulses behind contemporary practices is essential to the work of overcoming colonial repressions in this age of transnationally deployed capital.

Jace Weaver was the first to pose the story of the Canaanite woman in Matthew as a proper location for an indigenous reading of the gospels. He has done that reading and more since, including his contribution here. The ironic histories, readings, and philosophies he attempts to dissolve therein provide an excellent lens through which to see the tremendous growth and development of Native American biblical studies over the past several years.

Through his work and that of people like Homer Noley, William Baldridge, Marie Therese Archambault, George Tinker, and others, a new relationship toward scripture appears to be taking hold among Native academic scholars.

Weaver's call to "we-hermeneutics" involves a strict grounding in the lives and experiences of Native people. Interestingly, he never asks that Christian experience be privileged. Rather, he suggests that the hermeneutical task is one of drawing out of the stories of internal colonization of Native people in this hemisphere the frame and the terms of an imagined and realized future. Weaver locates his hermeneutics and the future in the same place, communities, and argues for the need for scholars and others in position of power to trust the ability of communities to decide rightly their own way forward.

I have not mentioned all of the fine articles here, but I can say one thing about the entirety. That is, I am happy to see a clear distinction emerge herein as to the difference between post-modern and post-colonial criticism. I hesitate to offer much of a definition of either, but am willing to join the authors of this volume who sense that the embrace of post-modern criticism has become for too many people an embrace of futility and an invitation to inaction in the face of power. The post-colonial, on the other hand, seems for now to be the location from which to speak truth to power and to find like-minded people who seek ways to address the conditions of suffering under which our planet's majority exists.

RESPONSE TO THE *SEMEIA* VOLUME ON POSTCOLONIAL CRITICISM

Kwok Pui-lan
Episcopal Divinity School

On June 30, 1997, the world's attention will focus on Hong Kong, as a historical event is going to happen. But what will the world be looking at? For the Chinese government, it will be a moment of national pride as China exerts sovereignty over Hong Kong, ceded to the British after the infamous Opium War (1839–42). For the British, it will be a glorious retreat, as they argue that they have brought freedom, prosperity, and the rule of the law to Hong Kong. The event has also captured the attention of politicians in Washington because the return of Hong Kong provides an occasion to bring up issues concerning human rights in China.

These contested interpretations of June 30, 1997, fascinate me because I was born and grew up in Hong Kong. While these grand political narratives of nationalism, sovereignty, democracy, human rights, and civil society are deployed by politicians and the international mass media, I am more interested in the *minute* details of the cultural practices that need to take place to signify the complex decolonization process. For example, at 23.30 hours on June 30, the Hong Kong Royal Police will be given half an hour to change their caps (with new emblems). At 24.00 hours, the Provisional Legislature selected by Beijing's handpicked Selection Committee will assume power and authority. Meanwhile, there have been intense discussions on whether to change the names of King's College and Queen's College, how to deal with royal symbols inscribed on government buildings, and where to put Queen Victoria's statue once the British flag is lowered. All of a sudden, Hong Kong stamps bearing the Queen's head became prized souvenirs as Hong Kong people and merchants from China rushed to buy them at the post offices. Little replicas of old-fashioned postboxes with the logo "Her Majesty's Service" are selling very well because Hong Kong people want to possess "tactile remnants" (Peskowitz) of their "own" history.

Hong Kong, referred to as the "Pearl of Orient," was not built in one day. The colonization process and its internalization by the colonized often took a long time (Berquist). Decolonization of a colony involves not simply a political turn-over but also complicated, controversial, and contested changes in cultural and signifying practices. Decolonization of the mind and the imagination involves debunking the regimes of truth imposed by the colonizers and the collaborators, dislodging the mind from familiar thinking patterns, disintegrating seemingly coherent discourses, displaying silences and closures of texts, decomposing the garbage that has filled the brain cells for too long, and much more.

As a soon-to-be-but-not-yet "post-"colonial female intellectual, I read the articles of this volume with utmost interest because I am eager to learn from others what they have to say about postcolonialism and biblical hermeneutics. The articles reflect multiple subject positionings of the practitioners of postcolonial criticism and their diverse enunciative sites of discourse (Bhabha). Some authors (Berquist, Dube, Perkinson, Avalos) are more receptive to the insights of postcolonial theories, while Jace Weaver, writing from a Native American context, questions the applicability of postcolonial analysis.

The broad range of articles forces the reader to contend with the diversity of experiences included in the term "postcolonial." In what ways can the colonized experiences of Yehud under Persia illumine the struggles of colonized people in the last several centuries? In what sense are Botswana, Mexico, Australia, and the United States equally "postcolonial?" How do we differentiate between the relations of the colonized white-settlers to the Europeans at "the center" from that of the colonized indigenous populations to the Europeans? How should we avoid collapsing into the same the experiences of colonized peoples in the Third World, indigenous peoples of the Americas, and African people in diaspora (Shohat: 102)? How can we respond to the cry of Weaver that "Native Americans remain a colonized people, victims of internal colonialism?"

This volume on postcolonial hermeneutics calls into question the usefulness and limit of the term "postcolonial," an issue that is at the heart of the debate among postcolonial theorists today (Chambers and Curti). Without overlooking the current debate, these diverse authors demonstrate that the introduction of postcolonial discourse into biblical criticism offers new avenues to interrogate the Bible as a cultural product, the formation of canon, and the politics of biblical interpretation. Collectively, they re-read colonization as "part of an essentially transnational and transcultural 'global' process" (Hall: 247). Without homogenizing the postcolonial experiences, their postcolonial readings of the Bible analyze the myriad ways the Bible has been used in the colonial discourse and offer concrete examples of reading strategies from the marginalized communities.

These postcolonial critics challenge the Orientalist reading of the Bible, still widely practiced in academia in Europe and North America. This Orientalist reading privileges the study of the classical text (in this case the Bible) over the living communities that interact with the text. The Bible is constituted as a frozen artifact of a classical age long past, and its meaning can only be activated and re-presented by the experts in the metropolitan centers in their lineage of scholarship. Under the rubric of "objectivity" and "scientific inquiry," this Orientalist reading circumscribes the range of issues that can be brought to the texts and suppresses reading strategies by the so-called natives.

De-mystifying the epistemic violence constructed by the colonial discourse and de-bunking the truth claims of metropolitan experts, these authors re-trace the diasporic and transcultural interaction of the Bible with diverse cultures and histories. Berquist re-reads the process of canonization against Persian imperial history; Dube and Avalos lift up the voices of Mositi Torontle and Vicente Leñero; Boer excavates the literary site of Sretan Bozic; Connor and Weaver explore the use of the Bible in marginalized communities in United States; Perkinson stages a multicultural dialogue on the story of the Syro-Phoenician woman; and Peskowitz interrogates biblical maps, tourist guidebooks, and travel advertisements.

For some time ideological criticism of the Bible has challenged the apolitical reification of the Bible as the Word of God. For example, Itumenleng Mosala (193) has clearly stated that the Bible is "the product, the record, the site, and the weapon of class, cultural, gender, and racial struggles." Postcolonial critics, as evident in the articles of Berquist and Dube, further raise the question of the influences of colonial experiences of the Jews under the Persian and Roman Empires in shaping the formation of canon and the production of biblical texts. Instead of treating the canon and the texts as fixed, stable, and privileged points of "origin," postcolonial critics examine the cultural and historical processes that call them into being. Claiming the Hebrew canon as an example of postcolonial literature, Berquist demonstrates the ways the Bible is "doubly inscribed," subverting the old, simple, and binary thinking of the colonizing and the colonized (Hall: 246–7). He says: "The canon can never be a truly Persian text; it never becomes a truly imperial artifact. Yet at the same time it is not equivalent to the colony; it does not speak the local vision as the locals would themselves voice it. The canon is part of the mediation between colonizer and colonized, but it is a troubled mediation, not a smooth dialectic synthesis."

Precisely because the canon and the biblical texts are contested sites, inscribed with different layers of racial, class, and gender politics, postcolonial criticism helps to illumine how the tensions and conflicts have been deployed by European colonizers in their empire-building. Dube explores how the travel of Jesus and the encounter with the Samaritan woman in John 4 play out in imperializing ideologies during the colonization of African countries. Weaver challenges the use of the Bible in justifying the genocide of Native Americans and the destruction of Native cultures and social organizations.

But these authors are not contented with simply critiquing the West (cautioned by Weaver), because they also provide examples of reading strategies for decolonization. I will highlight several examples that particularly fascinate me in this volume. Several years ago, I worked on the story of the Syro-Phoenician woman (Kwok: 71–83). I was interested in how the Gentile woman was inscribed in the master discourse of the Gospels and how the story was used to justify anti-Judaism, colonialism, and sexism. I welcome Perkinson's contribution to the ongoing dialogue and his application of postcolonial discourse theory to analyze the discursive nexus between the Syro-Phoenician woman and Jesus. Postcolonial critics have discussed the tension and ambivalence in claiming the master's language as one's own, especially in an unequal power relationship. Perkinson shows that the woman, through a witty *reiteration* of what Jesus has said, opens room for herself as a speaking subject and subverts the exlusionary insider/outsider binary logic that Jesus' speech has constructed.

Several authors interrogate the constructions of space, geography, travel, and the imperial gaze. In her fascinating exploration of the tropes of travel, Peskowitz elucidates the desire and violence in people's "irresistible compulsion" to claim the Holy Land as home. Such nostalgic desire, she argues, "contains the assumption that one belongs wherever one imagines one's home to be, no matter who else is displaced in the process." Dube's article displays the hidden interests inscribed in the travel of Jesus into the land of Samaria. Of particular interest is her close reading of the gender politics in the construction of the hierarchical geographic spaces. She writes: "In a mission story, a narrative that authorizes traveling to and entering into foreign lands and places, that she becomes a first point of contact is significant . . . Like the woman who represents them [the inhabitants], the foreign land must be entered, won, and domesticated." Boer's reading of Joshua 9 also discusses space and travel and the story is complex and multilayered. The Gibeonites pretended to have travel a long distance to come to the Israelites, who had traveled from Egypt some time ago. Boer's reading raises the perplexing question of who were the indigenous inhabitants and who were the colonial invaders. The possibility of multiple and shifting subject positions in the biblical text allows Boer to read it intertextually with Bozic's writings and to open avenues to discuss postcolonial Australian identities.

Avalos and Connor offer another reading strategy that can be termed "cultural translation" (Hall: 247). They elucidate the fascinating transcultural process when the Bible was brought to interact with Mexican and African American cultures. Instead of treating the Bible as *fetish* as the colonizers and the experts have done, they offer an image of the Bible as *diasporic adventure*[1] Avalos discusses Vicente Leñero's re-inscribing Jesus as Jesucristo Gómez and observes that Leñero "feels free to change any historical contexts in order to extract the essential messages of each of the episodes of the Gospels

---

[1] I am indebted to Adam Phillips for his insight: "the opposite of a fetish is an adventure," (*Terrors and Experts* [Cambridge, MA: Harvard University Press, p. 85]).

that he paraphrases." Instead of beginning with "in the days of King Herod of Judea" (Luke 1:5), Leñero starts with "in the final years of Luis Echeverria Alvarez's presidency." This simple change writes the postcolonial time and space into the story at once. From another context, Connor investigates the aural/oral hermeneutics implicit in the cultural imagination of African American spirituals. She shows that the spirituals became sites for the negotiation and mediation of the slaves' double consciousness: freedom/bondage, African religion/Christianity, this world/the world to come, humiliation/protest, and lament/celebration.

The volume also raises the question of subject position and the politics of representation in postcolonial criticism. Several authors offer information about themselves, while others do not. Is it important for the readers to know the social locations of the writers on postcolonial biblical hermeneutics? Would knowing something about the author's background contribute to or influence our reading? Who can or cannot represent the postcolonial situation? Can Caucasian American men and women speak for or contribute something to the discussion on decolonization of the Bible? Why and why not?

I think the answers to these questions are not simple, as we have learned from postcolonial critics to interrogate the binary logic: can/cannot, should/should not, white/black, and here/there. Instead of settling for an easy answer (a kind of closure), it may be more helpful to display the complex issues involved by asking more questions. Let us use a few examples from this volume to illustrate. Berquist does not tell us whether he is Jewish or not. If he is Jewish, would it add more weight to his argument because he is speaking as an insider to that history? Conversely, if he is a Christian, would he be labeled as anti-Jewish because he challenges the conventional notion of the canon and discusses the ways Jewish people internalized colonization? If he is a Buddhist, say from Asia, would we say that he is approaching this ancient history of the Jews with objectivity and fairness? Why would knowing the background of the author matter? If it indeed matters, is it because of the author, or is it because of Jewish history?

Let us use Connor as another example because again the author does not offer information about her class, race, culture, and religion. Would it affect our reading if we know the race of this particular author? Can we tell from her writing and language whether she is African, Asian, Hispanic/Latino, or Caucasian American? Would her argument be less appealing if, let us say, she tells us right from the beginning that she is a Caucasian American? Do African American spirituals belong to people who are descendants of slaves? Is it true that the spirituals are used in many churches besides the Black churches? Can Asia, Hispanic/Latino, Native American, or Caribbean Christians contribute to the interpretation of spirituals? Can Caucasian Americans do so too? Would the answers to this set of questions be different if the outcome of Connor's analysis is exactly the opposite. What if she had said the spirituals are other-worldly opium that lead the slaves away from the struggles of this world?

This brings me to the final example of Perkinson. Toward the end of the article, Perkinson volunteers to tell his identity: "a white male." What is the difference between a "white" male and a "pale" male (Boer)? Furthermore, should a person's race and gender be decisive in discussing the myths of origin? Why does Perkinson think he has an obligation to tell the reader he is "a white male" when he tries to bring out the implications of the Syro-Phoenician woman's story for the present? The way he tells it also demands attention: "For me, as a white male, the word of the woman as 'Canaanite' begs juxtaposition to voices either 'black' or 'Indian.'" Alas, what about the Hispanic/Latino and the Asian American, and people of mixed races like Tiger Woods? The omission of "Asian" is especially strange, since the land of Canaan is in West Asia.

Given the fact that Perkinson and Connor are both Caucasian Americans, does their racial identity affect the way we receive their work? Do we conceive them as white allies to the postcolonial struggles or do we think they have appropriated resources and scholarship from the marginalized communities? To complicate the question even more, would it matter if Peskowitz is Hungarian, Russian, and not American? Would it make a difference if she is Jewish American? If she is Jewish American, would it make a difference if I (her reader) am not from Hong Kong, but have come from the West Bank?

The publication of this volume is a cause for celebration because of the quality of the essays and the numerous questions the volume raises. I hope this volume will become a foundation for staging more postcolonial dialogues in the near future.

Works Consulted

Bhabha, Homi K.
    1994   *The Location of Culture*. New York: Routledge.

Chambers, Iain, and Lidia Curti
    1996   *The Post-Colonial Question: Common Skies, Divided Horizons*. New York: Routledge.

Hall, Stuart
    1996   "When Was 'the Post-Colonial'? Thinking at the Limit" Pp. 242–60 in *The Post-Colonial Question: Common Skies, Divided Horizons*. Ed. Iain Chambers and Lidia Curti. New York: Routledge.

Kwok, Pui-lan
    1995   *Discovering the Bible in the Non-Biblical World.* Maryknoll, NY: Orbis.

Mosala, Itumenleng
    1989   *Biblical Hermeneutics and Black Theology in South Africa.* Grand Rapids, MI: William B. Eerdmans.

Shohat, Ella
    1992   "Notes on the 'Post-Colonial.'" *Social Text* 31/32:99–113.

THE ETHICS OF POSTCOLONIAL CRITICISM

Mark G. Brett
Whitley College, Melbourne

It might be tempting to propose that postcolonial criticism trades in theoretical concepts that would be anachronistic in studies of the ancient world. Biblical studies, some might think, should be shielded from yet another faddish movement in the humanities. Indeed, some of the debates about whether any particular society is "postcolonial" would have little relevance for biblical studies. But Hector Avalos, following Elleke Boehmer, has set us on the fruitful path of defining postcolonial study as the critical scrutinization of colonial relationships, and there is no reason to exclude the study of ancient colonial relationships within which the bulk of biblical material was produced—whether the coloniser was Egyptian, Assyrian, Babylonian, Persian, Hellenistic, or Roman. We should also confess that much biblical interpretation, ancient and modern, has been enabled or constrained by imperialist social systems. The present volume of *Semeia*, among other recent biblical studies influenced by Edward Said (e.g. Sugirtharajah; Whitelam), should be evidence enough that biblical scholars need to be full participants in this wider movement of literary criticism.

I want to focus on the ethical questions raised by the papers in this volume. What intrigues me most about postcolonial criticism is its ethics of interpretation, or rather, its implied ethics. Jon Berquist introduces this subject by talking of postcolonial interpretation as a "moral act of commitment" [p.32], a commitment which is not satisfied with simply exposing the cultural bricolage of canonical texts but goes further "to construct interpretations which have decolonizing effects in the contemporary world" [p.29]. The question remains: what kinds of social ethics inform these decolonizing effects?

Laura Donaldson's study of William Apess, a nineteenth-century Pequot Indian, illuminates one of the complexities of this question, since Apess both absorbed and contested the values of the colonising culture. He engaged with a reading of the Bible, articulated especially by Daniel Webster, which made the Bible a source of civil liberty, individual responsibility, human dignity and equality (Donaldson: 36). This framework of political values was actually fabricated more by Enlightenment philosophers than by the Bible, but it was grafted by Webster on to early American nationalism. Apess apparently responded to this intertextual alchemy by creating a counter-nationalism for native Americans and a more radical, colour-inclusive egalitarianism inspired by the Methodists. As in Jim Perkinson's account of the Canaanite woman, Apess reinscribed his particular concern for Indian dignity precisely *within* the sphere of the colonising discourse that had excluded it.

The critique of Apess formulated by Randall Moon is one which has been deployed, in different ways, in many contestations of aboriginal identity: Apess writes, we are told, "too much like a white person and is too Christianized to be recognized as an 'authentic' representative of native America" (Moon: 52). This replays what Gareth Griffiths has called the "myth of authenticity," a myth much loved in the white Australian media and used to create a hierarchy of aboriginal voices which separates the "authentic, traditional pure-bloods" from urban aboriginal activists who have learned enough Latin to know that *terra nullius* was a British legal fiction.[1] The myth of authenticity is a kind of neo-foundationalism, riven with moral ambiguity since it proclaims a concern for the subaltern voice while at the same time effectively silencing it. The discourse of authenticity suspects even the resisting voice insofar as that voice adopts the language of the coloniser; according to this nostalgic version of authenticity, if the subaltern speaks a creole, the subaltern does not speak.

Laura Donaldson's defence of Apess convincingly places him in a frontier zone between complicit and oppositional postcolonialism. There is a wealth of critical concepts which could be used to explicate this dynamic: mimicry, mimetic circulation, iteration, and double-voiced revision, all of which can be understood as hybrid forms of cultural resistance. The notion of hybridity has contributed to a revision of an older theory which suggested that postcolonial societies necessarily pass through a phase of nativist nationalism (see Ahmad; Amuta; Bhaba; Brett, 1995). Among others, Homi Bhaba has argued for the necessity of hybridized identities and stressed the futility of a concept of culture conceived as stable and unitary.

The irony in this situation has been well articulated by Marshall Sahlins, who has recently pointed out that the self-conscious defence of "culture" has reached new political heights just when the very notion of culture is "condemned for its excessive coherence and systematicity, for its sense of boundedness and totality. Just when so many people are announcing the existence of their culture, advanced anthropologists are denying it" (13). According to Sahlins' account, the self-conscious use of "culture" as an anticolonial strategy originated in Germany in the late 18th century, in defiance of the global pretensions of English and French models of "civilization" (11, following Berlin).[2] The strategy was conceived in a Romanticist climate in

---

[1] Cf. Whitelam's account (43–45) of modern biblical historians who have also adopted the rhetoric of an "empty land," seeing ancient Palestine as empty of a population capable of political organization.

[2] See Herder's comment, "Only a real misanthrope could regard European culture as the universal condition of our species," quoted in Barnard: 24.

which cultures were seen to have essential, if ineffable, unity. Yet fidelity to culture is a moral principle now advocated by Indians, Maoris, Kashmiris, Aborigines, and so on, in a postmodern context which undermines all essential unities. Thus, the ethical issues need to be formulated more precisely: is it possible to separate fidelity to a *culture* from fidelity to a *people group* whose solidarity is always mediated by culture? Or to formulate the question as an outsider: is it possible to separate *respect* for a culture from respect for a people group?

The answer is yes and no. The terms of this partial separation between culture and people group were set out in Fredrik Barth's classic essay in *Ethnic Groups and Boundaries: The Social Organization of Culture Difference.* There Barth made the important claim that "cultural" contents can vary

> without any critical relation to the boundary maintenance of the ethnic group. So when one traces the history of an ethnic group through time, one is not simultaneously, in the same sense, tracing the history of "a culture": the elements of the present culture of that ethnic group have not sprung from the particular set that constituted the group's culture at a previous time, whereas the group has a continual organizational existence with boundaries (criteria of membership) that despite modifications have marked off a continuing unit. (38)

This thesis can be well illustrated by the Hebrew Bible, where we find the literary expressions of a people who have been clearly influenced by a range of ancient cultures. Yet we also find attempts to construct a continuity of peoplehood, even through the disjunctures of history. Whatever the discontinuities and contestations, Barth's main argument still stands: any unity an ethnic identity achieves is not simply to be equated with the continuity of a "culture."

If Barth is correct, as I think he is, then there are implications for the formulation of any ethic of postcolonial study: attempts to preserve a "culture" do not, *ipso facto*, preserve the identity or dignity of an ethnic group. Clearly, the dignity of social groups is usually entwined with wider issues of economics and politics, but it is also important to recognize ethnic identity can still be preserved in spite of cultural changes and influences. In short, people groups are culturally permeable, and it is the people rather than the culture who are the moral agents.

Etienne Balibar (21–23) argues that many anthropologists who have been involved in the struggle to preserve minority or dominated cultures have taken the view that the mixing of cultures is a contravention of nature; every culture is seen to be equally valuable and has a natural right to separate existence. The unintended consequence of this view is the expectation that interethnic exchanges will inevitably be characterized by defensiveness and aggression. What was originally an anti-imperialist strategy has ironically been turned by recent right-wing movements in Europe into xenophobia: since every culture has a right to separate existence, so this response goes, people of other cultures should keep their distance. There is an obvious parallel here between the resurgence of right-wing movements in Balibar's France and the old apartheid system in South Africa.

Building on the work of Balibar, Daniel Boyarin has distinguished, in his book *A Radical Jew*, between rightist racism and liberal racism: the political goals of rightist racism entail the subjugation or the expulsion of other "races"; liberal racism, on the other hand, tends to advocate the construction of new states within which the ethnic-nationalist aspirations for sovereignty may be fulfilled. The latter option, for Boyarin, simply reinscribes homogeneity, and the basic intolerance towards difference is replicated (247–50). Although Boyarin has no detailed discussion of Fredrik Barth, it is clear that this approach would make no sense unless one presumed something like Barth's account of how culture and ethnicity overlap, yet are distinct phenomena—ethnic identity *with* cultural permeability (see further, Brett, 1996). In articulating his model of postmodern, diasporic Judaism, Boyarin suggests that there is nothing wrong with ethnocentricity (a) when it is 'polyphonic,' and above all (b) when it is a strategy of survival amongst subordinate groups. In short, ethnocentrism is only malign when it is combined with homogenizing political power. Ethnocentrism cannot be treated in modernist fashion as a universalizable vice; on the contrary, it can be justifiable in contextual terms and therefore may require reframing in terms of a postmodern ethic of difference.

Boyarin's work allows us to focus the question of the relationship between postmodernism and postcolonialism. Clearly, the two movements have conspired together to recover marginal discourses. Yet, as Sahlins has suggested, there are some forms of postmodernism in which the thoroughgoing deconstruction of any attempt at representation would destroy the possibility of postcolonial identity (see also During: 32). Some analyses of colonial discourse might lead one to the ethical conclusion that the practice of representing *others* ought to be, as much as possible, avoided (e.g. May: 13). Dwight Furrow goes further to argue that even within a particular tradition there are many rival histories, and any one account of a tradition renders invisible the people and events that do not fit the patterns prescribed by the chosen account (65). He concludes that

> the self, whether we understand it individually or collectively, is a topography of lost and missing pieces cobbled together by a systematically distorted narrative of the remains. The quest for social identity is just one more vain search for the solace of origins, perpetually contested and itself the source of injustice. (192)

In this strand of postmodernism, no ethic can rely on the representation of social or cultural identities.

Many other critics have found an intersection of postmodernism and postcolonialism in the literary genre of "magic realism," or "marvellous realism," within which the myths and legends of a particular cultural tradition are recovered in responses to oppression (Dash; Hutcheon). This version of postmodernism has given license for "re-mythologization," rather the de-mythologisation that Hector Avalos has described in Leñero's *The Gospel of Lucas Gavilán*. The practice of re-mythologization suggests a community-forming, hybrid discourse which lays no claim to homogenous epistemological foundations, transparent identities, or stable collectivities. It suggests a mode of representation, and even of resistance, which juxtaposes marginal elements of tradition in dialogue with the voices of contemporary experience. While some may doubt whether this project should still be called "representation," it does at least indicate (*contra* Furrow) that there may still be life in a concept of cultural identity understood as permeable pastiche; culture and identity need not be entirely irrelevant to the quest for postcolonial ethics.

Given that postcolonialism and postmodernism can be read, at their intersections, as committed to dialogical identities and to the recuperation of subjugated discourses, we may now ask the specifically ethical question of how inclusive this dialogue should be. If we say that the dialogue should ideally be *completely* inclusive, then the model of ethics presupposed might ironically be something like the reconstructed modernism of Habermas's discourse ethics (Habermas, 1990, 1993; Rogerson). Followers of Habermas argue that openness to the particularity of the other requires that one "first defends the universalist idea that every subject in his or her individuality should get the chance of an unconstrained articulation of his or her claims" (Honneth: 307). Thus, the recuperation of subjugated discourses would be driven by principles of equal treatment and procedural justice.

Even so, postmodern ethicists have been suspicious of the project of universal commensurability and have argued for a politics of difference (Baumann). They would suggest that dialogue can and should proceed without the global pretensions of universalizability. Derrida has recently suggested that there are basically two different types of moral concern, and they conflict fundamentally. The first type is indeed the solidarity of justice which aims to treat everyone equally. The second type is an infinite care for the irreducibly particular other. The conflict between the two versions of moral concern is revealed by the fact that a form of care which is boundless would be compromised if it were constrained by the principle of equal treatment (Derrida, 1990).

Postmodern perspectivism confesses that we are always embedded in our own location—family, people group, traditions, and contextual dialogues—and there is an inevitable sacrifice of others. Thus, Derrida can write:

> By preferring my work, simply by giving it my time and attention, by preferring my activity as a citizen or as a professorial and professional philosopher, writing and speaking here in a public language, French in my case, I am perhaps fulfilling my duty. But I am sacrificing and betraying at every moment all my other obligations: my obligations to the other others whom I know or don't know, the billions of my fellows ... who are dying of starvation or sickness ... every one being sacrificed to every one else in this land of Moriah that is our habitat every second of every day. (69)

In short, postmodern ethics seems to lead in the direction of polyphonic ethnocentrism. Boyarin's work adds an important qualification to this point, since he only defends ethnocentrism as a form of resistance, i.e. when it does not possess the machinery of state. Unless every people group is to have its own government, a scenario Boyarin rightly rejects, we are committed to multicultural states. And states, unless they are to replicate the imperialist structure of centre and periphery, require a principle of equal treatment. The implied ethics of postcolonial studies cannot therefore do without modernism, it would seem, even if the ethics of resistance are postmodern.

One final caveat should be added: it is not clear to me that Habermas's particular version of modernist ethics has the potential to deliver decolonizing effects for multicultural states. While it does contain a principle of equal treatment, and it does promote actual conversation amongst all those affected by political decisions, it does so in a manner that seeks to bracket the particularities of cultural identity. Habermas attempts to distinguish on the one hand between universalizable norms, rules, and justice (what he calls "moral-practical" discourses), and on the other hand values or ends shaped by particular cultural identities (in his technical vocabulary, "ethical-existential" discourses). In his most recent work, for example, he writes:

> Moral-practical discourses, by contrast, require a break with all of the unquestioned truths of an established, concrete ethical life, in addition to distancing oneself from the contexts of life with which one's identity is inextricably interwoven. (1993:12)

In might be argued that Habermas's account reflects the moral consequences of separating "culture" from "people group," as I advocated in the discussion of Fredrik Barth. But while it is clear that people groups are culturally permeable, and it is the people rather than the culture who are the moral agents, the identity of a people cannot be grasped independently of culture. Most importantly, many of the most vexed questions of public justice turn precisely on the question of how particular people can achieve recognition *as a culturally defined group* (cf. Taylor). Accordingly, it is not clear to me how Habermas's account of discourse ethics can deliver public justice on these questions when it excludes precisely the identities that are at issue.

Lest it be thought that these questions have strayed too far from biblical studies, one need only refer to Whitelam's disturbing account of how "biblical archaeology" has consistently "imagined"[3] Israel in ways which—wittingly or unwittingly—contribute to the displacement of Palestinian identity within the modern state of Israel. Whitelam reveals, in quotation after quotation, how competing archaeological explanations of the "Israelite settlement" have actually been united in their failure to recognize the problem of indigenous rights. The most recent accounts, which see the proliferation of highland settlements in the early Iron Age as largely "indigenous," still uses the vocabulary of "Israel" and refuses to speak of a "Palestinian" population. Even Mendenhall and Gottwald's theories of an internal revolt are faulted for thinking that the indigenous system was corrupt and could "only be transformed by Israel and its religious and political ideology which comes from *outside*" (Whitelam: 113).

Whitelam's book is clearly driven by an *ethical* motive, emphasizing indigenous rights. One might even venture to say that his ethics are postmodern insofar as he doubts the commensurability of competing ethical claims about Palestine. Thus, against Philip Davies' claim to neutrality (Whitelam: 246, citing Davies: 23), he agrees with Edward Said that "there is no neutrality; there can be no neutrality or objectivity about Palestine" (Said: 30). Still, Whitelam's case seems more Romantic than postmodern insofar as he fails to consider the problems of cultural permeability and instability, theorized especially in postcolonial criticism. If his concern is focussed on what he calls the "population" of ancient Palestine (Whitelam: 36, 247 n. 11 and n. 20), then that population was surely free, as William Apess was, to engage with contiguous cultures; cultural hybridity is potentially a feature of all ethnic groups. Unless one is to fall back on to the nostalgic "myth of authenticity," there is no reason to assume that ancient Palestinian culture was incorrigible.

But in spite of the lack of clarity in his ethical stance, Whitelam has articulated for us an extremely important set of questions about the politics of naming. The jars and shards of archaeology are neither "Palestinian" nor "Israelite" until they are placed by hermeneutical imagination within larger narratives. And those narratives do indeed provide legitimating structures which underlie the competing national imaginations of Palestine and Israel. The emerging realization that "early Israelites" *were* "Palestinians" only

---

[3] Whitelam cites Benedict Anderson's well-known definition of nationhood as "imagined political community" and argues that the discourse of biblical studies has been monopolized by a nationalist imagination which silences Palestinian history (22). On the same page he footnotes approvingly Ernst Gellner's argument that nationalism "*invents* nations where they do not exist" (Gellner: 169). Unfortunately, Whitelam has clouded his argument by failing to notice Anderson's critique of Gellner: by conflating imagination, invention, and falsity, Gellner implies that there have been "true" communities which are somehow natural (Anderson: 6).

serves to illustrate Homi Bhaba's point that "hybridity is never simply a question of the admixture of pre-given identities or essences" (314): neither Israelis nor Palestinians can lay essentialist claims to pure identities in hoary antiquity. Nonetheless, it does not follow that hybridized identities need to be excluded from the business of ethics (a conclusion, ironically, upon which both Habermas and Furrow converge). At least at the level of state politics, postcolonial ethics would combine a principle of equal treatment with a recognition of cultural particularities.

Works Consulted

Ahmad, Aijaz
    1987   "Jameson's Rhetoric of Otherness and the 'National Allegory.'" *Social Text* 17:3–25.

Amuta, Chidi
    1989   *The Theory of African Literature*. London: Zed.

Anderson, Benedict
    1991   *Imagined Communities*. 2d ed. London: Verso.

Balibar, Etienne
    1991   "Is there a 'Neo-Racism'?" In *Race, Nation, Class: Ambiguous Identities*. Ed. Etienne Balibar and Emmanuel Wallerstein. London: Verso.

Barnard, Frederick
    1969   *J. G. Herder on Social and Political Culture*. Cambridge: Cambridge University Press.

Barth, Fredrik, ed.
    1969   *Ethnic Groups and Boundaries: The Social Organization of Culture Difference*. London: Allen & Unwin.

Bauman, Zygmunt
    1993   *Postmodern Ethics*. Oxford: Blackwell.

Berlin, Isaiah
    1976   *Vico and Herder*. New York: Vintage.

Bhaba, Homi, ed.
    1990   *Narrating Nations*. London: Routledge.

Boehmer, Elleke
    1995   *Colonial and Postcolonial Literature: Migrant Metaphors*. New York: Oxford University Press.

Boyarin, Daniel
    1994   *A Radical Jew: Paul and the Politics of Identity*. Berkeley: University of California Press.

Brett, Mark G.
1995 "Nationalism and the Hebrew Bible." Pp. 136–63 in *The Bible in Ethics*. Ed. John W. Rogerson, Margaret Davies, and M. Daniel Carroll R. JSOTS 207. Sheffield: JSOT.

1996 "Interpreting Ethnicity: Method, Hermeneutics, Ethics." Pp. 3–22 in *Ethnicity and the Bible*. Ed. Mark G. Brett. Leiden: Brill.

Dash, Michael J.
1974 "Marvellous Realism: The Way out of Négritude." *Caribbean Studies* 13:57–70.

Davies, Philip
1992 *In Search of 'Ancient Israel'*. JSOTS 148. Sheffield: JSOT.

Derrida, Jacques
1990 "Force of Law." *Cardoza Law Review* 11:919–1045.

1995 *The Gift of Death*. Chicago: Chicago University Press.

Donaldson, Laura
1996 "Son of the Forest, Child of God: William Apess and the Scene of Postcolonial Nativity." Paper read at the Annual SBL Meeting, New Orleans, November 1996. Forthcoming in *Postcolonialism and American Culture*. University of Illinois.

During, Simon
1987 "Postmodernism or Postcolonialism Today." *Textual Practice* 1:32–47.

Furrow, Dwight
1995 *Against Theory: Continental and Analytic Challenges in Moral Philosophy*. London: Routledge.

Gellner, Ernst
1964 *Thought and Change*. London: Weidenfeld and Nicholson.

Griffiths, Gareth
1994 "The Myth of Authenticity." In *DeScribing Empire*. Ed. C. Tiffin and A. Lawson. London: Routledge.

Habermas, Jürgen
1990 *Moral Consciousness and Communicative Action*. Oxford: Polity. Translation C. Lenhardt and S. Weber Nicholsen of *Moralbewusstsein und kommunikatives Handeln*. Frankfurt: Suhrkamp, 1983.

1993 *Justification and Application*. Oxford: Polity. Translation by C. Cronin of *Erläuterungen zur Diskursethik*. Frankfurt: Suhrkamp, 1981.

Honneth, Axel
1995 "The Other of Justice: Habermas and the Ethical Challenge of Postmodernism." Pp. 289–323 in *The Cambridge Companion to Habermas*. Ed. Stephen K. White. Cambridge: Cambridge University Press.

Hutcheon, Linda
1989 "Circling the Downspout of Empire: Post-colonialism and Postmodernism." *Ariel* 20:149–75.

May, Todd
    1995   *The Moral Theory of Poststructuralism.* University Park: University of Pennsylvania Press.

Moon, Randall
    1993   "William Apess and Writing White." *Studies in American Indian Literatures* 5:45–54.

Rogerson, John W.
    1995   "Discourse Ethics and Biblical Ethics." Pp. 17–26 in *The Bible in Ethics.* Ed. John W. Rogerson, Margaret Davies, and M. Daniel Carroll R. JSOTS 207. Sheffield: JSOT Press.

Sahlins, Marshall
    1995   *How "Natives" Think about Captain Cook, for Example.* Chicago: Chicago University Press.

Said, Edward
    1986   "The Burdens of Interpretation and the Question of Palestine." *Journal of Palestine Studies* 61:29–37.

Sugirtharajah, R. S.
    1996   "Orientalism, Ethnonationalism and Transnationalism." Pp. 413–29 in *The Bible in Three Dimensions.* Ed. Mark G. Brett. Leiden: Brill.

Taylor, Charles
    1992   "The Politics of Recognition." Pp. 25–73 in *Multiculturalism and the Politics of Recognition.* Ed. Anne Gutman. Princeton: Princeton University Press.

Whitelam, Keith
    1996   *The Invention of Ancient Israel: The Silencing of Palestinian History.* London: Routledge.

Mapping the Hybrid World: Three Postcolonial Motifs

Susan VanZanten Gallagher
Seattle Pacific University

The multiple identities and conflicting voices of postcolonial theory unmistakably emerge in this stimulating collection of essays exploring the relationship of postcolonialism and biblical studies. Most literary critics would admit to recognizing postcolonial theory when they saw it, but few are the brave souls who attempt to define or explain it. The editor of one of the most recent postcolonial readers (the publication of which has suddenly become a booming business), admits

> Students in a range of disciplines, whether they are studying in Lagos or London, New Delhi or New York, are increasingly confronted with the term 'postcolonial.' At first sight it seems straightforward but problems of definition soon appear. Does the term refer to texts or to practices, to psychological conditions or to concrete historical processes? Or does it perhaps refer to the interaction of all of these? Those who find themselves puzzling about such issues should take heart, for such puzzlement suggests *not* that they are failing to grasp what postcolonial theory and criticism involve but rather that they have already begun to engage with the powerful contending forces and disputes which swirl around the term and its uses. (Mongia: 1)

Such engagement continues in this collection of essays, in which biblical studies joins other disciplines such as philosophy, history, sociology, anthropology, and political science in considering the impact of postcolonial theory. Although that theory has been developed primarily by literary critics, postcolonial theory has truly become an interdisciplinary project and, as such, an important aspect of a new concern with "cultural studies."

The variety of topics and approaches represented in this collection demonstrate the vast scope and uncertain contours of the postcolonial theoretical map. Rather than attempting to chart that map in more detail, I have chosen to engage and reflect on three significant postcolonial motifs that appear in this collection. The various contributors draw on and elaborate these motifs in differing, sometimes conflicting, ways, and their applications serve to expand the postcolonial conversation in useful directions. Although many more motifs can be identified, I shall consider three that are of particular interest to me: 1) the universalizing tendency of postcolonial theory; 2) the prevailing trope of topography; and 3) the central notion of hybridity.

1. The Postcolonial Metanarrative

For some postcolonial literary theorists, several of the essays in this volume would have little, if any, critical validity. Defined in historical terms, *postcolonialism* refers to the period of time beginning in 1947 when nineteenth-century European nation-states encountered numerous forms of indigenous resistance in the lands they had colonized and subsequently withdrew from formal legal governance. Consequently, new politically independent nations were formed. Within this definition, applying postcolonial theory to the Babylonian, Persian, or Roman conquests, the Johannine community's expansionist vision, or any biblical pericope is anachronistic and ahistorical. Musa Dube's discussion of a contemporary African writer's revisionary biblical discourse in "Reading for Decolonization," however, would be appropriate, as would Miriam Peskowitz's account of the colonial engagements of nineteenth-century biblical scientists and archaeologists in her "Tropes of Travel."

Other postcolonial literary definitions move beyond the Middle East, Africa, and Asia to include literature from Canada, the United States, Australia, and Latin America—all previously politically colonized land masses, some presently economically colonized societies. The etymology of *postcolonial* implies a time *after* colonialism, an assumption that makes some uneasy, erasing, as it were, the continuing economic after-effects of colonialism in much of Latin America and Asia as well as overlooking the marked differences in the postcoloniality of a former colony such as the United States in comparison with the former colony of the Belgian Congo, now Zaire. Furthermore, the instances of flourishing settler colonies with remnants of surviving indigenous people, such as Native Americans and Australian aborigines, pose difficult paradoxes for those who would speak of a temporally or politically defined postcolonialism. Several of the contributors to this volume wrestle with these issue. Jace Weaver, in "From I-Hermeneutics to We-Hermeneutics: Native Americans and the Post-Colonial," notes, "for much of that 2/3 of the world colonialism is not dead.... Native Americans remain a colonized people, victims of internal colonialism" (ms. 19). And in discussing the conditions under which black Africans enslaved in the United States crafted a new literary genre, Kimberly Rae Connor claims, "the creators of the spirituals were practicing a postcolonial biblical discourse long before it was ever identified as such" (ms. 3).

Weaver and Connor, as most of the other essayists included here, understand postcolonialism less as a historical marker than as a political or philosophical marker, *post* as in *opposed to* a certain practice called *colonialism*. For literary theorists, such opposition usually leads to an examination, unveiling or deconstruction, and revision of the discourses that produce and reinforce oppression. Stephen Slemon, for example, focuses on the function of postcolonial theory to assume "a specifically anti- or *post*colonial *discursive* purchase in culture" (6). Postcolonial theory subversively refuses the discourses and theories of the colonizer; it embodies and enables anticolonial discourse; it "critiques . . . the process of production of knowledge about the Other" (Williams and Chrisman: 8), in an attempt to answer the question that Edward Said first posed in *Orientalism:* "How can we know and respect the other?" Such a political, discourse-oriented approach is found in Hector Avalos's "*The Gospel Of Lucas Gavilán* as Postcolonial Biblical Exegesis," in which colonialism is defined in a broader way as "any form of social, political, or economic subjugation undertaken by a state and its allied institutions" and postcolonial literature as "writings that scrutinize critically the colonial experience, whether past or present: (ms. 2). Similarly, Dube's wide-ranging discussion of imperialism and those cultural strategies that support imperialistic movements picks up on Said's recent terminology in *Culture and Imperialism,* which, though it concentrates on the "unique coherence and special cultural centrality" of British, French, and American imperialism, acknowledges the existence of many other imperial projects, such as the Austro-Hungarian, Russian, and Ottoman Empires (xxii). "Decolonizing," Dube maintains, "defines awareness of imperialism's exploitative forces and its various strategies of domination, the conscious adoption of strategies of resisting imperial domination as well as the search for alternative ways of liberating interdependence between nations, races, genders, economics and cultures" (ms. 3) A more general concentration on oppression, exploitation, and resistance enables Jon L. Berquist to consider the early stages of Hebrew Bible canonization as part of the imperialistic discourse of the Persian Empire in "Postcolonialism and Imperial Motives for Canonization," as well as clears a discursive space for many of the contributors to reflect on biblical texts, hermeneutics, and a historically broad range of revisionary discourses. A similar tactic of expansion was used in the 1992 special issue of *Social Text* on postcoloniality, which discussed the Incan, the Ottoman, and Chinese empires, as well as contemporary forms of colonialism such as Indonesia's oppressive rule of East Timor.

The implication of such moves, however, is to universalize certain patterns of oppression and resistance. Although in popular usage *imperialism* and *colonialism* are often used interchangeably, historians and political theorists more commonly distinguish among imperialism, colonialism, and neocolonialism. The colonial phase, most notoriously in the European "Scramble for Africa," is one highly specific part of the complex on-going drama of imperialism, and the ever-widening historical and geographical expansion of postcolonial theory to encompass the imperialistic impulses of both Alexander the Great and General George Armstrong Custer raises troubling questions. On the one hand, Russell Jacoby had lamented the "marginal returns" of a postcolonial theory that "claims four centuries and most of the planet as its domain" (30). One can only imagine his dismay at the further historical extensions of the theory suggested by Berquist or Dube. What isn't postcolonial? Other theorists criticize postcolonialism's own imperialism, which envelops all local specificity in what can only be termed a metanarrative, the metanarrative of oppression, resistance, and freedom. Aijaz Ahmad comments, "Colonialism thus becomes a transhistorical thing, always present and always in process of dissolution in one part of the world or another, so that everyone gets the privilege , sooner or later, at one time or another, of being coloniser, colonised and postcolonial. . . . The fundamental effect of constructing this globalised tranhistoricity of colonialism is one of evacuating the very meaning of the word and dispersing that meaning so wide that we can no longer speak of determinate histories of determinate structures such as that of the postcolonial state . . ." (283). Ahmad is working from a Marxist position that understands colonialism in specific economic terms, but there are other positions from which to object to the totalizing tendency of postcolonialism. Padmini Mongia notes, "If the impact of colonialism in understood as having produced equal and common effects, so that, for instance, the USA shares the same space as Kenya, postcolonial criticism no longer intervenes in Europe's grand narratives of progress and civilization but becomes itself another grand narrative. Socio-historic, cultural and racial differences are elided as colonialism itself becomes a privileged historical marker" (6–7). The ahistorical, universalizing, homogenizing effects of postcolonial theory, as Weaver warns, may not provide a politically useful analysis for those cast as Others in a specific time and place (ms. 18).

I do not mean to suggest that the contributors to this volume have fallen prey to the dangers of de-historicizing or de-contextualizing their discussions of colonial and anti- or post-colonial discourses, positions, and strategies. Indeed, the essays are rich with context-specific details of Canaanites, Persian-period Yehudites, Syro-Phoenicians, and Samaritans, among other people, cultures, and times, Yet the cumulative content and critical direction of the collection points to some kind of central experience of "colonization" and "resistance" that has manifested itself in human history over countless centuries and in all-too-many cultures, appearing in certain identifiable patterns. I believe that one of the more significant contributions of postcolonial theory may be to demonstrate the limitations of the postmodern resistance to metanarrative. Perhaps that resistance might better be directed toward particular narratives, such as the Enlightenment myth of progress or the Stalinist myth of communism. As Hispanic theologian Justo Gonzáles has noted, if no metanarrative exists, the marginalized people of the world have even less protection from the powerful, who are free to impose their power at will. At the same time, we must recognize that without concrete historical grounding, a postcolonial metanarrative dismantling the colonial myth is an elusive abstraction, airless and impotent. We can talk about colonialism and postcolonialism as universal concepts only by means of specific manifestations in particular times and places, and it is only in those particular discussions, grounded in particular discourses, that strategic postcolonial moves can take place.

THE TOPOGRAPHICAL TROPE

One of the most frequently employed metaphors in postcolonial discourse (including my own in the previous section) is that of map making. The topographical trope dominates postcolonial theory, with recurring terms such as terrains, territories, geography, borders, centers, peripheries, places, and homes. Spatiality joins temporality as a primary structure of thought and analysis in postcolonial theory. Although neo-colonialism most typically takes economic forms, nineteenth-century colonialism involved a physical appropriation of land, such as when hundreds of Gikuyu peoples were ejected from their fertile Kenyan farms to make way for British settlers. In *The Empire Writes Back,* Ashcroft, Griffiths, and Tiffin state, "place and displacement . . . are major concerns of post-colonial people" (24). The Cherokee Trail of Tears, the destruction of South Africa's Sophiatown and District 6, the forced removal of Palestinians—colonized people from a variety of historical locations have undergone physical displacement from the land that they identify as home.

Such physical appropriation of land was paralleled in discursive appropriation, as maps were constructed to chart the contours of the newly formed colony/region/province, replete with new European names for age-old landmarks. Thus, maps are especially productive means to interrogate and reinterpret colonial representation, as they concretely reveal and assert lines of power and linguistic impositions. Conrad's famous account in *Heart of Darkness* highlights the conjunction of map-making, exploration, and power: "Now when I was a little chap I had a passion for maps," his narrator Marlowe relates,

> I would look for hours at South America, or Africa, or Australia and lose myself in all the glories of exploration. At that time there were many blank spaces on the earth and when I saw one that looked particularly inviting on a map (but they all look that) I would put my finger on it and say: When I grow up I will go there. . . . there was one yet—the biggest—the most blank, so to speak—that I had a hankering after. True, by this time it was not a blank space any more. It had got filled since my boyhood with rivers and lakes and names. It had ceased to be a blank space of delightful mystery—a white patch for a boy to dream gloriously over. It had become a place of darkness. (11–12)

The blankness of the spaces on the maps suggests a corresponding blankness of culture or society. Eventually such empty spaces on the earth are filled in as

European explorers and mapmakers arrive, plotting the dimensions and affixing names—such as Stanley Falls and Lake Victoria—to the geographic features. Maps as a genre, says Rita Bernard, project an "ideological blueprint" on the land (46).

Peskowitz's engaging essay on "Tropes of Travel" examines how maps of the Middle East, along with Holy Land theme parks and travel advertising, "have led people of the West to occupy, visit, celebrate and claim as home a part of the world they would otherwise (and sometimes simultaneously) denigrate as 'the Orient' and 'the East'" (ms. 3). Nineteenth-century colonial projects made the mapping of Palestine possible in the first place, but the resulting maps, in turn, functioned as a means of extending and defining colonial control. Miniature replicas, popularized in the nineteenth century, gave Americans both the opportunity to embody colonialism literally as they towered over the diminutive versions of Jerusalem, the River Jordan, and the Dead Sea, as well as the opportunity to feel at home in the midst of the unfamiliar. Peskowitz chronicles these phenomena in entertaining detail, but her critique is the most pungent when she associates the numerous "tropes of travel" generated by colonial exploration and archeology with the development of biblical studies as an academic discipline, charging, "Without conscious and committed attention to the entangling of biblical studies and colonial culture, Biblical Studies continues within these foundations, and continues within its colonial legacy" (ms. 4). Tracing the origin of including maps in Bibles to the Protestant Reformation and its emphasis on the literal, as opposed to symbolic, truth of the text, Peskowitz notes how the "science" of maps reinforces the "truth" of the text: "the proliferation of maps assumes that access to the literal truth of biblical words is possible" (ms. 19). This analysis of Reformation map-making suggests how hermeneutics, in addition to the impact of colonial exploration and archeology, might have contributed to the late-nineteenth and early twentieth-century mania for biblical maps. In the face of increasing challenges from Darwinian science and higher biblical criticism, nineteenth-century American hermeneutics and apologetics increasingly relied on rational proofs, scientific evidence, and literal interpretation. The concrete, scientific nature of biblical maps designating, for example, the God-ordained separation of people into separate races by means of differing map colors, played a key role in the eventual development of American fundamentalism.

Besides Peskowitz's extended consideration of maps, replicas, and tourism as examples of dream topographies, several other contributors evoke the geographic trope. In his essay, Avalos takes the trope literally, as he identifies the particular setting of *The Gospel of Lucas Gavilán* in modern-day Mexico as an attempt to validate a specific geographic space of the "Third World" or "periphery" (ms. 5). Connor takes a more imagistic approach in her account of the frequent use of spatial metaphors of movement in spirituals, with sailing, walking, riding, rowing, climbing, all being employed as methods of travel. "The spirituals actually and symbolically moved a people towards liberation," she elaborates, as the Promised Land becomes a metaphor that stops off in the northern states before moving on to the transcendent one. Perhaps the most intriguing riff on the topographical trope is Weaver's discussion of the relative importance of spatiality rather than temporality for Native American thought. In theological terms, then, creation is significant not in terms of *when* it happened but rather in terms of *where* it happened: God created the world *here*, forming a particular land and particular people. Thinking spatially also invokes new readings of the concepts of the kingdom of God, human relationships to the earth, and the question of ownership of land. Thus we have come full circle, back to the concrete dispossession of the land, as Weaver asserts, "A post-colonial hermeneutic must take account of Native land claims" (ms. 31).

Physical and dream topographies demonstrate the significant conjunction between the control of space and discourse, of place and rhetoric, of land and maps. The slippery and often imprecise movement from metaphor to reality in such discussions suggests the inherent connection of the two. A colleague of mine who is a geographer recently finished editing a book of essays written by a number of Russian and American geographers. "Getting the contributors to discuss disagreements civilly in the text was one thing," she says, "rhetoric can always be toned down. But when it came to drawing the maps, we had some major battles." As discursive symbols, maps both represent and embody power.

3. Hybridity and Syncretism

One of the most frequently occurring and significant terms in postcolonial theory is *hybridity*, coined, elaborated, and popularized by Homi Bhabha (who ironically was lauded in *Newsweek* in 1997 as one of "100 Americans for the Next Century"). Bhabha's discussion of hybridity refers to the numerous, and at times paradoxical, identities of the postcolonial subject. Deconstructing "the binary logic through which identities of difference are often constructed-Black/White, Self/Other," Bhabha suggests that "interstitial passage[s] between fixed identifications open . . . up the possibility of a cultural hybridity that entertains differences without an assumed or imposed hierarchy" (4). Postcolonial identity and representation are far more complex than the simple dichotomies of colonizer and colonized initially introduced by theorists such as Frantz Fanon or Abdul JanMohammed: "Terms of cultural engagement, whether antagonistic or affiliative, are produced performatively. The representation of difference must not be hastily read as the reflection of *pre-given* ethnic or cultural traits set in the fixed tablet of tradition. The social articulation of difference, from the minority perspective, is a complex, on-going negotiation that seeks to authorize cultural hybridities that emerge in moments of historical transformation" (Bhabha: 3, 2). In performance, Bhabha claims, new kinds of hybrid identities are strategically claimed and exerted.

Such hybridity emerges from the syncretic nature of postcolonial societies, cultures, and discourses. Resisting a movement toward nativism, a futile, romantic attempt to return to a pristine, pre-colonial culture, writers such as Nigerian Nobel Prize winner Wole Soyinka, Guyanese novelist Wilson Harris, and West Indian poet E. K. Brathwaite recognize, affirm, and draw on the cultural hodgepodge of their postcolonial worlds. Soyinka thinks that the search for an authentic African culture is "Neo-Tarzanism" and asserts that his Africa includes "precision machinery, oil rigs, hydroelectricity, my typewriter, railway trains (not iron snakes), machine guns, bronze sculpture, etc." (38). Diana Bryden refers to the syncretic nature of postcolonial experience in her image of a multirunnered rhizome (a wisteria bush or a bean tree) in which numerous shoots cross and re-cross each other, pollinating each other, producing a riot of branches and blossoms—a trope that replaces the imperial metaphor of tree trunk and subsidiary branches, mother country and colonies, the colonial and the colonized (3). Postcolonial discourse, then, locates, investigates, and celebrates such hybridity, such cross-pollination. Williams and Chrisman perceptively suggest that while a good deal of colonial discourse has been analyzed for the ways in which it constructs the subaltern, other rhizomes have been neglected: "What has been less explored is the extent to which the subaltern may have played a constitutive rather than a reflective role in colonial and domestic imperial discourse and subjectivity. . . . In other words, the movement may have been as much from 'periphery' to 'centre' as from 'centre' to 'periphery'" (16). Some of the more recent instances of postcolonial literary analysis have begun to move in this direction, examining the development of a global twentieth-century culture. In *Colonial and Postcolonial Literature*, Elleke Boehmer, for example, examines "the entry of once-colonized Others into the West . . . [and] how these different cultures have continued flamboyantly to mix and mingle with one another, a development which has permanently transformed the English literary canon, and which has blown the English language, as once was, to the four winds" (7).

In the current collection, Roland Boer's "Green Ants and Gibeonites" while discussing nominalism and essentialism evokes these issues of hybridity, although his move away from essentialism ends up not in what Ashcroft, Griffiths, and Tiffin call "cross-culturality" (36) but rather in a "staged" performative identity that appears to float completely free of historic and social reality. The opposite course is taken by Jace Weaver, who cites Stuart Hall's claim that "colonisation has made ethnic absolutism an increasingly untenable cultural strategy" only to refute it: "One must nevertheless admit that there is something real, concrete, and centered in Native existence and identity" (ms. 21). Perhaps the reality for many Native Americans is much more of a bricolage of contending images, values, and objects. Weaver's essay ultimately points in this direction, in his analysis of William Apess's "signification," in which he employs the norms, language, and tools of Christianity in order to expose Amer-European's racism. Weaver's appreciation for the contributions of native world-views in reading biblical texts and his project of a "we-hermeneutic" are concrete steps in exploring the role that the colonized can play in constituting the discourse of the dominant culture. Kimberly Rae Connor sees similar signifying going on in African-American spirituals, as she elaborates in "'Everybody Talking About Heaven Ain't Going There': The Biblical Call for Justice and the Postcolonial Response of the Spirituals." Her discussion of the historical, pre-colonial African consciousness that lies behind the presence of biblical language and her insistence that the encounter with Christianity was not the only factor in the creation of the spiritual form acknowledges the genre as a true cross-cultural hybrid. The issue that remains to be addressed is how the theology and aesthetics of spirituals have informed the Euro-American Christian tradition, enriching the liturgy and theology of the church in another instance of cross-fertilization.

Jon Berquist, in "Postcolonialism and Imperial Motives for Canonization," takes a much broader historical view of the syncretic and hybrid nature of colonialism in his account of the early stages of Hebrew Bible canonization during the reign of the Persian Empire in colonial Yehud. Berquist argues that the canon was "a politically constructed document for the purposes of advancing an imperializing ideology," but he also locates canonical texts and moments that can be used against the imperializing ideologies (ms. 9). In recognizing that both the Judean experience as well as the massive economic military, social, and ideological forces embodied in the Persian Empire contributed to postexilic religion and the establishment of the canon, Berquist acknowledges the complex hybridity of historical circumstances. However, in identifying the canon as "a bricolage that presented and presents multiple views and ideologies," Berquist turns to deconstructive rather than postcolonial theory: "The canon ... cannot be considered complete, coherent, or consistent [because of] the impossibility of creating systems (including texts and ideologies) that are both complete and coherent, as shown variously by Godel and Derrida. The nature of language and even thought is such that complete coherence is impossible" (ms. 21). Rather than cultural encounters, exchanges, and affects, we are left in the chaotic prisonhouse of language where a continuous babble of voices interspersed with silences becomes coherent only when the reader imposes a form on it.

By far the most sustained discussion of hybridity occurs in Jim Perkinson's "A Canaanitic Word in the Logos of Christ: Or the Difference the Syro-Phoenician Woman Makes to Jesus." Besides examining the complex hybrid identities of the Syro-Phoenician woman, the Canaanite appellation used by Matthew, and the *logos* of Jesus, Perkinson, like Weaver, points to the need for a postcolonial hermeneutic in which a "Canaanite trace" affects "Jewish/Christian discourse." Examining the affects of the Syro-Phoenician woman's reiteration of Jesus's own discourse, Perkinson identifies the exchange as pedagogic for Jesus and, perhaps, a foreshadowing of the transformation of a localized Jewish sect into a multicultural world mission. The woman's *logos*, Perkinson claims, is a trace of messianic power operating for a brief moment against Jesus; there is "a hybridity within the word of deliverance that eludes the control of even Jesus himself." The final conclusion of this closely argued and complex essay points in a direction similar to Weaver's: "I am arguing that mainstream Eurocentric christologies must attend to the *formal possibility* of such a displacement, whatever its actual historical content, as part of the on-going reiteration of the word of salvation in various local contexts and discourses" (ms 14).

Perkinson's brief reference to the Syro-Phoenician woman's story as an early mission text raises a final topic on which many of the contributors touch—the question of Christian missions. Are the biblical mission texts inherently imperialistic? Dube strongly argues that they are, but counter-readings of the story of the Samaritan woman, Pentecost, or Paul's extension of the proclamation of the good news to non-Jews and insistence on Christian plurality (Romans 12, 1 Corinthians 12) might demonstrate the postcolonial nature of mission texts. Further discussion of these texts in the light of postcolonial theory would be useful.

Additional questions related to missions arise with respect to the specific applications of these texts in nineteenth-century missionary movements; for example, Dube, Weaver, and Peskowitz all touch on the negative impact upon indigenous cultures of the biblical Christianity proclaimed by missionaries. The African proverb that serves as an epigraph to Dube's essay represents the way that colonialism and Christianity are seen as synonymous, with biblical texts prompting, endorsing, and sustaining the colonial project. Undoubtedly, the agents and agencies of nineteenth-century Christianity were often deeply implicated in colonial oppression, as numerous works of literature as disparate as Chinua Achebe's *Things Fall Apart*, Herman Melville's *Omoo*, and Peter Mattheissen's *At Play in the Fields of Our Lord* also explore.

Yet too often the missionary movement has been interpreted in simplistic, binary terms that ignore the historical differences and specificities of distinct missionary projects. As Lamin Sannah comments, the missionary project most often is seen as either an act of the most rampant cultural imperialism or as a supernaturally blessed and providentially ordained plan. In *Encountering the West: Christianity and the Global Cultural Process*, Sannah refrains from "the handy rhetoric of caricature or hagiography," claiming, "what is really historically interesting about missions has little to do with either of those opposing positions, but rather with the unintentional and unpremeditated consequences of practice and conduct" (18). Sannah's challenging book explores both the way that the biblical texts affected indigenous peoples, as in providing new moral and cultural resources to oppose the excesses of colonialism, as well as the way that indigenous peoples, cultures, and languages affected the biblical text and Western understandings of that text. In the African missionary project, unlike the American missions to Native Americans discussed by Weaver, particular care was paid to translating the biblical text into indigenous languages, preserving vernacular usage, indigenous names for God, and idiomatic forms. Sannah writes, "Such a detailed attention to indigenous particularity fostered unprecedented cultural pluralism within the general scheme of world Christianity. For example, indigenous hymns, prayers and invocations, laden with older religious attitudes, sentiments and ideas, were now transcribed and incorporated into Christian use where ecumenical interest gave them international range" (146). In addition to further consideration of the biblical mission texts, the hybridity of mission-encounters is another fruitful field of future research. This collection of essays is only the first word in what could become an animated conversation about the complex, hybrid interactions among biblical studies, colonialism, and postcolonialism.

WORKS CONSULTED

Ahmad, Aijaz
    1996   "The Politics of Literary Postcoloniality." Pp. 276–93 in *Contemporary*
    [1995]   *Postcolonial Theory: A Reader*. Ed. Padmini Mongia. London: Arnold.

Ashcroft, Bill, Gareth Griffiths, and Helen Tiffin
    1989   *The Empire Writes Back: Theory and Practice in Post-Colonial Literatures*.
              London: Routledge.

Bernard, Rita
    1994   "Dream Topographies: J. M. Coetzee and the South African Pastoral."
              South Atlantic Quarterly 93:33–58.

Bhabha, Homi K.
    1994   *The Location of Culture*. New York: Routledge.

Boehmer, Elleke
    1995   *Colonial and Postcolonial Literature: Migrant Metaphors*. Oxford: Oxford
              University Press.

Bryden, Diana
    1987   "The Myths that Write Us: Decolonizing the Mind." *The Journal of Commonwealth Literature* 10:1–14.

Conrad, Joseph
    1988   *Heart of Darkness*. New York: Norton. [1899]

Fanon, Frantz
    1967   *Black Skin/White Masks*. Trans. Charles Lam Markmann. New York: Grove Weidenfeld.

Gonzáles, Justo
    1997   "The Whole Truth: Minority Scholars, The Academic Community, and the Church." Unpublished paper, delivered at "Reviving the Christian Mind" Conference. Wheaton College, Wheaton, IL.

Jacoby, Russell
    1995   "Marginal Returns: The Trouble with Post-Colonial Theory." *Lingua Franca* 5:30–37.

JanMohammed, Abdul R.
    1986   "The Economy of Manichean Allegory: The Function of Racial Difference in Colonialist Literature. Pp. 78–106 in *"Race," Writing, and Difference*. Ed. Henry Louis Gates, Jr. Chicago: University of Chicago Press.

Mongia, Padmini
    1996   "Introduction." *Contemporary Postcolonial Theory: A Reader*. Ed. Padmini Mongia. London: Arnold.

Said, Edward W.
    1978   *Orientalism*. New York: Pantheon.
    1993   *Culture and Imperialism*. New York: Knopf.

Sannah, Lamin
    1993   *Encountering the West: Christianity and the Global Cultural Process*. Maryknoll, NY: Orbis Press.

Slemon, Stephen
    1989   "Modernism's Last Post." *Ariel* 23:3–17.

Soyinka, Wole
    1976   *Myth, Literature, and the African World*. Cambridge: Cambridge University Press.

Williams, Patrick and Laura Chrisman, eds.
    1994   *Colonial Discourse and Post-Colonial Theory: A Reader*. New York: Columbia University Press.

www.ingramcontent.com/pod-product-compliance
Lightning Source LLC
Chambersburg PA
CBHW021808220426
43662CB00006B/221